"The Christian worldview has gotten short shrift in recent years in the public square. But now evangelical Christians are fighting back, none more vigorously and uncompromisingly than Brannon Howse. He makes a strong case for the involvement of motivated Christians and Christian values in public affairs."

— Fred Barnes, Executive Editor, *The Weekly
Standard,* Fox News Channel Commentator,
Cohost of "The Beltway Boys"

"At one time the question for America's judges was how to read the Constitution; but under today's liberal, postmodern, man-centered worldview, the question too often is whether to read the Constitution. Brannon Howse insightfully documents the tragic consequences that judicial tyranny, legal positivism, and the humanist worldview are having upon our faith, family, and freedoms."

— The Honorable Edwin Meese III, Former
Attorney General, Reagan Administration

"Brannon Howse grasps the underlying roots of the culture war raging in America, which involves two diametrically opposing worldviews. *One Nation under Man?* uncovers the source of America's political and cultural divisions, something many media and political pundits do not understand."

— David Limbaugh, Author of Two
New York Times Best-Selling Books,
Nationally Syndicated Columnist

"In *One Nation under Man?,* Brannon Howse explains the current worldview war that is raging in America between those who believe there is a Creator and those who do not. Because of the deep and far-reaching implications of a belief in God, or a rejection of Him, every American must choose which side of the battle he or she is on. There is a great deal at stake, and we can be sure that the victorious side in this war of ideas will dramatically impact every American institution and every aspect of American life from the cradle to the grave."

— United States Congressman Jim Ryun,
Three-time Olympian and Former
World-record Holder in the Mile

"Brannon Howse, in his book *One Nation under Man?*, reveals with laserlike clarity the truth that if we want God to bless the USA we must remember and obey His precepts, follow the original intent of the Founders, and be one nation under God not one nation under man."

> — Lee Greenwood, Best-selling Recording
> Artist, Writer and Performer of the Song
> "God Bless the USA"

"For years many of us have urged Brannon Howse to put his seminar into print. He has an excellent grip on the worldview of the Left and has shown it clearly to be deficient when compared with 'the wisdom of God' worldview taught in God's Word."

> — Dr. Tim LaHaye, Coauthor,
> "Left Behind" Series

"American professors teach tolerance for the terrorists of 9/11, proclaim acceptance for same-sex marriage, partial birth abortion, active euthanasia, hedonism, situational ethics, moral relativism, and the virtue of being one nation under man. Is it any wonder that twelve to eighteen months after high school graduation is the most dangerous time, both spiritually and intellectually, for students? There is a worldview war for the hearts and minds of our youth taking place in America, and the front line is today's college campus. . . . Brannon's book reveals as false and dangerous the politically correct, secular, and relativistic worldview of millions within America and why true conservativism is based on a Christian worldview. And for that I say 'Thank you!'"

> — Josh McDowell, Best-selling Author

"Many Americans live in a fog when it comes to understanding the real issues facing this country, and the evidence for this is all around us. In his book *One Nation under Man?*, Brannon Howse marvelously dispels the fog and enables the readers to understand the real underlying issues that are tearing America apart, and it should be required reading for every American."

> — D. James Kennedy, Ph.D., President,
> Coral Ridge Ministries TV and Radio

"Much ink has been spilled on the differences between red states and blue states. Brannon Howse gets to the foundational worldview issues and shows the relevant distinctions between the two major worldviews of our time. He then shows us how to apply a Christian worldview to the key issues of the twenty-first century."

> — Kerby Anderson, National Director of Probe,
> Host of "Point of View"

"Brannon has hit a grand slam with this book! The secular left is the enemy of America and the enemy of Christianity, and we have to fight back to save our country from becoming like modern-day Europe."

> — Tim Wildmon, President, American
> Family Association and Radio Network

"Your own honest heartfelt answer to the question of whether America is one nation under God or one nation under man will determine your views on judicial appointments, embryonic stem cell research, involvement with the United Nations, the war on terrorism, separation of church and state, economic and social policy, and every other issue facing America today. Brannon demonstrates that not only do ideas have consequences but that worldviews shape ideas. For those who believe that this is one nation under God, this book is invaluable."

> — David Barton, Best-selling Author,
> President of Wallbuilders

"Brannon Howse not only takes on the major dogma of the humanists but drives home the point that secular humanism is, for all intents and purposes, our nation's new national religion. It certainly is as religious as Christianity, and its Darwinian fish symbol speaks volumes. I highly recommend Brannon's book for all age groups but especially young adults in our nation's high schools and colleges."

> — David A. Noebel, Coauthor of *Mind Siege*,
> Summit Ministries

ONE NATION
under man?

BRANNON HOWSE

ONE NATION
under man?

THE WORLDVIEW
WAR BETWEEN
CHRISTIANS AND THE
SECULAR LEFT

BROADMAN
&HOLMAN
PUBLISHERS

NASHVILLE, TENNESSEE

© 2005 by Brannon S. Howse
All rights reserved
Printed in the United States of America

13-digit ISBN: 978-0-8054-3185-8
10-digit ISBN: 0-8054-3185-3

Published by Broadman & Holman Publishers,
Nashville, Tennessee

Dewey Decimal Classification: 302
Subject Headings: SOCIAL PSYCHOLOGY \ CHRISTIAN LIFE
                       SOCIOLOGY——FOREIGN OPINION

Unless otherwise noted, Scripture quotations have been taken from the Holman
Christian Standard Bible®, © 1999, 2000, 2002, 2003 by Holman Bible Publishers.
Another translation quoted is NIV, the New International Version, © 1973, 1978,
1984 by International Bible Society.

1 2 3 4 5 6 7 8 9 10 09 08 07 06 05

This book is dedicated to my wife Melissa,
whom I love to love and who is my biggest fan, supporter,
and my best friend.

To my children Landon, Libby, and Logan,
I love you and want to preserve America's Christian history
and freedoms, which are gifts from God, so you and your
children's children and beyond can freely live out the Christian
worldview and create a Christian dynasty that will impact
America and the world for eternity.

To my father George and my mother Jeanne,
I love you and am so grateful that you raised me in a home
of love and where the Christian worldview was inculcated
into me from the earliest of ages.

Contents

Foreword

My father, President Ronald Reagan, said, "If we ever forget that we are one nation under God, then we will be a nation gone under."

While on the one hand, millions of Americans believe in God, the moral law, and in applying the Christian worldview to all areas of life, the unyielding efforts of others on the secular Left have moved America steadily down a road of rejecting the laws of God in favor of the fickle, sound-bite-based laws of men. Our actions as a nation speak loudly about our collective belief system. Babies are aborted because ultrasound images reveal minor birth defects. Nearly full-term infants can be legally exterminated, their brains sucked out during a partial-birth abortion, and our courts have rendered both Congress and the president impotent to stop the practice. Same-sex sexual relationships are sanctioned, and Christian symbols are removed from government emblems while pagan ones remain.

Yet, Christians believe that violating moral laws is an offense to God. It is sin.

And yes, I did say *sin!* The secular Left moans at that word. It's so . . . archaic. To the enlightened elitists in left-leaning media and academia, and to postmodern wise men of the ACLU, the NEA, the Democratic National Committee, and our Federal courts, "sin" doesn't fit. The idea itself offends the worldview of an America where the U.S. Supreme Court has ruled everyone has the right to create their own reality. We have been assured now of a country where each person does what is right in his or her own eyes.

Not long ago, I faced the unpleasant task of putting my dog to sleep. I used a hypodermic needle, and he simply dozed off and died.

Had I done to my dog, though, what Michael Schiavo did to his wife—starve the animal to death—I would have been arrested. Florida prohibits the inhumane treatment of animals, and thus the starvation of one's pet is a criminal act. However, the courts ruled that it was legal to kill Terri Schiavo by starving and dehydrating her. So now, in addition to partial-birth abortion, America has added active euthanasia to her national sins.

Indeed, America is engaged in a worldview battle between Christians and the secular Left. Many believe there is no such thing as God, or that if, by chance, He should happen to exist, He is doubtless a politically correct Figure that tolerates all and passes judgment on no one.

The "anything goes" worldview of the secular Left is becoming mainstream philosophy, largely due to federal judges who have rejected moral law—the laws of nature and nature's God—for man-made law. The U.S. Supreme Court has engineered the secularization of America.

One of the remaining voices of moral reason on the High Court, Justice Antonin Scalia, predicted what would be the result of the U.S. Supreme Court's striking down of Texas's sodomy law in the June 2003 *Lawrence* case. In his dissenting opinion, Scalia wrote that the Court's ruling "effectively decrees the end of all morals legislation. If, as the court asserts, the promotion of a majoritarian sexual morality is not even a legitimate state interest," laws criminalizing "fornication, bigamy, adultery, adult incest, bestiality and obscenity" cannot survive future court rulings. In other words, now anything does go.

These are symptoms of the moral rot that occurs when a people reject God and His laws. They descend into a slime pit of secularism and will eventually endure the horrors of the resulting governmental tyranny.

The Bible points out that a man cannot serve two masters, for he will hate one and love the other. America is divided between those who want to serve and honor God by following His laws as encouraged by America's Constitutional Republic and those who want to serve and honor themselves through implementing man-made rules and the religion of secularism.

Speaking of an America divided North and South, Abraham Lincoln proclaimed that a house divided cannot stand. Today we face a division of worldview rather than geography and economics, and in this watershed book, Brannon Howse exposes the broad front in a worldview war for the heart and soul of America. The outcome of this conflict will determine the destiny of our land. Brannon's insightful writing demonstrates why he has served as education reporter for *The Michael Reagan Show* since 1993 and why he is a frequent guest host of my show. In the pages that follow, my friend Brannon serves his country by dramatically waving a warning of the consequences America will reap if we continue our headstrong detour toward the cliff of secularism.

Will America come back to being one nation under God or will we, as my father cautioned, become a nation gone under because we rejected the One who created the inalienable rights we hold dear? Will we devolve into a huddled mass of men and women with no one but each other as guide and arbiter of our freedoms?

I hope my father's words were not a prophecy of what will be. I fear, though, that they may not bode well—that one day we will have nothing greater to pledge ourselves to than one nation under man.

— MICHAEL REAGAN

Preface

Put Your Worldview to the Test

In 2004, I developed the nation's first free, online test that provides an instant score to help people determine how closely their worldview aligns with biblical Christianity. Nearly twenty-five thousand people took the test in its first twelve months online. I encourage you to go to the Web site www.worldviewweekend.com and take the test before you read this book.

Upon taking the test, you'll get an immediate score showing your worldview in the areas of law, economics, civil government, religion, social issues, sociology (family issues), education, and science. The rating will show whether you are a: Strong Christian Worldview Thinker (True Conservatism), Moderate Christian Worldview Thinker, Secular Humanist Worldview Thinker (Radical Liberalism), Socialist Worldview Thinker, or Communist/Marxist/Socialist/Secular Humanist Worldview Thinker. It will also show how your worldview compares with others in your age category and those with a similar background. The report is very informative, so I encourage you to complete all the pre-test background questions.

Some that score poorly have complained that the test does not so much evaluate a person's worldview as whether one is a Republican. However, if the results look more like the platform of one party than another, it is simply because one comes closer to embracing a Christian worldview than the other. The issues facing our nation were worldview issues long before there was a Republican or a Democratic party. And if you happen to think some of the test questions have nothing to do with Christianity, that is all the more reason to read this book. As a guide to thinking through the test, I've included a copy of the complete test in the appendix. (For additional worldview help, I invite you to attend a Worldview Weekend. Go to www.worldview weekend.com, and you'll see the cities, dates, and speakers for each of our upcoming seminars.)

This test is meant to show where your worldview is strong and where it needs improvement. Whatever your score, don't be frustrated. The good news is you can always improve. That's what this book is for.

So as we start our worldview thinking together, I'll thank you for putting your worldview to the test.

— Brannon S. Howse
President and Founder
Worldview Weekend

Acknowledgments

I want to thank my publisher and particularly David Shepherd who believed in my vision for this book and its message. Special thanks to my editor, Greg Webster, for his assistance in helping me make editorial decisions on the book's content. And thanks to Lisa Parnell, project editor, for her patience in taking my last-minute changes.

For assistance in research I thank Steve Crampton, lead attorney for the Center for Law and Policy, author and researcher Jerry Newcombe, and David Barton of Wallbuilders for historical and judicial research and content review. Thank you Scott Lindsey at Logos Bible Software for setting me up with their top-of-the-line Scholar's Library Silver and many other great theological titles for my research. Having more than one thousand scholarly books on my computer made research for this book so much easier.

Thanks to Tim Wildmon, president of the American Family Association, for listening to me read chapters of this book to him over the phone, giving me words of encouragement and e-mailing me articles and data that proved valuable in my research and writing. Tim, I thank you most of all for your loyal friendship and faithful perseverance and example of the Christian life.

Kerby Anderson, thank you for all the e-mails you sent me with the latest cutting edge polls, surveys, and cultural analysis. David Noebel, Kerby Anderson, and Mike Busak: Thank you for reading the manuscript form of this book and giving me your feedback.

Introduction

Without a doubt, America is a divided nation, and the 2004 presidential election revealed just how divided we are. While the electoral map shows more red states than blue, that does not reveal the whole picture because the candidate that wins the majority of the votes in a given state gets all the electoral votes in that state. When we look at the straight vote count, we see that 55.1 million Americans voted for John Kerry and 58.6 million Americans voted for President Bush, a difference of only 3.5 million votes. That certainly suggests a clear division.

So just what is dividing Americans? Why can we not agree on the issues of our day? What is the driving force that causes both sides to be so committed to their beliefs, ideas, and opinions? Why is the battle between these two opposing groups as important as the battle between the colonies and the British troops during the Revolutionary War? What will be the outcome for the winners as well as the losers? Whether you are a Christian, conservative, atheist, liberal, moderate, or even if you don't know what you believe, this book will reveal the real state of the Union and the two predominate opposing worldviews that will determine the fate of America.

The 2004 election defines clearly those who want to be one nation under the rule of man—with moral relativism and secular humanism* as the foundation—and those who want to be one nation under God—with the absolute moral truth of God's law as the foundation. While liberals reside in both the Democratic Party and the Republican Party, the platform of the Republican Party has traditionally reflected conservative

---

*Humanism is the belief there is no supernatural world and thus no God of the Bible. Humanism promotes the primacy of man and man as the center of all things, for man is god. Thus radical liberals desire to be one nation under man, not one nation under God.

positions such as respect for the life of the unborn, marriage defined as between one man and one women, and opposition to euthanasia.

Polling data shows that many who embrace the liberal policies of the Democratic Party are less religious than those who support the pro-life, traditional marriage policies of the Republican Party. This divide first became apparent with the 2000 election in which those who attended religious services more than once a week supported Bush by a margin of 2 to 1 while those who never attended religious services supported Gore by the same margin.[1]

Thomas Edsall, writing in the *Washington Post,* also documents the religious worldview battle going on in the voting booth: "Pollsters are finding that one of the best ways to discover whether a voter holds liberal or conservative values is to ask: How often do you go to church? Those who go often tend to be Republican; those who go rarely or not at all tend to be Democratic."[2] The election numbers affirm that the same religious-practice divide of 2000 was again present in 2004, and that it extended across ethnic, gender, and age lines. In this election, 61 percent of Bush's vote came from people of all faiths who attend services weekly. Conversely, Kerry received the support of 62 percent of Americans who never attend worship, and among occasional churchgoers, voters were split almost evenly between Republicans and Democrats.[3]

The reaction of modern-day liberals to the reelection of George W. Bush has been very instructive to the worldview battle that is raging in America:

- Democratic leaders such as Lawrence O'Donnell and Bob Beckel (as well as many rank-and-file Democrats) are making noise about secession. The proposed map they are circulating on the Internet demonstrates their understanding of the cultural divide in this election: they propose that the blue states won by Kerry join with Canada to form the "United States of Canada" and that the remaining thirty-one red states be named "Jesusland."
- Radio personality Garrison Keillor, host of the popular National Public Radio show "A Prairie Home Companion" and a Democrat, claims he is on a quest to take away the right of born-again Christians to vote, saying their citizenship is actually in heaven,

not the United States. Keillor made the comments during a speech at Chicago's Rockefeller Memorial Chapel and during his radio monologue the Saturday after the election. According to a transcript of the Saturday show, Keillor said, "I am now the chairman of a national campaign to pass a constitutional amendment to take the right to vote away from born-again Christians. [enthusiastic audience applause] Just a little project of mine. My feeling is that born-again people are citizens of heaven. That is where their citizenship is, [laughter] in heaven; it's not here among us in America." Earlier, in the Chicago speech the day after the election, Keillor also described his reaction to the reelection of President Bush: "I am a Democrat—it's no secret. I am a museum-quality Democrat," Keillor said. "Last night I spent my time crouched in a fetal position, rolling around and moaning in the dark." According to a report in the University of Chicago's *Chicago Maroon*, Keillor told the audience, "If born-again Christians are allowed to vote in this country, then why not Canadians?"[4]

Many in the media claimed President Bush won reelection in the fall of 2004 because of the "values vote." Liberals seemed unable to understand how "values" could override the issues of the economy and the war in Iraq. Yet, one voter in five said moral values were the most important issue driving the vote, and almost eight out of ten of those backed Bush.[5]

Strikingly, liberals talk about the values vote only when referring to those who voted for President Bush. Of course, those that voted for John Kerry also were voting on the basis of values of a different sort—and how those values align with John Kerry's thinking about abortion on demand, same-sex marriage, and so forth. Modern-day liberals have a value system, too, but it is based on a different foundation than that of conservatives. Liberal values are built squarely on moral relativism.

One Democrat argues that his party needs to make up for its "God-gap," as if a party that is overwhelmingly committed to abortion and same-sex marriage, to name only two pertinent issues, could fool the public into thinking they actually care about what matters to God—to say nothing of the implications that Democrats are hooked at the hip with the American Civil Liberties Union, radical homosexual groups, the National Education Association, Planned Parenthood, and the United Nations, all of which make no secret about their hatred of the God of the Bible and His laws. What many modern-day liberals don't understand is that everyone's worldview is the foundation of their values, and this worldview is the motivator behind a person's conduct.

The "values vote" was a worldview vote because the voters that oppose same-sex marriage, abortion, euthanasia, and the secularization of America do so based on the Christian worldview on which their values are founded. Voters that openly embrace the Christian worldview and voters that are even moderately committed to a Christian worldview went to the polls in record numbers in the 2004 elections. President Bush received 78 percent (21.2 million) of the evangelical vote. Nearly 12 million more evangelicals voted in 2004 than in 2000. There was an 80-percent increase in the number of evangelicals voting from the 2000 elections.[6] This surge in evangelicals showing up at the polls returned President Bush to the White House.

The phrase "culture war" is often invoked to describe the values battle between liberals and conservatives, but a more fitting term would be worldview war. While Pat Buchanan invoked the term culture war in 1992, he went on to describe a war of worldviews: "There is a religious war going on in this country, a culture war as critical to the kind of nation we shall be as the Cold War itself, for this war is for the soul of America."[7]

Political writers, seemingly without even knowing it, are agreeing with the premise of this book, which is that modern-day liberalism is based on a humanistic worldview and the associated morally relativistic foundation. Thomas Edsall, writing in the *Atlantic,* puts it this way: "Whereas elections once pitted the party of the working class against the party of Wall Street, they now pit voters who believe in a fixed and universal morality against those who see moral issues, especially sexual ones, as elastic and subject to personal choice."[8] Whether Edsall recognizes it or not, he is describing a worldview battle between Christianity and secular humanism.

Political writer and commentator Michael Barone understands that the issues of today are far more than political. He describes a worldview battle between those that knowingly or unknowingly embrace secular humanism and those that are influenced to some degree by the Christian worldview: "What demographic factor separates voters more than any other? The answer is religion. . . . The two Americas evident in the 48 percent [to] 48 percent 2000 election are two nations of different faiths. One is observant, tradition-minded, moralistic. The other is unobservant, liberation-minded, relativist."[9] Notice that Barone also describes the desire of liberals to be liberated—from any notion, laws, and worldview that restrict their freedom to do as they please.

Today's modern-day liberals desire to free themselves and America from God and the Christian worldview, the foundation of conservatism as well as our republic itself. They concern themselves less with America's war on terror than their own personal war on Christianity. Former secretary of labor in the Clinton administration, Robert B. Reich, echoes their perspective when he declares:

> The great conflict of the 21st century may be between the West and terrorism. But terrorism is a tactic, not a belief. The underlying battle will be between modern civilization and anti-modernist fanatics, between those who believe in the primacy of the individual and those who believe that human beings owe blind allegiance to a higher authority; between those who give priority to life in this world and those who believe that human life is no more than preparation for an existence beyond life; between those who believe that truth is revealed solely through scripture and religious dogma, and those who rely primarily on science, reason, and logic. Terrorism will disrupt and destroy lives. But terrorism is not the only danger we face.[10]

Do you realize what this former high-ranking U.S. government official has declared is equal to terrorism and is a foundational threat to America? That's right, conservative Christians.

Reich says today's worldview battle is "between modern civilization and *anti-modernist fanatics.*" If you don't believe, accept, and value postmodernism and its belief that all truth is created by man and not God, you are an anti-modernist fanatic. Reich himself acknowledges that today's worldview war is between secular humanists and Christians, "between those who believe in the primacy of the individual [secular humanism] and those who believe that human beings owe blind allegiance to a higher authority." He goes on to attack those that believe in life after death as well as the authority and validity of the Bible. If Reich and his radical liberal friends have their way, there may one day be a division in the U.S. Department of Homeland Security dedicated to monitoring not only terrorists but also tracking and prosecuting Christians that openly live out their Christian worldview.

In 2002, Charles Kimball, a college professor at a prominent university, wrote *When Religion Becomes Evil,* in which he suggests that one indication a religion has become evil is when it makes claims of absolute truth: "When zealous and devout adherents elevate teachings and belief of their tradition to the level of absolute truth, they open the door to the possibility that their religion will become evil."[11]

Ironically, Professor Kimball misses the point that, by his own definition, he is evil. Kimball maintains a religious worldview whether he cares to admit it or not. There is no such thing as a nonreligious worldview. All worldviews uphold some perspective about God and truth. The professor is practicing an evil religion by forcing on his students his absolute belief that Christians are evil.

The political arena is similarly awash in an anti-Christian point of view. In September of 2004, former vice president Al Gore showed his anti-Christian colors when he attacked the faith of President George W. Bush. In a twelve-thousand-word profile on his "life and times" in the *New Yorker* magazine, Gore revealed how the liberals like to preach tolerance but are the most intolerant. Here's what Gore had to say about the faith of President George W. Bush: "It's a particular kind of religiosity. It's the American version of the same fundamentalist impulse that we see in Saudi Arabia, in Kashmir, in religions around the world: Hindu, Jewish, Christian, Muslim."

Al Gore equated Wahhabi Islam—which has fostered beheadings, massacres, the September 11 attacks, the killing of children, and countless horrors—with the president's evangelical Christian faith. When was the last time an evangelical Christian beheaded someone, blew up a building filled with innocent people, flew a plane into an office tower, or slaughtered children in the name of God? Secularists may try to paint conservative Christians and radical Muslims with the same brush, but the facts mitigate against such attempts. Their worldview led Christians, instead, into "radical" activities like founding the American Red Cross, the Salvation Army, the first American hospitals, the first rescue missions for homeless people, and pro-life clinics that provide health-care and adoption services, which save thousands of babies from abortion each year.

President Bush may well have offended the postmodern crowd when he called the terrorists evil and sought to bring capitol punishment to bear upon them through the use of military force, but he has stated clearly in several interviews that he cannot separate his Christian faith from his job as president. That, as you no doubt know, drives the secularists crazy.

It is the worldviews of people like Al Gore, John Kerry, Ted Kennedy, Robert Reich, and their liberal, humanist compatriots that pose the real threat to America. Their worldview has resulted in the taking of innocent life through abortion and now active euthanasia in the case of Terri Schiavo.

The precursor to Adolf Hitler's annihilation of Jews and Christians was his murder of 275,000 handicapped individuals.[12] The worldview by which Al Gore and those of his ilk justify legislation and policies that allow for and fund the killing of unborn babies is the same worldview that allowed Hitler, Stalin, and Mussolini to justify the murder of millions. Hitler's paganism and hatred of Christianity fueled his vile regime. The Fuehrer once proclaimed, "The heaviest blow that ever struck humanity was the coming of Christianity." Heinrich Himmler, the brutal head of the Gestapo, dictated the policy that followed from Hitler's view: "We shall not rest until we have rooted out Christianity."[13]

Hitler's atrocities were birthed from a worldview that rejected God and His laws—a rejection that humanists in America share. The twentieth century was the bloodiest of all centuries, and humanism—the worldview of Robert Reich, the Third Reich, Al Gore, and Charles Kimball—was the foundation for those committing the atrocities. Such a comment may seem extreme to some Americans, but facts are facts. It has been the godless worldview of America's radical liberals that has permitted, encouraged, funded, and profited from *our* nation's holocaust—the slaughter of forty million unborn babies and counting. And now picking up steam in America is the liberal's barbaric love affair with active euthanasia.

As humanist liberals decry Christianity, they undermine the very worldview upon which America was founded, thus making themselves the true enemies of America. Founding father Dr. John Witherspoon would certainly agree with my analysis, for it was he who wrote, "[H]e is the best friend to American liberty who is most sincere and active in promoting true and undefiled religion and who sets himself with the greatest firmness to bear down on profanity and immorality of every kind. Whoever is an avowed enemy of God, I scruple not [do not hesitate] to call him an enemy to his country."[14]

Americans must realize that it is the worldview of humanistic liberals that poses the real threat to our American way of life. How can our nation long survive if the worldview of the secular humanists is allowed to permeate every American institution? According to William Provine of Cornell University, a prominent evolutionary biologist, the following are five foundational beliefs of a secular humanist: "There's no evidence for God, there's no life after death, there's no absolute foundation for right and wrong, there's no ultimate meaning for life, and people don't really have free will."

So who is promoting a false and dangerous worldview for America? Conservatives that desire to continue as one nation under God or liberals who daily move us closer to becoming one nation under *Man?*

In this book I will demonstrate that modern-day liberalism is anti-American and is based on the lying, evil religion of humanism. I will prove that your presuppositional worldview—that God is or that God is not—is the foundation of your worldview, upon which your values and actions are built. I will refute many popular untruths of the Left and reveal how humanism will cause America's inevitable demise if it continues to permeate our nation's public schools, universities, courts, legislatures, laws, and churches.

Conservatives are mistaken if they think we cannot lose this worldview war—and America with it. Although God is sovereign, He does not wear an American flag pin on His lapel. He can and will judge America if Christians don't stand up. I am tired of pious Christians that justify sitting in their easy pew, completely uninvolved in the battle because they claim simply to be "trusting God." Apathy is not trust. It is sin. As James 4:17 points out: "For the person who knows to do good and doesn't do it, it is a sin."

When the lines are this clear between those who want to be one nation under God and those who want to be one nation under man, how can any Christian *not* see his or her need to at least vote? I take God at His Word, and, as a result, I know He will allow America to be lost—sooner rather than later—if Christians don't do what they know is right.

God told Abraham He would not destroy Sodom and Gomorrah if He found only a few righteous. And perhaps God will spare America if enough Christians continue to oppose evil and faithfully fight the worldview battles of abortion, euthanasia, and same-sex marriage. In the fall of 2004, the issue of same-sex marriage was on the ballot in eleven states. All reaffirmed the definition of marriage as "one man with one woman," and of the eleven, ten were red states. Only Oregon "went blue" for John Kerry.

Had people who value a Christian worldview not voted on what they saw as religious-based issues, George W. Bush would not have been reelected in 2004. The crucial state of Ohio perhaps provides the best example. Phil Burris of Citizens for Community Values collected signatures to get Amendment 1—defining marriage as between one man and one woman—on the state's ballot. In the process, his organization also registered fifty-three thousand voters. Without Amendment 1, it is likely Christians would not have turned out as heavily as they did. Thus, President Bush would have lost Ohio and the election.

Winston Churchill once said, "If you will not fight for right when you can easily win without blood shed; if you will not fight when your victory is sure and not too costly; you may come to the moment when you will have to fight with all the odds against you and only a precarious chance of survival. There may even be a worse case. You may have to fight when there is no hope of victory, because it is better to perish than to live as slaves." Unless Americans recognize that liberal humanists hate truth, the U.S. Constitution, the Bill of Rights, and Christianity, we will soon be enslaved by the anti-Christian worldview they are implementing to varying degrees in every area of American life.

Do you doubt their hatred? Consider the following article by Dan Whitcomb of Reuters:

A California teacher has been barred by his school from giving students documents from American history that refer to God—including the Declaration of Independence.

Steven Williams, a fifth-grade teacher at Stevens Creek School in the San Francisco Bay area suburb of Cupertino, sued for discrimination on Monday, claiming he had been singled out for censorship by principal Patricia Vidmar because he is a Christian.

"It's a fact of American history that our founders were religious men, and to hide this fact from young fifth-graders in the name of political correctness is outrageous and shameful," said Williams' attorney, Terry Thompson.

"Williams wants to teach his students the true history of our country," he said. "There is nothing in the Establishment Clause (of the U.S. Constitution) that prohibits a teacher from showing students the Declaration of Independence."

Williams asserts in the lawsuit that since May he has been required to submit all of his lesson plans and supplemental handouts to Vidmar for approval, and that the principal will not permit him to use any that contain references to God or Christianity.

Among the materials she has rejected, according to Williams, are excerpts from the Declaration of Independence, George Washington's journal, John Adams' diary, Samuel Adams' "The Rights of the Colonists," and William Penn's "The Frame of Government of Pennsylvania."[15]

In 1776, a group of good men decided to fight because they believed in God-given rights, liberty, individualism, prosperity based on hard work and honesty, the right to keep and own what you work for, freedom of religion, freedom of speech, freedom from socialism, and a totalitarian repressive government. On a warm July 4, 1776, in Philadelphia, fifty-six brave men signed their names to the Declaration of Independence, stating, "With a firm reliance on the protection of Divine Providence, we mutually pledge to each other our lives, our fortunes, and our sacred honor."

Many of these were men of means. They owned land, livestock, homes, and businesses, and they risked it all for the one thing they could not buy—liberty. Freedom had to be earned. Even though it could not be purchased with money, liberty for America and these men came at a high price. Of the fifty-six, few were to get by for long without severe hardship. Five were captured by the British and tortured before they died. The homes of twelve—from Rhode Island to Charleston—were looted, occupied by the enemy, or burned. Two lost their sons in the war. Two sons of another were captured. Nine of the fifty-six died in the war that followed their courageous stand.

Those brave and noble men pledged and lost either their lives or the lives they had known. Though their fortunes may have been destroyed, their honor has remained intact to this very day. Will we be able to say the same of ourselves? Will our honor stand, or will our children and grandchildren ask why we did not follow the example of our founders? Will they wonder why, in our timidity, we allowed God to be kicked out of America? Will we be the generation in which we finally become one nation under *Man?*

Chapter 1

One Nation under God: Why It Really Matters

In July 1995, *Newsweek* magazine reported that nearly half of all Americans believe the United States will not exist in a hundred years. Such a notion alarms me to the core. As I see it, there is no reason to assume the United States of America shouldn't continue as a vibrant, healthy nation for centuries to come. But I also see that the doomsaying half of our citizenry may be disturbingly prophetic. If their prophesy comes true, it will result from the determined efforts of the most destructive force ever unleashed against America: the ideology of the liberal Left.

If Americans continue to allow radical liberals to use the courts as well as state and federal policy to undermine parental authority and religious liberties, to redefine marriage, and to eliminate America's national sovereignty, America as a free nation will indeed cease to exist, and it won't take the full one hundred years predicted. I believe it can happen within the lifetimes of many people reading this book today.

Your Presuppositional Worldview Matters

America is embroiled in a worldview war between those who want to be one nation under God and those campaigning to be one nation under man. This war between the conservative Right and the secular

Left begins with the presuppositions of each group. At the heart of each worldview is the question of whether God is or is not.

Christians start with the presuppositional worldview that God is alive and well and that God's moral law, which is a reflection of God's character and nature, is instilled in the laws of nature and engraved on the hearts and conscience of every person. Thus, it serves as the compass and foundation of all values, beliefs, ideas, and behavior.

The secular Left begins with the presuppositional worldview that God does not exist or that He doesn't matter; and thus instead of maintaining values, beliefs, ideas, and behavior based on the moral law of God, they trust in the minds of men and women. The secular Left believes individuals create their own reality and their own standards, and conduct their lives accordingly.

Individuals such as HBO's Bill Maher, former governor of Minnesota Jesse Ventura, and Americans United for the Separation of Church and State head Barry Lynn regularly bemoan, attack, and rail against people who believe in God. They consider us to be dangerous and, most likely, outright crazy. Bill Maher, host of *Real Time with Bill Maher*, explained in February 2005 on MSNBC's *Scarborough Country* just how wacko he believes Christians to be:

> We are a nation that is unenlightened because of religion. . . . I think that religion stops people from thinking. I think it justifies crazies. I think that flying planes into a building was a faith-based initiative. I think religion is a neurological disorder. If you look at it logically, it's something that was drilled into your head when you were a small child. . . . When you look at belief in such things—as do you go to heaven, is there a devil—we have more in common with [Muslim countries] Turkey and Iran and Syria than we do with European nations and Canada and nations that, yes, I would consider more enlightened than us.[1]

Maher said he wasn't speaking only of evangelicals but included all religious people. He noted that he agrees with Jesse Ventura "who had that quote about religion is a crutch for weak-minded people who need strength in numbers."[2]

What Maher, Ventura, Lynn, and other radical, secular liberals don't recognize is that—even as they bemoan the religion of others—

they are proclaiming their own. For the secular Left to say they do not have religious beliefs is to say they don't have any beliefs at all, that they don't have any assumptions, ideas, values, or thoughts. A religion, after all, is simply a collection of beliefs. One would have to be deceased not to have *any* beliefs, and thus I can proclaim confidently that every living human being holds religious beliefs of some sort.

Liberals use their liberal organizations, media outlets, the courts, legislatures, and government agencies to degrade or outlaw Christianity in public, while the government funds the religion of secular humanism in America's public schools. They have effectively deceived the majority of Americans into believing secular humanism is not a religion.

If this country had been founded by today's secular Left, not only would they have established a nation based on their religious worldview and presupposition that God is not; they would have created a government that does not allow for the public practice of Christianity or any other belief system incompatible with the elites who run things. The Left seeks to remove "under God" from the Pledge of Allegiance and eliminate congressional chaplains. They want to prohibit servicemen from saying "God bless you" at military funerals and to make sure no crosses are engraved on tombstones in a national cemetery.

Americans are embroiled in a religious worldview war for the very heart and soul of America. Our Founding Fathers knew whose side they were on. They built a strong foundation and left us a godly legacy on which to build our future. They primed us with everything we need to stand for God, and the battle is now ours to lose.

No Doubt about Who the Founders Were Under

Was America really founded as a "nation under God"—a *Christian* nation? Was there a biblical reason why our founders created a constitutional republic rather than a pure democracy? Or was America actually a secular endeavor by secular men? Was the American Revolution perhaps even contrary to the principles of Christianity?

To answer these questions, we'll examine the writings of the Founding Fathers themselves. But first, I want to cite two sources not known for being conservative. What have *Newsweek* and *Time* magazines had to say about the religious foundation of America?

In December 1982, *Newsweek* did a cover story examining the influence of the Bible on America. The story also discussed the fact that Ronald Reagan and the U.S. Congress declared 1983 the year of the Bible. *Newsweek* writes, "For centuries [the Bible] has exerted an unrivaled influence on American culture, politics, and social life. Now historians are discovering that the Bible, perhaps even more than the Constitution, is our founding document: The source of the powerful myth of the United States as a special, sacred nation, a people called by God to establish a model society, a beacon to the world."[3] Although I don't agree that it is any kind of myth, America was founded by men called by God, and I am pleased *Newsweek* acknowledged that the Bible was an intricate part of the foundation upon which the nation was built.

On May 25, 1987, *Time* published an article entitled "Looking to Its Roots" in which we read, "Ours is the only country deliberately founded on a good idea. That good idea combines a commitment to man's inalienable rights with the Calvinist belief in an ultimate moral right and sinful man's obligation to do good. These articles of faith, embodied in the Declaration of Independence and in the Constitution, literally govern our lives today."

Any American who wants to know whether America was founded as a nation under God only needs to spend a few hours reading the writings of the Founders. They were such prolific writers that, even today, handwritten letters and diaries by some of the Founders have not been read and studied. However, the thousands of personal writings, letters, journals, and speeches that have been examined reveal a far different picture than what the liberal revisionist historians want you to think.

After reviewing an estimated fifteen thousand items, including newspaper articles, pamphlets, books, monographs, and so on, written between 1760 and 1805 by the fifty-five men who signed the Constitution, professors Donald S. Lutz and Charles S. Hyneman presented their findings in a 1984 *American Political Science Review.* Their article, "The Relative Influence of European Writers on Late Eighteenth-Century American Political Thought," revealed that the Bible, especially the book of Deuteronomy, contributed 34 percent of all quotations used by our Founding Fathers.[4]

The other sources cited include:
- Baron Charles Montesquieu, 8.3 percent
- Sir William Blackstone, 7.9 percent
- John Locke, 2.9 percent
- David Hume, 2.7 percent
- Plutarch, 1.5 percent
- Beccaria, 1.5 percent
- Trenchard and Gordon, 1.4 percent
- Delolme, 1.4 percent
- Samuel von Pufendorf, 1.3 percent
- Cicero, 1.2 percent
- Hugo Grotius, 0.9 percent
- Shakespeare, 0.8 percent
- Vattel, 0.5 percent.

These additional sources also took 60 percent of their quotes from the Bible. Including both direct and indirect citations, the majority of all quotations referenced by the Founders come from Scripture.[5]

This is not surprising because many of the Founders were the top religious leaders of their day. Consider, for instance, the backgrounds of those who signed the Declaration of Independence (half of whom held seminary degrees):

- *Rev. Dr. John Witherspoon* was responsible for two American translations of the Bible, including America's first family Bible.
- *Charles Thompson* was responsible for *Thompson's Bible*.
- *Benjamin Rush* not only published the first mass-produced Bible in America, but he also founded America's first Bible Society and the Sunday School movement.
- *Francis Hopkins,* a church music director, produced the first purely American hymnbook.[6]
- *John Langdon* and *Charles Cotesworth Pinckney* founded the American Bible Society.
- *Rufus King* was founder of the New York Bible and Common Prayer Book Society.
- *James McHenry* founded the Maryland Bible Society.

- *Alexander Hamilton* formed the Christian Constitutional Society to elect people to office who would support Christianity and the Constitution of the United States.[7]
- *John Adams* wrote to Thomas Jefferson on June 28, 1813, "The general principles on which the fathers achieved independence were . . . the general principles of Christianity. . . . I will avow that I then believed, and now believe, that those general principles of Christianity are as eternal and immutable as the existence and attributes of God."
- *Thomas Jefferson* in 1774, while serving in the Virginia Assembly, personally introduced a resolution calling for a day of fasting and prayer. Later, while serving as the governor of Virginia (1779–81), Jefferson decreed a day of "Public and solemn thanksgiving and prayer to the Almighty God."
- *John Jay,* the original chief justice of the U.S. Supreme Court and one of the men most responsible for the Constitution, wrote, "Providence has given to our people the choice of their rulers, and it is the duty—as well as the privilege and interest—of our Christian nation to select and prefer Christians for their rulers."[8]
- *George Washington* in his Farewell Address argued for the vital role of religion and morality in our nation: "Of all the dispositions and habits, which lead to political prosperity, religion and morality are indispensable supports. In vain would that man claim the tribute of patriotism, who should labor to subvert these great pillars."[9] And also: "without such a firm foundation, liberties and freedoms were at risk: Let it simply be asked, 'Where is the security for life, for reputation, and for property, if the sense of religious obligation desert?'"[10]
- On June 28, 1787, frustrations were running high at the Constitutional Convention when Benjamin Franklin, arguably one of America's *least* religious founders, admonished his colleagues: "If a sparrow cannot fall to the ground without His notice, is it probable that an empire can rise without His aid? We've been assured in the sacred writing that 'Except the Lord build the house, they labor in vain that build it.'"[11]

How to Maintain a Utopian Paradise

John Adams, who served as our nation's first vice president under George Washington and then as the second president of the United States, so believed in the relevancy of the Bible that he wrote the following in his diary on February 22, 1756: "Suppose a nation in some distant region should take the Bible for their only law book, and every member should regulate his conduct by the precepts there exhibited! Every member would be obliged in conscience to temperance, frugality, and industry; to justice, kindness, and charity towards his fellow man; and to piety, love, and reverence toward Almighty God. . . . What a Utopia, what a Paradise would this region become?" He also noted, "We have no government capable of dealing with an irreligious people." In other words, those who disregard religion are disregarding what makes America the nation that it is.

I could fill hundreds of pages with quotes from our Founding Fathers proving that most of them, both publicly and privately, believed in the Christian worldview. Many of them were convinced that as long as we, as a nation, hold onto and protect our Christian heritage, we will flourish. Likewise, they also believed that if we deny and reject that heritage it will be the death of this nation they so loved.

To that end, George Washington wrote, "We ought to be no less persuaded that the propitious smiles of Heaven can never be expected on a nation that disregards the eternal rules of order and right, which Heaven itself has ordained."

Similarly, in his inaugural address on March 4, 1809, President James Madison declared, "We have all been encouraged to feel in the guardianship and guidance of that Almighty Being, whose power regulates the destiny of nations."

The Founders believed that Christianity's influence on this world would produce at least five tangible benefits:
1. A civilized society
2. Self-governing individuals
3. Good citizens
4. Elevated academic achievements
5. A stable society with a common values base.[12]

While extreme liberals denounce America's Christian heritage and history, many Christians have succumbed to revisionist history. Some who are conservative in their worldview and sound in their theology actually question whether or not America was founded with the approval of God and His providential assistance.

God, the Declaration of Independence, and the U.S. Constitution

If our founders were so intent on founding America as a secular nation as liberals claim, why did they reference God and the Bible throughout our nation's founding documents?

In the Declaration of Independence, God is mentioned four times:

1. "The Laws of Nature and of Nature's God." The "laws of nature" refer to the natural laws God instilled in man and creation. The laws of nature's God is a reference to God's laws as found in the Bible.
2. "All men are created equal, they are endowed by their Creator with certain unalienable Rights." The word *Creator* is a reference to the Creator God.
3. "Appealing to the Supreme Judge of the World for the Rectitude of our Intentions." The Supreme Judge of the World is a reference to God.
4. "With a firm Reliance on the Protection of Divine Providence. . . ." This is a reference to God's power, wisdom, and sovereignty.

Many liberals point out that neither God nor the Bible is mentioned in the U.S. Constitution. Because the Declaration of Independence was already established, however, the foundational role of God and the Bible had been laid. What liberals don't want you to understand is that the Declaration of Independence and the U.S. Constitution are equally important—the Declaration lays the foundation for the Constitution.

As Constitutional historian and legal expert John Eidsmoe points out:

> The Declaration has been repeatedly cited by the U.S. Supreme Court as part of the fundamental law of the United States of America. The *United States Code Annotated*

includes the Declaration of Independence under the heading "The Organic Laws of the United States of America" along with the Articles of Confederation, the Constitution, and the Northwest Ordinance. Enabling Acts frequently require states to adhere to the principles of the Declaration; in the Enabling Act of June 16, 1906, Congress authorized Oklahoma Territory to take steps to become a state. Section 3 provides that the Oklahoma Constitution "shall not be repugnant to the Constitution of the United States and the principles of the Declaration of Independence."[13]

Eidsmoe goes on to describe the relationship between the Declaration and the Constitution: "The Declaration is a statement of the basic American values or principles: equality, God-given rights. The Constitution is the means by which these rights are to be secured: a federal republic consisting of a federal government and state governments, with certain powers delegated to the federal government and others reserved for the states, with those powers separated into legislative, executive, and judicial branches. The Declaration is the foundation; the Constitution is the structure built on that foundation."[14] The Constitution is built on the Declaration of Independence, and the Declaration finds practical expression in the Constitution. Neither can be fully understood without the other.[15]

Why You Should Vote for People Who Believe in God

The American Civil Liberties Union (ACLU) and its allies believe themselves to be fighting Christian fundamentalists who want to create a theocracy by violating the so-called "separation of church and state." The ACLU's caricature of Christian motives aside, what we *are* fighting for is a principle the Founders understood well. If our nation rejects God's authority, we will be allowing ourselves to accept the only alternative, which is "man"—and the resulting government—as the ultimate authority.

The Declaration of Independence states, "All Men are created equal and are endowed by their Creator with certain unalienable Rights." The actions of our government should be based on whether or not it is fulfilling the purpose for which government was created: to protect our God-given rights. According to the Declaration, "to secure these Rights, Governments are instituted among men."

Clarence E. Manion, professor of constitutional law and dean of Notre Dame College of Law, was quoted in Verne Paul Kaub's book, *Collectivism Challenges Christianity*:

Look closely at these self-evident truths, these imperishable articles of American Faith upon which all our government is firmly based.

- First and foremost is the existence of God.
- Next comes the truth that all men are equal in the sight of God.
- Third is the fact of God's great gift of unalienable rights to every person on earth.
- Finally to preserve and protect these God-made rights of God-made man.[16]

A Firm Belief in a Power above Us

Benjamin Franklin contended, "Only a virtuous people are capable of freedom. As nations become corrupt and vicious, they have more need of masters."

In 1854 the U.S. House Judiciary Committee wrote: "Laws will not have permanence or power without the sanction of religious sentiment and without a firm belief that there is a Power above us that will reward our virtues and punish our vices."

If our leaders don't understand they will be held accountable in this life and the next to a deity above our governments, there is no accountability to rule with justice and mercy and to defend the righteous and punish the wicked. History has proven this point well. Hitler, Stalin, Mussolini, and many other tyrants who were professing atheists became our world's greatest mass murders.

If There Is No God or Creator

- If there is no God or creator, then everything happens by chance or by mistake.
- If there is no God, then man was not created in His image.
- If there is no God, then there is no right or wrong.
- If there is no God, there is only the natural world.

- If there is no God, then man does not have an eternal soul and there is no life after death.
- If there is no God, life has no meaning.
- If there is no God, man does not have a free will, for he is the product of his environment.

Yale University history professor Donald Kagan acknowledges the consequences of the worldview that says "God is dead." Based largely on the writings of Fredrick Nietzsche, this philosophy is often called nihilism. Kagan writes, "[A] vulgar form of Nihilism has a remarkable influence in our educational system through our universities. The consequences of the victory of such ideas would be enormous. If both religion and reason are removed, all that remains is will and power, where the only law is that of tooth and claw."[17]

If the government is the highest authority—and all rights are given to us by the government—then what the government *gives* the government also can take away. On the other hand, if our rights are given to us by the Creator, then they are "inalienable," for all people, for all times, and for all places. It remains possible, of course, that our rights can be infringed or violated, but they cannot rightly be taken away. If Americans would embrace this eternal truth, they would eagerly support the election of leaders who acknowledge God and their accountability to Him for how they lead.

Not only must we elect people of such commitment and character, but Americans must earnestly fight attempts by the ACLU and other humanist organizations and by liberals who try to eradicate God from our country. If Americans allow the Source of freedom, liberty, and justice to be removed or downplayed, then we will receive our just reward—enslavement at the hands of men and women of power.

In his 1961 inaugural address, President John F. Kennedy intoned, "The rights of man come not from the generosity of the state but from the hand of God."

On February 15, 1959, at an Attorney General's Conference, President Harry S. Truman warned, "If we don't have a proper fundamental moral background, we will finally end up with a totalitarian government which does not believe in rights for anybody except the State."

My friend Bill Federer, a prolific historian, correctly connects a leader's religious beliefs to the actions of the government:

> Thus it follows, that as long as a person is doing "actions," they have thoughts preceding those actions—and that collection of thoughts is that person's "system of belief" or "religion." As long as the government is doing "actions," the government has thoughts preceding those actions—and that collection of thought is the government's "system of belief" or "religion." So there can never really be a separation of "religion" and government—as long as the government is doing "actions" there are thoughts or beliefs underlying those actions. The ACLU is not trying to be "religion" neutral, but, in fact, it is promoting a religion —a "non-deity based" secular humanism system of belief.[18]

Hitler, Stalin, and Mussolini demonstrate the destruction that results when a leader doesn't believe in God, life after death, heaven, hell, or a judgment day on which he will be held accountable by the righteous Judge. In their atheistic worldviews, they were the highest authority. As a result, Hitler killed as many as six million Jews and five million non-Jews during his Holocaust; and while Stalin was the dictator of the Soviet Union, he killed some 20 to 40 million people according to experts. The twentieth century was the most murderous of any century in history, due largely to tyrants and dictators who did not acknowledge any authority higher than themselves. The *Congressional Record* wrote that 135 million people were killed by Communists in the twentieth century.[19]

Our Founders so believed in the importance of elected officials believing in a deity higher than government to which they were accountable that Benjamin Rush, known as the Founding Father who promoted the establishment of schools in America, said, "Such is my veneration for every religion that reveals the attributes of the Deity, or a future state of rewards and punishments, that I had rather see the opinion of Confucius or Mohamed inculcated upon our youth than see them grow up wholly devoid of a system of religious principles. But the religion I mean to recommend in this place is that of the New Testament."[20]

Benjamin Rush understood that religion—or a belief in God—made for great citizens. He also knew that if America's future educators were not firm in their belief in the Deity who rewards good and punishes evil, then our republican form of government would not last.

As we will explore later, the very form of government our Founders created required that not only the population but, moreover, those in the executive, legislative, and judicial branches of government acknowledge God and their accountability to Him. This belief was so central to early American leaders that even the individual states adopted constitutions that acknowledge God. Let's look at a few examples:

- *Maryland,* 1776 Preamble: "We the people of the state of Maryland, grateful to Almighty God for our civil and religious liberty . . . ."
- *Pennsylvania,* 1776 Preamble: "We, the people of Pennsylvania, grateful to Almighty God for the blessings of civil and religious liberty, and humbly invoking His guidance . . . ."
- *South Carolina,* 1778 Preamble: "We the people of the State of South Carolina . . . grateful to God for our liberties, do ordain and establish this Constitution. . . ."
- *Minnesota,* 1857 Preamble: "We, the people of the State of Minnesota, grateful to God for our civil and religious liberty, and desiring to perpetuate its blessings. . . ."
- *Alabama,* 1901 Preamble: "We the people of the State of Alabama, . . . invoking the favor and guidance of Almighty God, do ordain and establish the following Constitution. . . ."
- *Alaska,* 1956 Preamble: "We, the people of Alaska, grateful to God and to those who founded our nation and pioneered this great land . . . ."

I hope that before we forfeit our God-given rights to an increasingly powerful central government, Americans will once again grasp the need to acknowledge the Deity higher than the state, to reject the lies of those who oppose Him, and to cease voting for those that put themselves above God.

The Christian Worldview Reason for a Constitutional Republic

The Founders could have chosen among any number of forms of government. There were quite a variety of governing philosophies and worldviews floating around at the time of America's founding. However, the Founders deliberately chose a government they believed would best insure the preservation of the core, unchanging standards of liberty.

If asked, most people will say America was founded as a democracy. And, in truth, that is the way we typically refer to our nation—as "a democracy." It is crucial to understand, however, that America was—and is—a constitutional republic, not a democracy. A pure democracy would actually be bad news. Unfortunately, we are sliding quickly that way and are reaping the consequences. Let me explain.

In the Pledge of Allegiance, we affirm our loyalty "to the republic for which it [the flag] stands. . . ." Yet, many think of "a democracy" and "a constitutional republic" as interchangeable terms. In his book *The Church at the End of the 20th Century,* the late Christian philosopher Francis Schaeffer called democracy "the dictatorship of the 51 percent."

And in a U.S. War Department Training Manual published in 1928, we find the U.S. government's telling definition of a democracy: "A government of the masses. Authority derived through mass meeting or any other form of 'direct' expression. Results in mobocracy [mob rule]. Attitude toward property is communistic-negating property rights. Attitude toward law is that the will of the majority shall regulate, whether it be based upon deliberation or governed passion, prejudice, and impulse, without restraint or regard to consequences. Results in demagogism [trying to stir up people by appeals to emotion or prejudice in a attempt to establish a new leader], license, agitation, discontent, anarchy."[21]

The Founders spent countless hours studying various forms of government from all over the world and deliberately chose not to establish a democracy. In fact, the framers of the U.S. Constitution believed so strongly in the dangers of democracy that they included a provision in the Constitution requiring that "each State maintain a republican form of government."[22]

The Dangers of a Democracy

In a pure democracy, the majority rules—and has its way—on everything. The Founders characterized the dangers of such a government in no uncertain terms.

- Fisher Ames said, "A democracy is a volcano which conceals the fiery materials of its own destruction. These will produce an eruption, and carry desolation in their way."[23]
- Benjamin Rush said, "A simple democracy is the devil's own government."[24]
- John Adams said, "Remember, democracy never lasts long. It soon wastes, exhausts, and murders itself. There never was a democracy yet that did not commit suicide."[25]
- Noah Webster said, "In democracy . . . there are commonly tumults and disorders. . . . Therefore a pure democracy is generally a very bad government. It is often the most tyrannical government on earth."[26]
- John Witherspoon said, "Pure democracy cannot subsist long nor be carried far into the departments of state—it is very subject to caprice and the madness of popular rage."[27]

So if a democracy is so bad and America—thankfully—is not one, then what exactly is a "constitutional republic"?

Turning back to our 1928 U.S. War Department Training Manual, we read the following about a republic:

Authority is derived through the election by the people of public officials best fitted to represent them.

Attitude toward property is respect for laws and individual rights and a sensible economic procedure.

Attitude toward law is the administration of justice in accord with fixed principles and established evidence, with a strict regard to consequences. A greater number of citizens and extent of territory may be brought within its compass.

Avoids the dangerous extreme of either tyranny or monocracy——results in statesmanship, liberty, reason, justice, contentment, and progress. . . . Our Constitutional fathers, familiar with the strength and weakness of both autocracy and democracy, with fixed principles definitely in mind, defined a representative form of government. They made a very marked distinction between a republic and a democracy and said repeatedly and emphatically that they had founded a republic.[28]

Noah Webster told us the firm foundation and fixed principles of this republic must be that, "[O]ur citizens should early understand that the genuine source of correct republican principles is the Bible, particularly the New Testament, or the Christian religion."[29]

The Differences between a Republic and a Democracy

In his book *Keys to Good Government*, historian David Barton states, "The difference between a republic and a democracy is the source of its authority. In a democracy, whatever the people desire is what becomes policy. If a majority of the people decides that murder is no longer a crime, in a democracy, murder will no longer be a crime. However, not so in our republic: in our republic, murder will always be a crime, for murder is a crime in the Word of God. It is this foundation which has given our republic such enduring stability."[30]

John Adams said, "The very definition of a republic is 'an empire of laws and not of men.'"[31] The Founders chose a constitutional republic because they understood the heart of man was evil, and left to our own desires and intents people, over time, would naturally choose to do that which is wrong. The Bible clearly tells us that every way of a man is right in his own eyes (Prov. 21:2), that the heart is deceitful above all things and desperately wicked (Jer. 17:9), and that evil men and seducers shall become worse and worse, deceiving and being deceived (2 Tim. 3:13).

Alexander Hamilton in *The Federalist* poses the question and answers why we have government to begin with: "Why has government been instituted at all? Because the passions of men will not conform to the dictates of reason and justice without constraint. . . . [T]he infamy of a bad action is to be divided among a number, than . . . to fall singly upon one."[32]

America's Blueprint for the Law

So just what was the constraint the Founders considered to be the foundation of this republic? It is overwhelmingly documented that the base was the Bible, in which we find the principles and standards for every area of life. The foremost legal authority of the Founders' day was William Blackstone. *Blackstone's Commentaries* on the laws was introduced in 1766, and it became the law book of the Founding Fathers. In fact, *Blackstone's Commentaries* formed the basis of American law until 1920. Reflecting on our need to keep our laws consistent with God's laws, *Blackstone's Commentaries* states, "To instance in the case of murder: this is expressly forbidden by the Divine. . . . If any human law should allow or enjoin us to commit it, we are bound to transgress that human law. . . . But, with regard to matters that are . . . not commanded or forbidden by those superior laws such for instance, as exporting wool into foreign countries; here the . . . legislature has scope and opportunity to interpose."

This was also the worldview articulated by Alexander Hamilton when he wrote, "[T]he law . . . dictated by God Himself is, of course, superior in obligation to any other. It is binding over all the globe, in all countries, and at all times. No human laws are of any validity if contrary to this."[33]

Founder Rufus King backed up his friend Alexander Hamilton when he contended, "[T]he . . . law established by the Creator . . . extends over the whole globe, is everywhere and at all times binding upon mankind. . . . [T]his is the law of God by which He makes His way known to man and is paramount to all human control."[34]

Concerning American Christians and their belief in laws based on biblical truth and the need to adhere to and promote such laws, contemporary researcher George Barna writes, in his report *Practical Outcomes Replace Biblical Principles as the Moral Standard*, "In several instances there is a large gap between what people say is morally acceptable and what they say should be legal. This reflects the shift away from biblical principles and Christian values as the basis of modern law. Increasingly, Americans are looking for the law to reflect their personal preferences and desires rather than a universal set of absolutes based on God's dictates. If this trend continues then it stands to reason that we will inevitably experience increased instability in our laws, relationships and marketplace experiences."[35]

When asked why this change has occurred, Barna states that

religious institutions have failed to present a compelling case for the biblical basis of moral truth: "Most people do not believe there is any source of absolute moral truth. Even [self-professing] born-again individuals are abandoning the notion of law based on scriptural principles. Families, who hold a major responsibility for shaping the moral values and attitudes of children, are ill-equipped to do that job in relation to a Christian worldview or on the basis of a comprehensive and coherent notion of faith-based truth. The result is that busy people, regardless of their faith affiliation, wing it when it comes to moral decisions."[36]

Barna reveals that many Americans do not possess a knowledge of how God desires for us to live and to conduct the affairs of our nation. In another report, *Americans Are Most Likely to Base Truth on Feelings*, he notes: "The virtual disappearance of this cornerstone of the Christian faith—that is, God has communicated a series of moral principles in the Bible that are meant to be the basis of our thoughts and actions, regardless of our preferences, feelings or situations—is probably the best indicator of the waning strength of the Christian Church in America today."[37] We as a nation are continuing our downward spiral into lawlessness and disorder. The weakening and deterioration of America's freedoms and liberties will continue because we lack the key component for restoring them—a people who possess the knowledge and understanding of biblical truths necessary to support a republic.

David Barton underscores this concern in his book, *Original Intent*: "The Founders understood that Biblical values formed the basis of the republic and that the republic would be destroyed if the people's knowledge of those values should ever be lost. . . . Understanding the foundation of the American republic is a vital key toward protecting it. Therefore, in analyzing public policy remember to ask, 'Is this act consistent with our form of government?' and support or oppose the policy on that basis."[38]

Maintaining a Republic

Maintaining a republic is hard work and requires the election of individuals who understand the unique nature of our republic. To preserve the republic, we must elect men and women who have an understanding of God's instructions on how we are to live. This is why I'm so troubled that many pastors refuse to encourage church members to get involved in the political process and to vote in every election, whether local, state, or national. The likely reason is that many of our nation's pastors are products of liberal universities and seminaries and have bought into the "separation of church and state" myth. It's astounding that anyone who takes the time to understand the goals and philosophy of a constitutional republic as articulated by our Founders would believe the lie of separation.

The battle to display the Ten Commandments in America's courtrooms, for instance, is not only a religious battle but a battle to maintain the very foundation of America's form of government. Without the moral law of the Bible and without a Christian worldview, there is no foundation for the American republic. To separate our biblical worldview from our form of government would mean that we abolish the form of government intended by the Founders. And clearly, just such an abolition is the goal of groups such as the American Civil Liberties Union and other socialistic, communistic, or humanistic organizations that oppose the biblical worldview and distort America's godly heritage.

Education expert and founder Benjamin Rush believed the Bible should be a textbook in America's schools. A central reason was that the Bible presents the only worldview consistent with perpetuating the form of government chosen by the Founding Fathers. Rush argues, "We profess to be republicans, and yet we neglect the only means of establishing and perpetuating our republican forms of government; that is, the universal education of our youth in the principles of Christianity by means of the Bible. For this Divine Book, above all others, favors that equality among mankind, that respect for just laws, and those sober and frugal virtues which constitute the soul of republicanism."[39]

Dr. Jedidiah Morse, another Founding Father who believed Christianity to be the foundational worldview of America's republic, proclaimed, "Whenever the pillars of Christianity shall be overthrown, our present republican forms of government, and all the blessings which flow from them, must fall with them."[40]

It is clear, then, in order for our constitutional republic to flourish, elected officials must be convinced of the need to preserve our biblical foundation. A key responsibility is to appoint and confirm judges who share the desire to properly protect the republic. Correspondingly, we (the people) should demand the impeachment of elected officials and judges who do not uphold theirs oaths to adhere to our founding documents.

The Founders warned us repeatedly that we could not expect God's blessing or protection—and could very well face His wrath—if we ever make a practice of violating His principles. Engraved on the Jefferson Memorial in Washington, D.C., are these words of Thomas Jefferson, author of the Declaration of Independence and our third president: "God who gave us life gave us liberty. And can the liberties of a nation be thought secure when we have removed their only firm basis, a conviction in the minds of the people that these liberties are the gift of God? That they are not to be violated but with His wrath? Indeed, I tremble for my country when I reflect that God is just; that His justice cannot sleep forever."

Similarly, George Washington wrote, "We ought to be no less persuaded that the propitious smiles of Heaven can never be expected on a nation that disregards the eternal rules of order and right which Heaven itself has ordained."[41]

George Mason, the Father of the Bill of Rights, speaking at the Constitutional Convention, declared, "As nations cannot be rewarded or punished in the next world, so they must be in this. By an inevitable chain of causes and effects, Providence punishes national sins by national calamities."[42]

In *Original Intent,* David Barton again drives home the very important point that a nation's respect for God will be reflected in its laws, legislation, and policy: "Of course, considering the spiritual implications of a policy is important only if there is a God, only if He has established transcendent rights and wrongs, and only if He responds on that basis. However, if one accepts these 'ifs,' then public policy must be analyzed accordingly."[43] Regardless of what some Americans may want, every law, every piece of legislation, and all public policy must be consistent with the teachings of Scripture, or we are not operating under the rules of a constitutional republic.

Again, let me quote Benjamin Rush, to whom the Founders looked for wisdom regarding passing laws that contradict the laws of God: "Upon these two foundations, the law of nature and the law of revelation [the law of nature's God], depend all human laws; that is to say, no human laws should be suffered to contradict these."[44]

The basis of our freedom lies not in the whims of the majority but in holding the will of the people in check—by holding the will of the people accountable to an unchanging standard and measuring whether that will is just or unjust, good or evil, right or wrong.

We, the Democracy—Dependency and Demise

A democracy makes it possible for the majority to implement national policies that contradict divine laws. It also opens the door to fiscal policy that breeds dependency of the people and the resultant demise of our society. In 1787—roughly the time our original thirteen states adopted the Constitution—Alexander Tyler, a Scottish history professor at the University of Edinborough, had this to say about "The Fall of the Athenian Republic" some two thousand years prior: "A democracy is always temporary in nature; it simply cannot exist as a permanent form of government. A democracy will continue to exist up until the time that voters discover that they can vote themselves generous gifts from the public treasury. From that moment on, the majority always votes for the candidates who promise the most benefits from the public treasury, with the result that every democracy will finally collapse due to loose fiscal policy, (which is) always followed by a-dictatorship."[45] That is why our forefathers founded the United States of America as a republic rather than a democracy.

The average longevity of the world's greatest civilizations has been about two hundred years. These nations always progressed through the following sequence:
- From bondage to spiritual faith
- From spiritual faith to great courage
- From courage to liberty
- From liberty to abundance
- From abundance to complacency
- From complacency to apathy

- From apathy to dependence
- And from dependence back into bondage.

Keeping that progression in mind, consider several striking observations by Professor Joseph Olson of Hamline University School of Law in St. Paul, Minnesota. About the 2000 presidential election, he relates these statistics:

- Population of counties won by: Gore–127 million; Bush–143 million
- Square miles of land won by: Gore–580,000; Bush–2,242,700
- States won by: Gore–19; Bush–29
- Murder rate per 100,000 residents in counties won by: Gore–13.2; Bush–2.1

Professor Olson overlays these facts with this stunning observation: "In aggregate, the map of the territory Bush won was mostly the land owned by the tax-paying citizens of this great country. Gore's territory mostly encompassed those citizens living in government-owned tenements and living off government welfare." Olson believes the U.S. is now somewhere between the "complacency and apathy" phase of Professor Tyler's definition of democracy; with some 40 percent of the nation's population already having reached the "governmental dependency" phase.[46]

Not surprisingly, the 2004 map was virtually identical in the Bush vs. Kerry race for the White House.

Our True Heritage

Armed with this knowledge and respectful of the dangerous trends upon us, we must take ownership of our great responsibility to instruct our children, friends, family members, and fellow Americans in the true heritage of our constitutional republic and to make clear the protection, liberty, prosperity, and blessing that comes from following God's plan for all areas of our lives and our civil government. It is crucial that we educate as many as possible in the truth of a biblical worldview so they might join in the protection and strengthening of our constitutional republic.

America is the longest-standing constitutional republic in the history of the world. Yet, if Americans continue to allow humanistic liberals to kick God out of our country, the foundation of our freedoms will be destroyed. Our end will be as President Ronald Reagan warned: "If we ever forget that we are one nation under God, then we will be a nation gone under."

Chapter 2

The Liberals' Big Lie: Separation of Church and State

The liberal humanist desire to kick God out of America has been forged by an outright myth propagated through the deliberate misinterpretation of the Founders' original intent. Americans have bought the lie that the Founders were secular men who built a nation on secular ideas and principles.

The Phrase that Never Was

Most Americans believe the term "separation of church and state" is found in the U.S. Constitution, but it is not. If you're looking for a constitutional source for the idea, however, you will find it in the constitution of the former Soviet Union: "In order to ensure to citizens freedom of conscience, the church in the U.S.S.R. is separated from the State, and the school from the church. Freedom of religious worship and freedom of anti-religious propaganda is recognized for all citizens."[1]

Consistent with the intentions of those who framed the Soviet constitution, today's secular humanist liberals use the concept to enforce the belief that the religion of God should have no part in American civil government, policy, or laws at any level—local, state, or federal.

But what is the origin and true intent of the phrase "separation of church and state" here in the United States of America? It originated in a letter written by Thomas Jefferson on New Year's Day 1802, to the

Danbury Baptist Association. The Baptists had shared with Jefferson their fear that the government might establish a state church. In his letter, Jefferson reassured the group of clergyman that the First Amendment prohibits the U.S. Congress from establishing a state church. To clarify the intent, Jefferson declared that a wall of separation between church and state should be maintained in order to *keep the government* from interfering with the free exercise of religion: "I contemplate with solemn reverence that act of the whole American people which declared that their legislature should 'make no law respecting an establishment of religion, or prohibiting the free exercise,' thus building a wall of separation of Church and State."[2] In other words, the law is intended to place restrictions on the government, not upon the people!

It is disheartening to note that in 1947, and on numerous occasions thereafter, the U.S. Supreme Court took the phrase "separation of church and state" from Thomas Jefferson's letter and (shamelessly!) inverted the intended meaning of the phrase. As a result, Thomas Jefferson is now inaccurately perceived as an aggressive deist who wanted a secular America and who wanted to "keep the church in its place." Both ideas are gross misrepresentations of the truth.

Thomas Jefferson's Worldview

We've already touched on Thomas Jefferson's beliefs, but because his statement—however misused—is central to today's church/state issue, it is extremely important that we have an accurate understanding of this especially influential Founder. Let's take a look at his worldview.

He evidently believed in the real interaction between God and people in daily affairs. We mentioned earlier that, while serving in the Virginia Assembly, Jefferson called for the Day of Fasting and Prayer.[3] Later, while serving as the governor of Virginia (1779–81), Jefferson decreed a day of "public and solemn thanksgiving and prayer to Almighty God."[4] It was also he who penned in the Declaration of Independence the following statements:

- "We hold these truths to be self-evident that all men are created equal. That they are endowed by their creator with certain unalienable rights, that among these are life, liberty and the pursuit of happiness. . . ."

- "We, Therefore, the Representatives of the United States of America, in General Congress, Assembled, appealing to the Supreme Judge of the world for the rectitude of our intentions. . . ."
- "And for the support of this Declaration, with a firm reliance on the protection of Divine Providence, we mutually pledge to each other our Lives, our Fortunes, and our Sacred Honor."

Do these sound like the words of a man hostile to Christianity, someone who wanted a secular nation?

Another of Jefferson's acts is also very revealing. After the signing of the Declaration of Independence, a committee was organized to create a state seal that would reflect the new nation's worldview. Jefferson recommended, "The children of Israel in the wilderness, led by a cloud by day, and a pillar of fire by night."[5]

The words of Thomas Jefferson in 1798 leave little doubt that he would disapprove of the U.S. Supreme Court using—out of context—his separation phrase to justify "constitutional limits" on the religious liberties of Americans: "No power over the freedom of religion . . . [is] delegated to the United States by the Constitution."[6]

And for all those who say Thomas Jefferson would not have wanted America's students to pray in school, read the Bible, or invoke the name of God in their graduation speeches, consider another serious bit of evidence to the contrary. While serving as the third president of the United States, Thomas Jefferson chaired the school board for the District of Columbia. In that capacity, he wrote the first plan of education adopted by the city of Washington. His plan directs teachers to use the Bible and *Isaac Watts' Hymnal* as the primary books by which to teach reading.

Jefferson's writings and actions in favor of a biblical worldview are almost innumerable. Just to make sure there's no doubt in your mind where he stood, though, I'll list a few more examples.

- On March 23, 1801, Thomas Jefferson wrote to Moses Robinson: "The Christian Religion, when divested of the rags in which they [the clergy] have enveloped it, and brought to the original purity and simplicity of its benevolent institutor, is a religion of all others most friendly to liberty, science, and the freest expansion of the human mind."[7]

- On December 3, 1803, President Jefferson recommended that the U.S. Congress pass a treaty with the tribe of the Kaskaskia Indians. The treaty included one hundred dollars paid by the Federal treasury to a Catholic missionary.[8]
- President Jefferson also extended three times a 1787 act of Congress in which special lands were designated: "For the sole use of Christian Indians and the Moravian Brethren missionaries for civilizing the Indians and promoting Christianity."[9]
- President Jefferson signed bills which appropriated financial support for chaplains in Congress and in the armed forces.
- He signed the Articles of War on April 10, 1806, in which he, "Earnestly recommended to all officers and soldiers, diligently to attend divine services."[10]

So, you tell me. What would Thomas Jefferson say concerning federal judges prohibiting the state of Alabama from having a monument of the Ten Commandments in the lobby of the Alabama Supreme Court building? How would he react to a federal judge telling the students of Galveston, Texas, that they could not invoke the name of Jesus Christ in a graduation ceremony? What would Thomas Jefferson say to the U.S. Supreme Court that set national policy for every state in the union by ruling in 1962 the state of New York could not have students recite a prayer at the beginning of each school day? What would his position be on their 1963 ruling that made it illegal for Pennsylvania's students to begin each day by reading from the Bible? Where would Jefferson stand on their 1980 ruling that made it illegal for the state of Kentucky and every other state in the Union to post the Ten Commandments?

The answer is clear. He wrote a summary statement on January 23, 1808, to Samuel Miller:

I consider the government of the U.S. as interdicted [prohibited] by the Constitution from intermeddling with religious institutions, their doctrines disciples, or exercises. This results not only from the provision that no law shall be made respecting the establishment, or free exercise, of religion, but from that also which reserves to the states the powers not delegated to the U.S. [10th Amendment]. Certainly no power to prescribe any religious exercise or to assume authority in religious discipline has been delegated to the general government. It must then rest with the states as far as it can be in any human authority.[11]

If the humanistic, liberal, God-hating Americans actually knew and admitted what Thomas Jefferson believed, they would shift from using him as their secular "poster boy" to calling him a member of the religious right. Clearly, Thomas Jefferson—the very one upon whom they base their lie of church/state separation—would tell you what knowledgeable conservatives have been saying for years: the Federal government has no constitutional authority to tell the states what they can and cannot do when it comes to the free exercise of religion.

The truth is Thomas Jefferson believed America's form of government was supported by religion: "Deemed in other countries incompatible with good government and yet proved by our experience to be its best support."[12]

But what about the other Founders? Was perhaps a secular nation their intent?

The Founders, Christianity, and Government

Joseph Story served on the U.S. Supreme Court from 1811 to 1845, and in his commentaries on the Constitution of the United States, he wrote:

Now, there will probably be found few persons in this, or any other Christian country, who would deliberately contend, that it was unreasonable, or unjust to foster and encourage the Christian religion generally, as a matter of sound policy, as well as of revealed truth. In fact, every American colony, from its foundation down to the revolution, with the exception of Rhode Island, (If, indeed that state be an exception,) did openly, by the whole course of its laws and institutions, support and sustain, in some form, the Christian religion; and almost invariably gave a peculiar sanction to some of its fundamental doctrines. And this has continued to be the case in some of the states down to the present period, without the slightest suspicion, that it was against the principles of public law, or republican liberty.[13]

The reason Story mentions that some think Rhode Island should be an exception is that, in considering the place of the Ten Commandments in their system of law, "Rhode Island adopted the last six of the Commandments, but not the first four."[14]

The strategy of secular humanists is simple: If you say something often enough, people tend to believe it. So, in various forms, they repeat the myth that America's Founders held to a secular, deistic worldview.

Were the Founders Deists?

Deists generally do not believe the Bible is a book of supernaturally revealed truth from God to man. They also tend to believe God created the world and then "walked away"; the logical conclusion being that God does not govern in the affairs of men. So, knowing whether or not the Founders were deists is significant.

Dr. M. E. Bradford of the University of Dallas conducted a study of the Founders to look at this very important question. He discovered the Founders were members of denominations as follows: twenty-eight Episcopalians, eight Presbyterians, seven Congregationalists, two Lutherans, two Dutch Reformed, two Methodists, two Roman Catholics, and three deists.[15]

Notice Dr. Bradford's study found that only three out of fifty-five Founders were possibly deists. These are Hugh Williamson of North Carolina, James Wilson of Pennsylvania, and Benjamin Franklin of Pennsylvania. Hugh Williamson, though, was licensed to preach by the Presbyterian Church, which makes it questionable just how serious a deist he really was.

Benjamin Franklin clearly was a deist as a young man, but he later became disenchanted with deism. While Franklin probably never became a Christian in the orthodox sense, he came a long way from deism in his eighty-four years.[16] At the Great Convention it was Franklin who called for prayer, declaring that "God governs in the affairs of men."[17] (Remember, according to deism, God does not so intervene.)

Consider also this comment from Founder Noah Webster, author of *Webster's Dictionary,* who believed the rejection of a Christian worldview was at the root of all evil: "All the miseries and evils which men suffer from vice, crime, ambition, injustice, oppression, slavery, and war, proceed from their despising or neglecting the precepts contained in the Bible."[18]

Benjamin Rush, who helped found five schools and universities, wrote in 1791 about educational policy in which he discussed the danger of removing the Bible from America's schools: "In contemplating the political institutions of the United States, [if we remove the Bible from schools,] I lament that we waste so much time and money in punishing crimes and take so little pains to prevent them."[19]

Dr. Rush believed the best way to make sure our children become good citizens is to teach them to be good Christians by teaching them the Bible: "We profess to be republicans, and yet we neglect the only means of establishing and perpetuating our republican form of government; that is, the universal education of our youth in the principles of Christianity by means of the Bible. For this Divine Book, above all others, favors that equality among mankind, that respect for just laws, and those sober and frugal virtues which constitute the soul of republicanism."[20] He even lists specific reasons for using the Bible as a textbook in America's schools:

> Before I state my arguments in favor of teaching children to read by means of the Bible, I shall assume the five following propositions:
>
> I: That Christianity is the only true and perfect religion, and that in proportion as mankind adopts its principles and obeys its precepts, they will be wise and happy;
>
> II: That a better knowledge of this religion is to be acquired by reading the Bible than in any other way;
>
> III: That the Bible contains more knowledge necessary to man in his present state than any other book in the world;
>
> IV: That knowledge is most durable and religious instruction most useful when imparted in early life; and
>
> V: that the Bible, when not read in schools, is seldom read in any subsequent period of life.[21]

Robert Winthrop served as speaker of the House of Representatives and mentored Daniel Webster. Winthrop declared that when Christianity is practiced there is little need for stringent government; but if the Christian worldview were rejected, crime would increase and governmental force become more necessary. As a result, Americans would have less freedom:

> All societies must be governed in some way or other. The less they may have of stringent state government, the more they must have of individual self-government. The less they rely on public law or physical force, the more they must rely on private moral restraint. People, in a word, must necessarily be controlled, either by a power within them or by a power without them; either by the Word of God or by the strong arm of man; either by the Bible or by the bayonet. It may do for other countries and other governments to talk about the state supporting religion. Here, under our free institutions, it is religion which must support the state.[22]

President George Washington believed that it was impossible for a nation to be moral without religion: "[L]et us with caution indulge the supposition that morality can be maintained without religion. Whatever may be conceded to the influence of refined education on minds, . . . reason and experience both forbid us to expect that national morality can prevail in exclusion of religious principles."[23]

Rev. Dr. John Witherspoon, a signer of the Declaration of Independence and president of Princeton University (1768–76), so believed in the congruence of God and country that anyone who was not on the side of God was an enemy of America: "[H]e is the best friend to American liberty who is most sincere and active in promoting true and undefiled religion and who sets himself with the greatest firmness to bear down on profanity and immorality of every kind. Whoever is an avowed enemy of God, I scruple not [do not hesitate] to call him an enemy to his country."[24]

Founding Father Fisher Ames was responsible for the final wording of the First Amendment as passed by the House. And how did Ames feel about Christianity in America's schools? He was concerned that—even in his day—the Bible was taking a backseat to new text-books: "Why then, if these books for children must be retained, as they will be, should not the Bible regain the place it once held as a school book? Its morals are pure; its examples captivating and noble. The reverence for the Sacred Book that is thus early impressed lasts long, and probably, if not impressed in infancy, never takes firm hold of the mind."[25]

Even early outside observers could readily see the impact of Christianity on our country. Alexis de Tocqueville traveled from France to America to find out what made America great. Tocqueville shared his observations in his book, *The Republic of the United States* (sadly, the title of recent editions has been changed to Democracy in America). Tocqueville writes, "Upon my arrival in the United States, the religious aspect of the country was the first thing that struck my attention. And the longer I stayed there, the more did I perceive the great political consequences resulting from this state of things to which I was unaccustomed. In France, I had almost always seen the spirit of religion and the spirit of freedom pursing courses diametrically opposed to each other. But in America, I found that they were intimately united, they reigned in common over the same country."[26] Tocqueville did not perceive a separation between America's Christian religion and its institutions: "Religion in America . . . must . . . be regarded as the foremost of the political institutions of that country."[27]

Even into the middle of the nineteenth century, our leaders understood the inviolable connection between America's faith and its governing principles. On March 27, 1854, the U.S. Congress released a report stating, "Had the people, during the Revolution, had a suspicion of any attempt to war against Christianity, that Revolution would have been strangled in its cradle. At the time of the adoption of the Constitution, and the amendments, the universal sentiment was that Christianity should be encouraged, not any one sect. . . . In this age, there can be no substitute for Christianity. . . . That was the religion of the founders of the republic and they expect it to remain the religion of their descendants."[28] And two months later the U.S. Congress again declared, "The great, vital and conservative element in our system is the belief of our people, in the pure doctrines and the divine truths of the Gospel of Jesus Christ."[29]

The Ten Commandments in American Law

The deliberate use by our forefathers of the Ten Commandments as the foundation of America's legal system and constitutional republic is further evidence they never intended to create a secular nation or government. And they did not intend the First Amendment to be used as a tool to eradicate a religious foundation and religious expression and practices from American government.

Regarding the Ten Commandments, John Adams, Founding Father and second president of the United States, wrote, "The moment the idea is admitted into society that property is not as sacred as the laws of God, and that there is not a force of law and public justice to protect it, anarchy and tyranny commence. If 'Thou shalt not covet,' and 'Thou shalt not steal,' were not commandments of Heaven, they must be made inviolable precepts in every society, before it can be civilized or made free."[30]

His son, President John Quincy Adams, similarly declared, "The law given from Sinai was a civil and municipal as well as a moral and religious code, . . . laws essential to the existence of men in society and most of which have been enacted by every nation which ever professed any code of laws.[31] Vain indeed would be the search among the writings of profane antiquity [secular history] . . . to find so broad, so complete and so solid a basis for morality as this Decalogue [Ten Commandments] lays down."[32]

Noah Webster wrote that all governmental laws supporting justice and morality stem from the Christian religion and the Ten Commandments: "The opinion that human reason left without the constant control of Divine laws and commands will . . . give duration to a popular government is as chimerical [unlikely] as the most extravagant ideas that enter the head of a maniac. . . . Where will you find any code of laws among civilized men in which the commands and prohibitions are not founded on Christian principles? I need not specify the prohibitions of murder, robbery, theft [and] trespass."[33]

Without doubt, the Ten Commandments played a significant role in the development of American law. Even now, in his commentary, *The Ten Commandments in American Law and Government,* Matthew D. Staver writes, "When a governmental practice has been 'deeply embedded in the history and tradition of the country,' such a practice will not violate the Establishment Clause because the practice has become part of the 'fabric of our society.' (See *March vs. Chambers,* 463 U.S. 783, 786 [1983].) Similarly, the Supreme Court has often recognized the impact of the Ten Commandments on our system of law and government. (See *Griswold vs. Connecticut,* 381 U.S. 479, 529 n.2 [1965] Stewart, J. dissenting—most criminal prohibitions coincide with the prohibitions contained in the Ten Commandments.)"

Matthew Staver cites numerous federal cases that acknowledge the influence of the Ten Commandments on our nation. For instance:

- *McGowan vs. Maryland,* 366 U.S. 420, 450 (1961) (Frankfurter, J., concurring) ("Innumerable civil regulations enforce conduct which harmonizes with religious canons. State prohibitions of murder, theft and adultery reinforce commands of the Decalogue.")
- *Stone vs. Graham,* 449 U.S. 39, 45 (1980) (Rehnquist, J., dissenting) ("It is equally undeniable . . . that the Ten Commandments have had a significant impact on the development of secular legal codes of the Western World.")
- *Lynch vs. Donnelly,* 465 U.S. 668, 677–78 (1984) (describing the depiction of Moses with the Ten Commandments on the wall of the Supreme Court chamber and stating that such acknowledgments of religion demonstrate that "our history is pervaded by expression of religious beliefs").
- *Edwards vs. Aguillard,* 482 U.S. 578, 593–94 (1987) (acknowledges that the Ten Commandments did not play an exclusively religious role in the history of Western civilization).

That the Ten Commandments "did not play an exclusively religious role in the history of Western civilization" means their impact was not only for religious people and churches but for all of society.

Other courts and important leaders have similarly acknowledged the invaluable contribution of the Ten Commandments to our social order. In 1950, the Florida Supreme Court declared, "A people unschooled about the sovereignty of God, the Ten Commandments, and the ethics of Jesus could never have evolved the Bill of Rights, the Declaration of Independence, and the Constitution. There is not one solitary fundamental principle of our democratic policy that did not stem directly from the basic moral concepts as embodied in the Decalogue."[34]

In President Harry S. Truman's February 15, 1950, address before the Attorney General's Conference on Law Enforcement Problems in the Department of Justice, he declared, "The fundamental basis of this nation's laws was given to Moses on the Mount. The fundamental basis of our Bill of Rights comes from the teachings we get from Exodus and St. Matthew, from Isaiah and St. Paul. I don't think we emphasize that enough these days. If we don't have a proper fundamental moral background, we will finally end up with a totalitarian government, which does not believe in rights for anybody except the State!"[35]

Even leaders of other countries have been keenly aware of the role the Ten Commandments, God, and Christianity have played in America. Margaret Thatcher, former prime minister of the United Kingdom, said of America, "The Decalogue [Ten Commandments] are addressed to each and every person. This is the origin of our common humanity and of the sanctity of the individual. Each of us has a duty to try and carry out those commandments. . . . If you accept freedom, you've got to have principles and the responsibility. You can't do this without a biblical foundation. Your Founding Fathers came over with that. They came over with the doctrines of the New Testament as well as the Old. They looked after one another, not only as a matter of necessity, but as a matter of duty to their God. There is no other country in the world which started that way."[36]

In 1983 a United States district court in Virginia declared, "Further, biblical influences pervade many specific areas of law. The 'good Samaritan' laws use a phrase lifted directly out of one of Jesus' parables. The concept of the 'fertile octogenarian,' applicable to the law of wills and trusts, is in a large part derived from the book of Genesis where we are told that Sarah, the wife of the patriarch Abraham, gave birth to Isaac when she was 'past age.' In addition, the Ten Commandments have had immeasurable effect on Anglo-American legal development."[37]

In 1998, a Wisconsin appeals court quoted a 1974 Indiana Supreme Court opinion that stated, "Virtually all criminal laws are in one way or another the progeny of Judeo-Christian ethics. We have no intention to overrule the Ten Commandments."[38]

The True Meaning of the First Amendment

U.S. Supreme Court Justice Joseph Story explained succinctly the actual meaning of the First Amendment: "The whole power over the subject of religion is left exclusively to the State governments to be acted upon according to their own sense of justice and the State constitutions."[39]

The intent of the Founders was never to restrict religion. They were clearly concerned about the government's potential to interfere with religious freedoms, as can be seen in how they wrestled with the wording of the First Amendment. The original draft was introduced in the Senate on September 3, 1789, and stated, "Congress shall not make any law establishing any religious denomination." The second version stated, "Congress shall make no law establishing any particular denomination." The third version went a little further: "Congress shall make no law establishing any particular denomination in preference to another." The final version was even more sweeping: "Congress shall make no law establishing religion or prohibiting the free exercise thereof."[40]

By still another measure the Founders demonstrated their support for religious belief by requiring any territory applying for statehood to show respect for the "Northwest Ordinance." Article 3 of the ordinance declares, "Religion, morality, and knowledge, being necessary to good government and the happiness of mankind, schools and the means of education shall forever be encouraged."[41]

The Founders as individuals were committed to the Bible and Christianity, and for that reason as well, it stands to reason that the First Amendment was not intended to separate the Christian religion from the federal or state governments.

Protecting Religious Convictions

Joseph Story, who served on the U.S. Supreme Court (1811–45), believed the First Amendment was not written to suppress Christianity but to keep Christian denominations from vying for preference as the national religion. The Founders also did not want anyone—even if their beliefs were contrary to Christianity—to be persecuted for their convictions:

The real object of the First Amendment was not to coun-
tenance, much less to advance, Mohamedism, or Judaism,
or infidelity, by prostrating Christianity; but to exclude all
rivalry among Christian sects, and to prevent any national
ecclesiastical establishment, which should give to a hier-
archy the exclusive patronage of the national government.
It thus cut off the means of religious persecution (the vice
and pest of former ages), and of the subversion of the
rights of conscience in matters of religion which had been
trampled upon almost from the days of the Apostles to the
present age. . . . Probably at the time of the adoption of
the Constitution, and of the first amendment to it . . . the
general, if not the universal, sentiment in America was that
Christianity ought to receive encouragement from the State,
so far as was not incompatible with the previous rights of
conscience and the freedom of religious worship. An attempt
to level all religions and to make it a matter of state policy
to hold all in utter indifference would have created universal
disapprobation, if not universal indignation.[42]

Again, it is obvious that to "separate church from state" was
never the intent of the First Amendment. While the Founders clearly
were not secularists, the meaning of the amendment has been cor-
rupted by modern leaders who are and who want to re-create our
foundation.

The Tenth Amendment

The Tenth Amendment allows that the "powers not delegated
to the United States by the Constitution, nor prohibited by it to the
States, are reserved to the States respectively, or to the people."
Unfortunately, this amendment, too, has fallen victim to those who
want to secularize our world. Take for instance, the 1962 case *Engel
vs. Vitale*. The courts not only employed the "separation of church
and state" phrase but also violated the Tenth Amendment by telling
the state of New York it could not allow students to begin the school
day with a prayer. According to the Constitution, if the state of New
York wants their students to invoke a non-denominational prayer,

that is explicitly allowed under the Tenth Amendment. The state does have that right because the U.S. Constitution does not give the federal government the power to control the education or religious activities of any state in the Union.

Furthermore, even the First Amendment—supposedly represented by the "separation" concept—restricts only Congress from establishing a religion: "Congress shall make no law representing an establishment of religion, or prohibiting the free exercise thereof." Because the state of New York is not Congress, how could their state prayer policy be a violation of the First Amendment? Rightly interpreted, it simply is not. In truth, the U.S. Constitution leaves religious choices up to each individual and each state.

The original intent of the framers of the U.S. Constitution actually seems to have been that it was completely acceptable for any given state to establish a state religion if the people of that state so desired. In fact, attorney Ann Coulter points out, "It is a fact when the First Amendment was ratified, several states had established religions. Fortunately for the burgeoning minority religions in states, the established religions were things like 'Episcopalianism' and 'Congregationalism' rather than 'Liberalism.'"[43] So, the Founders thought religion was "OK enough" to allow states to establish an official religion if they thought that best. Quite a radical difference from where we find ourselves today!

Redefining "Church"

David Barton explains another striking reason why the 1962 U.S. Supreme Court ruling was so dangerous for every state and citizen in America: "In the 1962 case, the Court redefined the meaning and application of a single word: the word 'church.' For 170 years prior to that case, the word 'church'—as used in the phrase 'separation of church and state'—was defined to mean 'a federally established denomination.' However, in 1962 the Court explained that the word 'church' would now mean 'a religious activity in public.' This was the turning point in the interpretation of the First Amendment."[44]

Not only did the Court introduce a new meaning to the word *church,* but there was no historical precedent for such a radical move by the Court to strip states of their freedom of religion—to say nothing of a state's right to adopt a religious preference. Barton argues further: "The 1962 case which removed school prayer was the first case in Court history to use zero precedents. The Court quoted 'zero' previous legal cases. Without any historical or legal base, the Court simply made an announcement: 'We'll not have prayers in schools anymore; that violates the Constitution.' A brand new direction was taken in America."[45]

Hopefully about now you're scratching your head, trying to figure out how the U.S. Supreme Court managed to redefine the First Amendment and effectively nullify the Tenth Amendment just to force their own liberal worldview on the American people. Catch your breath. There's more.

The Liberals' Quiet Revolution

The changes that bloomed in the 1960s actually began about twenty years earlier. In 1947, the U.S. Supreme Court issued a ruling in the case of *Everson vs. Board of Education,* concerning whether it was constitutional for tax funds to pay for the transportation of students to a private, religious school. While it did not find it unconstitutional, the Court did, for the first time, use Thomas Jefferson's "wall of separation" phrase completely out of context. David Barton notes, "That Court, unlike previous courts, did not give the context of Jefferson's letter, and did not even mention that previous Supreme Courts had used Jefferson's letter to preserve religious values in public society. That 1947 Court was the first to use Jefferson's metaphor completely divorced from its context and intent."[46]

While it was troubling for the Court to use Jefferson's words out of context, the most disturbing part of the *Everson* case was the silent revolution the Court thus began. For all practical purposes, the justices held their own constitutional conventions in the 1940s (the first of a number of "Court conventions") in which they eliminated the Tenth Amendment and stripped every state in the Union of their constitutionally protected freedoms.

In *Original Intent,* David Barton explains the consequences America suffers to this day from the *Everson* decision:

In *Everson*, the Court took the Fourteenth Amendment (which dealt with specific State powers) and attached to it the First Amendment's federal provision that "Congress shall make no law respecting an establishment of religion."

The result of merging these two Amendments was two-fold: first, the Court reversed the bedrock constitutional demand that the First Amendment pertain only to the federal government; second, the Court declared that federal courts were now empowered to restrict not only the religious activities of the federal government but also those of States and individuals as well. The expansion of the Court's juris-diction in the *Everson* decision was accomplished only by direct violations of the purpose for which both the First and Fourteenth Amendments were enacted.[47]

U.S. Supreme Court Justice William Douglas, in *Walz vs. Tax Commission* (1970), comments on what he views as a "revolution" resulting from the unconstitutional linking of the First and Fourteenth Amendments: "reversing the historic position that the foundations of those liberties rested largely in State law. . . . [T]he revolution occasioned by the Fourteenth Amendment has progressed as Article after Article in the Bill of Rights has been [selectively] incorporated in it [the Fourteenth] and made applicable to the States."[48]

Turning the Bill of Rights on Its Head

Of the delegates that attended the Constitutional Convention in Philadelphia in 1787, only thirty-nine out of fifty-five signed the Constitution. Many of those who refused to sign the Constitution did so because they believed the Constitution did not contain the safeguards necessary to keep the central government in check. In addition, several states barely approved the Constitution, and North Carolina refused to ratify it until stricter limits were placed on the power of the federal government—to keep it from trampling the rights of the states.

In George Washington's first inaugural address, he asked Congress to amend the U.S. Constitution so as to further protect our freedoms, and on December 15, 1791, the first ten amendments—the Bill of

Rights—were ratified. These amendments were designed as ten hand-cuffs placed on the central government to limit its power and protect the God-given rights of the states and their people. In other words, the Bill of Rights was intended to protect the states from tyranny by the federal government.

Samuel Adams described this purpose when he wrote, "to see a line drawn as clearly as may be between the federal powers vested in Congress and distinct sovereignty of the several States upon which the private and personal rights of the citizens depend. Without such distinction there will be danger of the Constitution issuing imperceptibly and gradually into a consolidated government over all the States. . . . [T]he population of the U.S. live in different climates, of different education and manners, and possessed of different habits and feelings [and] under one consolidated government cannot long remain free."[49]

Beginning in 1940, in the case *Cantwell vs. Connecticut,* then in 1943, *Murdock vs. Pennsylvania,* and finally, in 1947, *Everson vs. Board of Education,* the U.S. Supreme Court re-defined the Fourteenth Amendment and laid the foundation for the silent revolution.

The Fourteenth Amendment

The damage done to the Fourteenth Amendment centers on this phrase: "All persons born or naturalized in the United States and subject to the jurisdiction thereof, are citizens of the United States and of the State wherein they reside. No State shall make or enforce any law which shall abridge the privileges or immunities of citizens of the United States."[50]

David Barton explains how the Court amended the Constitution and, by fiat, gathered unto itself unlimited—and unprecedented— power over every state in the Union: "In those decisions, the Court declared that the purpose of the Fourteenth Amendment was to limit the States not just on racial civil rights issues, but on the numerous items contained within the Bill of Rights. Under this reshaped purpose of the Fourteenth—and thereby under its new extended scope of power—the First Amendment would now limit every State and community, and no longer just the federal government as originally intended."[51]

With the 1940 (*Cantwell vs. Connecticut*), 1943 (*Murdock vs. Pennsylvania*), and 1947 (*Everson vs. Board of Education*) U.S. Supreme Court decisions, the Court took off the handcuffs that had restrained the federal government's power and placed those cuffs on the states. Now the federal courts were empowered to decide when and what rights the states could practice.

Stripping States of the Freedom of Religion (and More!)

Once the Fourteenth Amendment was misapplied by the Court— and Congress allowed it to stand—the Court was free to apply the Fourteenth Amendment to the First Amendment as it did in the *Everson vs. Board of Education*. What followed was a series of natural steps further in the direction of judicial tyranny.

In the 1963 case *Abington vs. Schempp*, the U.S. Supreme Court stated that this new national policy established by the 1947 *Everson* case settled the issue of the meaning of the First Amendment: "[T]his Court has decisively settled that the First Amendment's mandate that 'Congress shall make no law representing an establishment of religion, or prohibiting the free exercise thereof' has been made wholly applicable to the States by the Fourteenth Amendment. . . . The Fourteenth Amendment has rendered the legislature of the States as incompetent as Congress to enact such laws."[52]

In other words, by linking the First and Fourteenth Amendments, the Court declared that "Congress" is no longer simply a reference to the U.S. Congress. It now means a state through its legislature cannot allow, endorse, permit, or acknowledge any religious activities or symbols.

In 1970, U.S. Supreme Court Justice William Douglas openly acknowledged that the Court's 1947 decision infringed on state rights, and he recognized the revolutionary implications: "involved the imposition of new and far-reaching constitutional restraints on the States. Nationalization of many civil liberties has been the consequence of the Fourteenth Amendment, reversing the historic position that the foundations of those liberties rested largely in State law. . . . And so the revolution occasioned by the Fourteenth Amendment has

progressed as Article after Article in the Bill of Rights has been incorporated in it and made applicable to the States."[53]

As the Founders debated the First Amendment, they agreed the
First Amendment was crafted solely for the purpose of prohibiting the
federal government from establishing a church or national denomination. They were equally clear that if the people of any particular
state wanted to establish a state church of their own, the state government was free to do so. Supreme Court rulings from 1947 through
2000, though, have relentlessly attacked that freedom. The Court has
now succeeded in outlawing state-sponsored prayer in schools, Bible
reading, the posting of the Ten Commandments, and student-initiated
prayer. The Founding Fathers would be appalled that judges were
allowed to so ruthlessly use the Constitution to strip the states of
their God-given rights.

Ideas and Their Consequences

The courts are clogged with lawsuits filed by liberal groups such
as the ACLU and Americans United for the Separation of Church and
State (AU). Virtually every case is filed on behalf of someone or some
group alleging that another has violated the mythical separation
of church and state. Consequently, the separation lie has stripped
Americans of the right to openly practice the Christian faith anywhere
not approved by liberal judges. Several examples of the squashing of
religious freedom are worth noting:

- Patrick Cubbage was fired from the Brig. Gen. William C. Doyle
  Veterans' Memorial Cemetery in North Hanover, New Jersey,
  because the Department of Veteran Affairs did not want him to
  say "God Bless" when presenting the flag to veterans' families
  at funeral services.[54]
- A federal district court upheld a Washington high school's
  refusal to recognize a student Bible club as it had other student
  clubs. The Kent School District says other student clubs—
  including the Gay-Straight Alliance and Multicultural Student
  Union—are permissible, but a Bible club is not. The district has
  a non-discrimination policy that allegedly prevents all types
  of discrimination. However, the school actively discriminates

against the Bible club merely because it has a provision that voting members must actually believe in the Bible. While the Bible club is open to all students, it has a constitutionally protected right to establish voting membership qualifications in order to preserve the religious nature of the club. The Alliance Defense Fund is appealing the federal district court ruling.[55]

- A judge in Houston, Texas, ordered Harris County to remove a Bible from a monument outside its civil courts building, ruling that the display violates the constitutional separation of church and state.[56]

- A teacher's aide in Indiana County filed a federal civil rights lawsuit against her employer, saying she was unfairly suspended from her job for a year without pay for refusing to remove a small cross she wears as a necklace.[57]

- The Tennessee Department of Children's Services disapproves of the practice of a successful children's home taking its child residents to church each week. As a result, the state agency discontinued referring children to the care facility.[58]

- The ACLU successfully demanded that Breen Elementary School in Rocklin, California, remove a "God Bless America" sign posted after the attacks of September 11, 2001.[59]

Who's to Blame for Where We Are Today?

Some may shrug their shoulders and bemoan our predicament, assuming it got this way simply because there are no brakes on our runaway court system. That would suggest, though, that we are in an inevitable and unfixable situation—which we are not. The Founders anticipated such a problem by building "checks and balances" into the Constitution to keep the three branches of government operating within proper constraints. According to the Constitution, our legislative representatives are charged with the responsibility to counterbalance the power of the judicial branch, but, quite simply, the United States Congress has shirked its duty and utterly failed to restrain our overheating judiciary.

Congress has not required the judiciary to stay within the confines of its constitutional authority and responsibility. The final blame, however, does not rest even with the Congress. The primary reason legislators have not acted is because the American people have not demanded that Congress correct the mistakes of the U.S. Supreme Court and the liberal revolution that has stripped states and American citizens of religious liberty. Noah Webster warned that if America found itself in the shape we are today, it would be the fault of the people: "If [our] government fails to secure public prosperity and happiness, it must be because the citizens neglect the divine commands, and elect bad men to make and administer the laws."[60]

At one time, Americans were well versed in the Declaration of Independence, the Constitution, the Bill of Rights, and the *Federalist Papers*. We understood the civic process—how it works and why it is so important. Citizens knew the lessons of history well enough to assess current events by time-tested standards. Yet today, countless Americans are ignorant of even the most basic information such as the name of the vice president, the secretary of state, the attorney general, and the Speaker of the House.

If many Americans do not know who their most powerful leaders are, fewer still are familiar with laws being debated on Capitol Hill and argued before the courts, even though they impact Americans' faith, family, and freedoms. Most would not even recognize when freedoms are at risk because they don't know exactly what their God-given rights are and how the Founders intended to preserve them.

Riding the Fence

Among "we the people," there is one group which I think bears a special responsibility for the present state of our nation. Most of America's pastors have been virtually missing in action for years on substantive political issues. By contrast, pastors and religious leaders of the Founders' day preached not only the salvation message but also exhorted their congregations on the biblical response to the issues, whether it be slavery, gambling, drunkenness, voter participation, the biblical responsibilities of an elected official—including the type of judges we put into power—or the appropriate consequences for ungodly elected officials.

While America has pastors, priests, and religious leaders who stand tall, they are much too few and far between. The typical pastor in America today is liberal or leaning-liberal in their theology and politics. Even those who maintain a sound theology often are ignorant of how to apply biblical principles to the issues we face.

Many pastors do not realize the phrase "separation of church and state" is not found in the Constitution. They know next to nothing about our nation's founding and little of substance about the Christian worldview and how it applies to law, government, economics, education, and sociology. They do not recognize the threat of worldviews that compete with Christianity and that are stealing the souls of adults and young people alike in their churches. In many cases, these pastors not only have bought the "separation lie" but like doing so because accepting the lie makes life easier for them. They justify believing it by accepting the equally false notion of a dividing line between the "secular" and the "sacred." This way, pastors and religious leaders don't have to address topics in church that require them to pick a side instead of riding the fence. Most prefer this fence ride because it allows them to keep everybody happy while they fill pews and offering plates and build multimillion dollar churches as monuments to themselves and their success.

The problem fence-sitters try desperately to avoid is that as soon as a pastor embraces and practices a thoroughly biblical worldview that pastor is asking for controversy. Such a pastor must be willing to confront abortion, secular humanism in America's schools, and other controversial topics in sermons. Any firm stand is sure to offend a certain percentage of church members, who will simply take their money elsewhere and tell their friends about the narrow-minded church they just left.

This potential loss of a "paying customer" terrifies many church leaders. And if you don't think the majority of America's churches are run like businesses seeking to outdo the competition in order to garner more patrons, then walk the aisle of a Christian bookstore. Read the titles and back covers of the latest church growth propaganda, and a fairly clear picture will emerge. It's not pretty.

Because they are "up front," pastors are especially vulnerable but also especially responsible. A Christian worldview that acknowledges good and evil, right and wrong, and rejects our culture's worship at the new altar of tolerance, political correctness, moral relativism, and the New Age that says "all ways lead to God" will make waves.

Unfortunately, timid, whiney pastors are neither new nor uniquely American. Aside from a few German church leaders like Dietrich Bonhoeffer, who was executed in a Nazi concentration camp, the majority of pastors in World War II-era Germany did not have the courage of their convictions and did nothing to stop Adolph Hitler's murderous regime. The lesson, I believe, is that, aside from a handful of courageous pastors, most American church leaders will "go along to get along" right up until the day they find the doors to their churches chained and locked.

Why do I think the majority of America's Christian leaders are now more like castrated sheep than strong shepherds? Consider this: The Barna Research Group surveyed America's pastors and found "that only half of the country's Protestant pastors—51 percent—have a biblical worldview. Defining such a worldview as believing that absolute moral truth exists, that it is based upon the Bible, and having a biblical view on six core beliefs (the accuracy of biblical teaching, the sinless nature of Jesus, the literal existence of Satan, the omnipotence and omniscience of God, salvation by grace alone, and the personal responsibility to evangelize)."[61]

It's little wonder pastors are off base in their worldviews since most have been trained in institutions also stumbling toward liberalism. Aside from a few that still stand firm, America's Bible colleges and seminaries have been hijacked by religious liberals who themselves doubt America's godly heritage.

Many professors at our "Christian" colleges and universities are hostile to biblical faith even though the institutions in which they teach retain a Christian façade. They attack the authority and inerrancy of the Bible; they question the physical resurrection of Jesus Christ, His deity, His virgin birth; they take Bible verses out of context, and they completely ignore verses that call into question their preferred religion of tolerance, political correctness, and New Age spirituality.

What can you do about this issue? The first step is simple. If you're attending a church whose pastor would rather hide behind the "separation lie" than to face the implications of the real truth, then your part in solving our national crisis is to find another church.

Counter the Lie with Truth

The next step is to learn to counter lies with the truth. Memorize a few key points in this chapter, and the next time someone babbles about the "separation lie," set them straight. Don't be shocked if not everyone is open to hearing the truth, much less accepting and believing it. Overcoming years of brainwashing is not easy, particularly if the "lie" fits a person's liberal ideology and their desire to repress and eradicate the Christian worldview from America.

But I urge you to keep on keeping on—and to stay in keeping with our Founders.

Go ahead: Hold that school Bible study. Invoke the name of God or Jesus Christ in a graduation speech. Begin a city council meeting with prayer. Use your local park for a church service or patriotic concert that includes songs like "God Bless America" or "Amazing Grace," and be sure to find a local pastor who will offer a heartfelt, God-honoring prayer. Why not even have a student read a few verses from the Bible? Then when the liberals go nuts and threaten to sue, call up the American Family Association's Center for Law and Policy or Matt Staver's Liberty Counsel. These committed legal experts have argued cases all the way to the U.S. Supreme Court, and they do it for free because reversing the tide of judicial pollution is their mission. Believe me, if you call them with a solid case, you'll make their day.

Chapter 3

Modern-Day Liberalism Is Secular Humanism

Attorney and occasional Worldview Weekend speaker David Limbaugh is concerned about the same problem Ann Coulter, I, and many other conservative Americans find troubling: Modern-day liberalism is in fact the *religion* of secular humanism, but no one screams "separation!" when liberal, humanistic curriculum is continually used in American schools and funded by U.S. taxpayers. Limbaugh is clear: "If our self-professed separationists are truly motivated by the separationist principle, why don't they object when the government endorses values that are hostile to Christianity? Could it be their true motivation is a bias against Christian values?"[1]

To fully understand what is happening in the arena of humanism, we need to take a close look at the tactics—both blatant and stealthy—used by liberals to achieve their goals. (It may also be helpful for you to review the stark differences between the key elements of Christian and humanistic worldviews. I suggest you take a look at the summary chart in appendix 2 to give you quick access to the most important points.)

Let's begin by discussing how and where to recognize liberal humanism when you see it.

Not Every RINO Lives in Africa

When discussing politics, legislation, or judicial rulings, people often voice their approval or disapproval based on a general notion of whether they're liberal or conservative. The words do have specific meanings, however, and to make sure there is no confusion about what I mean when I say "liberal" and "conservative," I will define each term. But first, it is important to be aware that "Republican" and "Democrat" are not always synonymous with "conservative" and "liberal." Among Republicans, there are the RINOs—Republican In Name Only.

A RINO does not apply convictions based upon a biblical worldview to public policy. While they may say their worldview is Judeo-Christian, their endorsement of liberal social policies shouts otherwise.

Then there are the Log Cabin Republicans. Despite what they'd like you to think, their agenda bears no resemblance to anything the great Republican who grew up in a log cabin would stand for. These folks comprise a staunchly pro-homosexual group. The Log Cabins, RINOs, and those in the Republican Party who agree with their worldview are great examples of a decidedly liberal movement within the Republican Party. They're so left-wing that the Log Cabin Republicans, for instance, would not even endorse President George W. Bush for reelection in 2004 because of his strong support of traditional marriage.

Then there is Democrat and former governor and U.S. senator from Georgia Zell Miller. Senator Miller not only endorsed the reelection of President George W. Bush, but in his keynote speech at the Republican Presidential Convention in 2004, he slammed the Democratic Party for its radical liberalism, lack of common sense, and trampling of traditional values. While listening to Miller speak, I was reminded of some of the more liberal Republicans who are similar to the picture Miller painted of some Democrats.

Another Fence to Sit On

In addition to those within the traditionally conservative Republican Party who are not, there are people in both parties that swing left or right depending on shifts in the political wind. Rather than adopt a worldview approach, their position on any given issue sometimes seems more based on whim—or perhaps sound bite—

than on conviction. In fact, such moderates (sometimes called neo-conservatives) lack any deep conviction—religious or otherwise—thus making them a very interesting, or sad, case depending on how you look at it. Personally, I have more respect for the humanist who is truly committed to his definable worldview than for the moderate that simply has no strong convictions one way or the other.

Those with such a limp worldview are good only at adopting their values, ideas, and beliefs from whomever seems to be making the most persuasive case at the moment. They often check to see which way the wind is blowing or who else is following the parade before deciding what to think.

I also have little patience with neo-conservative Republicans who are passionate only about economic issues and the size of government while avoiding matters of underlying philosophy, ideology, or theology. To a true conservative the neo-conservative looks like an empty suit, an intellectual elitist absent without leave on the moral issues that make up the culture war—the worldview war.

What Is a Modern-Day Liberal?

So, if you can find liberals in both political parties, then what, exactly, is a liberal? My definition of a liberal is an individual whose worldview agrees with the following:

- Abortion on demand
- Doctor-assisted suicide and active euthanasia
- Man has no soul.
- Same-sex marriage
- Man is not accountable to the God of the Bible, and there will be no judgment day as in the Scriptures.
- There is no life beyond this world (but if there is, everyone will go to heaven or somewhere similar as long as they are sincere in their beliefs).
- Naturalistic, biological evolution
- Sex-education that includes educating children in kindergarten and up about tolerance for the homosexual lifestyle
- Redistribution of wealth through government programs, agencies, and policies

- The "separation of church and state," meaning Christians should sit down, shut up, and never be heard expressing their beliefs, convictions, or opinions based on a Christian world-view
- The growth of government
- The globalist agenda of the United Nations, especially such initiatives as the UN Convention on the Rights of the Child
- Absolute truth does not exist, thus everyone should act purely according to his or her own best interest (the only absolute is that there are no absolutes).
- People are basically good and do bad things solely because of their environment or social influences.
- The new tolerance movement that declares all ideas, life-styles, and beliefs must be accepted and valued. It claims all religions are equal, except Christianity, which is to be rejected as intolerant.
- Intolerance is defined as claiming to know what is right based on moral absolute truth.
- Radical environmentalism that infringes on free enterprise and private property rights
- A progressive tax system that punishes hard work, risk, and entrepreneurship
- The federal government should oversee all aspects of education from curriculum to testing.

Those committed to the liberal worldview are working, directly or indirectly, to undermine religious liberties in America because such freedom conflicts with their liberal philosophy. Modern-day liberalism effectively supports every facet of a secular humanist worldview.

What Is a Traditional Conservative?

By contrast, you could come up with a definition of conservative by simply taking the opposite side of each of the liberal proposi-tions. There are, however, conservative distinctives that bear a deeper explanation than that. Here's an outline of beliefs that define a conservative:

- The God of the Bible exists and created the world.

- God placed within each individual the ability to know right from wrong as defined by the moral law which the Bible articulates and says is also etched on the mind and conscience of every person.
- Absolute truth exists for all time, people, and places.
- Man was created in the image of God.
- Man has a soul that will live forever.
- Once a person leaves this world, he or she will be rewarded or punished based on how the person lived on earth.
- Man is responsible for his own actions and must be held accountable.
- Man has been placed on earth for a purpose that is larger and more important than self.
- America must defend and protect the sovereignty of the United States and oppose a one-world government and the globalist agenda.
- God is the creator of family, church, and civil government.
- Man has rights given to him by God that should not be infringed.
- There is no distinction between the secular and the sacred because all issues are religious issues.
- Marriage should be defined as "one man and one woman together for life."
- Free enterprise is the most effective system for freedom, liberty, and self-government.
- Limited and small government
- Freedom of religion
- The Constitution is a static document and should not be changed by judges legislating from the bench.
- Abortion is murder.
- Active euthanasia is murder.
- Parental authority is a biblical right and duty.
- Parents and local school boards should oversee the education of the children in their community.
- The ACLU definition of the separation of church and state is a lie.
- Public religious expression is not only constitutional but a benefit to society.

The foundation, then, on which a conservative bases his or her positions on important issues is the Christian worldview. Most conservatives, knowingly or unknowingly, have been influenced by the same biblical worldview on which the Founders based their structure for America's legal, governmental, economic, and ethical system.

A Christian worldview is also the basis on which conservatives battle our society's ongoing drift toward liberalism. Writing in one of his superb articles, "American Conservatism 1945–1995," Irving Kristol submits that Christians engage politically because of their overall commitment to a Christian worldview, a concern over the moral decline in America, and to combat our loss of religious freedoms:

Active religion-based conservatism did not become a political force in the United States because of either religion or conservatism. Its activism was provoked by militant liberalism and the militant secularism associated with it. This liberalism and this secularism, in the postwar years, came to dominate the Democratic Party, the educational establishment, the media, the law schools, the judiciary, the major schools of divinity, the bishops of the Catholic Church, and the bureaucracies of the "mainline" Protestant denominations. One day, so to speak, millions of American Christians—most of them, as it happened, registered Democrats—came to the realization that they were institutionally isolated and impotent. They quite naturally wanted their children to be raised as well-behaved Christians but discovered that their authority over their own children had been subverted and usurped by an aggressive, secular liberalism that now dominated our public education system and our popular culture. They looked at our high schools and saw that gay and lesbian organizations were free to distribute their literature to the students but that religious organizations were not. They saw condoms being distributed to adolescent teenagers while the Supreme Court forbade the posting of the Ten Commandments on the classroom wall. And so they rebelled and did the only thing left for them to do: They began to organize politically. In so doing they may very well have initiated a sea-change in American politics and American life.[2]

So, if conservatives base their worldview on the Bible, the Ten Commandments, and the writings of our Founders—who overwhelmingly based their beliefs, writings, and speeches on the Bible—then on what do liberals base their worldview?

Hint: Secular Humanism

John Dewey is one of the most honored humanists and socialists of all time. In one of his most definitive works, *Liberalism and Social Action,* he makes the case for socialism, humanism, and liberalism and bemoans the damage that will be done to liberalism if socialism's goal of redistributing wealth fails: "But the cause of liberalism will be lost for a considerable period if it is not prepared to go further and socialize the forces of production, now at hand, so that the liberty of individuals will be supported by the very structure of economics organization."[3]

This call for redistribution of wealth ("socialize the forces of production" is Dewey's euphemism), of course, is right out of *Humanist Manifesto I* (of which Dewey was a signer), *Humanist Manifesto II,* and *Humanist Manifesto* 2000.

John H. Bunzel, a former member of the U.S. Commission on Civil Rights, wrote an article, "Religion and Liberals," for the *Los Angeles Times* in which he openly admits what many have known for a long time—the Democratic Party is the comfortable home of humanistic atheists. Bunzel contends, "Millions of Americans do not believe in God. They do not invest moral authority in a transcendent source such as the Bible, or deal in absolutes of right and wrong, or dividing the world into simplistic categories of good and evil. Such people, and I include myself among them, have tended to find themselves more comfortable in the Democratic Party than in the Republican Party, where a marked strain of Christian fundamentalism runs strong."[4]

Even without God, humanists have crafted a sweeping, religious worldview. In an article from the *Journal of Higher Education,* Dr. Howard W. Hintz details the fact that secular humanism is a religion that forms the basis of liberal dogmatism:

Dr. Reed Bell, in his book, *Prescription Death: Compassionate Killers in the Medical Profession,* describes a bioethics course he attended at Vanderbilt University. The course, taught by John Lachs, was entitled "Individual Rights and the Public Good in the Treatment of Humans.:

On the first day of class, Lachs encouraged the students to be "open-minded" about the subject matter and to expect to change their mindset about the practice of medicine. Says Bell, "The professor's ethical discourse conveyed the primary message: that we should accept as ethical abortion, infanticide, condoned suicide, and euthanasia.

"After the first week," says Dr. Bell, "I approached the professor and asked him where these new ideas came from for the practice of medicine. He handed me a copy of the *Humanist Manifesto II* and told me this was the source of the New Ethic.

The Bible is censored from the classroom, only to be replaced by a new "Bible": *Humanist Manifestos, I, II, and 2000.*[5]

Organized (Secular) Religion

Which organizations are the largest repositories of liberalism in America today? Pretty much in order, it would be the Democratic National Committee (DNC), the ACLU, AU, and the National Education Association (NEA). Together, they've generated a system that makes me, like attorney Ann Coulter, sick and tired of having my tax dollars fund secular humanism masquerading as liberalism: "It's well past time for liberalism to be declared a religion and banned from public schools. Allowing Christians to be one of many after-school groups induces hysteria not just because liberals hate religion. It's because the public school is their temple. Children must be taught to love Big Brother, welcoming him to take over our schools, our bank accounts, our property and even our toilet bowls."[6]

But you don't have to take only Ann's—or my—word that secular humanism is the foundation of liberalism. I'll let the DNC, NEA, ACLU, and AU tell you in their own words. (There are, by the way, surprising connections between these organizations that may explain the success they've had in carrying out their liberal, dogmatic agenda. For instance, John Dewey, an avowed humanist, socialist, and celebrated liberal educator, helped establish the ACLU and was the honorary president of the NEA in 1932. And Barry Lynn, executive director of AU, worked for the ACLU for seven years.)

But back to letting the secularist, liberal organizations tell their own story. In 2003, for example, NEA federal policy manager Randall J. Moody announced plans to target sixteen states he thought the NEA could carry for a "pro-education" Democratic president against George W. Bush in 2004, and forty to forty-five House races where they could recruit "moderate" candidates. The NEA planned to raise funds for candidates, provide direct-mail services, and "turn out the vote."[7]

In the *Washington Times,* George Archibald discloses, "The president of the National Education Association acknowledges that the union is left-wing politically and 90 percent pro-Democrat but says he wants to reach out more to Republicans."[8]

And in a press release by the ACLU dated June 19, 2004, the ACLU writes, "The American Civil Liberties Union today asked the Democratic Party Platform Committee to include strong language in its 2004 platform to protect and promote civil liberties." (Using, of course, the ACLU's warped definition of "civil liberties.") The press release continues by quoting Laura W. Murphy, director of the ACLU Washington Legislative Office: "The time to take a stand is now, and the Democratic Party should take that stand with us."

The leanings of these organizations are no secret to outside observers, either. The NEA is so liberal it refuses to give quarter to any opinions of the conservatives who are forced to join in order to receive the necessary teacher liability insurance. Phyllis Schlafly notes, "The NEA accords no rights to the 30 percent of NEA members who are Republicans. Since 1976 when the NEA became a big player in national politics by supporting Jimmy Carter, the NEA has endorsed a Democrat for President in every election."[9]

Bill Bennett, the former U.S. secretary of education, made this comment regarding the NEA: "You're looking at the absolute heart and center of the Democratic Party."[10]

Both the NEA and the ACLU work closely with the DNC to further liberal policies in America. David Limbaugh observes, "It would be ludicrous for the NEA to deny its political activism. In 1996, it employed more political operatives than both major political parties combined. It would be just as ridiculous for it to deny its liberalism, but it does, claiming to be bipartisan. But since the NEA established its Political Action Committee in 1972, it has supported and endorsed every Democratic presidential candidate and has overwhelmingly supported Democratic candidates at the congressional level as well."[11]

In January 1999, *Investor's Business Daily* published an article delineating the NEA's liberal agenda and commitment to the liberal Democratic Party: "The nation's largest teacher union wants the U.S. to nationalize health care, start a nuclear freeze, adopt national energy policies and pass more gun-control laws. Yet it doesn't want teachers tested or schools privatized. . . . The NEA has long backed a left-wing political agenda. Many of its proposals seem far removed from improving teachers' working conditions. . . . The NEA's political action committee spent $6 million in the '96 election cycle; ninety-nine percent of its political action committee donations to candidates went to Democrats."[12]

Another test to see where an organization stands is to note who they consider to be their enemies. While the NEA is supposedly the great preserver of "the three Rs" in American education, its "public enemy number one" is the "two Rs." Yes, the NEA considers the Religious Right its nemesis. In 1997, the NEA published a guide for its members that explained how to oppose the "Radical Right" (as the NEA calls the Religious Right). So, allow me to say it clearly: The NEA, the ACLU, AU, and the DNC are specifically opposed to a Christian worldview.

I Survived the Anti-Christian Left

To the manifold observations of others, I can further the point by adding my own close encounter with the rabid intolerance of left-wing tolerance mongers. In March of 1996, I was invited by the Hamilton County School Board in (Chattanooga) Tennessee to offer the conservative opinion on a very liberal education plan under consideration.

The Public Education Foundation pitching the plan to Hamilton County was closely allied with Hillary Clinton, whose long-standing involvement with education policy dates back—even prior to being First Lady—to her stint as a board member of the National Center on Education and the Economy.

My appearance at the Hamilton County School Board meeting was so well advertised by parents who also opposed the liberal education plan that the event had to be moved to the largest school auditorium in the county. That night I spoke for over an hour to more than a thousand taxpayers and received several standing ovations as I aggressively criticized the wacky education plan. The education proposal had almost nothing to do with academics and everything to do with promoting outcome-based education, moral relativism, and political correctness. The plan even went so far as to give a new diploma to students who achieved the desired humanist and socialist worldview.

Not only that, first hiring preferences were to be given to these "achieving" students by local businessmen who might be looking for a dumbed-down, low-paid workforce that could perform menial tasks. Although I was well received by the common sense parents and taxpayers, local liberals from the NEA and its offspring, the PTA, attacked me viciously. In the next morning's Chattanooga newspaper, the local PTA president and NEA mouthpieces yammered, "Mr. Howse is an extremist comparable to that of the Ku Klux Klan and the black listings of the 1950s." Another NEA mouthpiece exploded, "Who will be the next speaker who comes to town, a terrorist with a gun in his belt?" For the next several days, NEA-lovers went after me with all they could in the local newspaper, television, and radio.

I must confess I wear that as a badge of honor. But as with winning any medal, it came with a price. Shortly after stepping off the stage to a standing ovation on the night of the board meeting, a livid supporter of the liberal education plan approached me and predicted I would be audited by the IRS. Although I shrugged off the comment at the time, to my amazement, within weeks, I received my audit notice from the IRS.

Looking back, I realize I shouldn't have been surprised. After all, I was opposing locally the very education plan the Clintons were trumpeting on a national level. Hamilton County was to be a test site—one of the first school districts in America to implement the Clinton education plan Hillary and her friends had been writing and speaking about when she was overseeing education in Arkansas. And because I was being critical not only of the Clintons' education agenda but also the NEA and PTA, I shouldn't have been shocked to be the focus of extreme and untrue insults, to say nothing of IRS harassment.

You see, liberal connections in education run deep. In December 1991, while angling for the presidency, Bill Clinton told the NEA candidate screening panel, "If I become President, you'll be my partners. I won't forget who brought me to the White House."[13]

Clinton kept his promise, and in 1993 while addressing NEA delegates, Clinton thanked the NEA for "the gift of our assistant secretary." The "gift" was former NEA staffer Sharon Robinson, who became the U.S. assistant secretary of education for the Office of Educational Research and Improvement. Clinton also reminded his allies, "I believe that the president of this organization [Keith Geiger] would say we have had the partnership I promised in the campaign in 1992."

The NEA's Commitment to Socialism and Humanism

The NEA's historical waters run deep, too. In 1929, John Dewey authored *Individualism, Old and New,* in which he wrote, "We are in for some kind of socialism; call it by whatever name we please, and no matter what it will be called when it is realized."[14]

That same year, after returning from the Soviet Union, Dewey published an article in the *New Republic.* In it, he fawned over the USSR's school system and the socialist worldview it instilled in its students: "the marvelous development of progressive education ideas and practices under the fostering care of the Bolshevist government . . . the required collective and cooperative mentality. . . . The great task of the school is to counteract and transform those domestic and neighborhood tendencies . . . the influence of home and church."[15]

After becoming one of the NEA's formative leaders as well as honorary president of the NEA, Dewey, in 1933, co-authored the *Humanist Manifesto.* And as if his position was still not quite clear enough, he wrote *A Common Faith* in which Dewey described his disdain for Christianity, its commitment to moral absolutes, and its contention about the sinfulness of man and need for a savior outside of himself. This John Dewey—the same one who traveled to Russia in the 1930s to help organize and implement the Marxist educational system there—is today known in America as the "Father of Progressive Education." And yes, this is the same John Dewey who, in 1935, became president of the League of Industrial Democracy, an organization originally called the Intercollegiate *Socialist* Society. To say the least, it puzzles me to think we should revere someone with such anti-American sentiments, and it should put us all on red alert against the rhetoric and influence of the NEA.

Reading Red-iness?

Even though a major one, John Dewey is *only one of many* Marxist influences in American education. As far back as 1940, a state of California senate committee investigated how various foundations were using their resources to promote certain philosophies and to control teacher training. The committee discovered the Rockefeller Foundation had spent millions of dollars rewriting history and creating new history books that undermined traditional patriotism and support for the free enterprise system.

The committee was shocked to discover that curriculum—which was funded by the Rockefellers and promoted by the NEA—taught blatantly socialist ideas. The committee reported, "It is difficult to believe that the Rockefeller Foundation and the National Education Association could have supported these textbooks. But the fact is that the Rockefellers financed them and the NEA promoted them very widely."

What is the motive behind the NEA removing traditional history from our schools? Quite simply: if our children do not know where they come from, they will not know where they are headed—or worse, they can be headed wherever the NEA wants to head them.

This approach is frighteningly parallel to Karl Marx's dictate: "Take away the heritage of a people and they are easily persuaded." Our heritage is decidedly on the side of individual freedom and

American sovereignty, and yet the NEA has actively promoted the United Nations and its global education plan. The NEA-supported, United States version of the UN plan goes by the euphemism, Goals 2000.

Although we think of it as a new idea, the globalization concept for education has a long pedigree among NEA socialists. In the January 1946 *NEA Journal,* editor Joy Elmer Morgan wrote an editorial entitled "The Teacher and World Government," in which she outlined a nefarious plan: "In the struggle to establish an adequate world government, the teacher . . . can do much to prepare the hearts and minds of children for global understanding and cooperation. . . . At the very top of all the agencies which will assure the coming of world government must stand the school, the teacher, and the organized profession."

Wow! Did you get that? One-world government starts in the classroom!

On a parallel track lies the educators' goal for eliminating free enterprise:

In the December 1933 *NEA Journal,* editor Morgan wrote an editorial calling for government control of corporations.

On June 29, 1938, the *New York Herald Tribune* reported on the NEA Convention being held in New York City: "Dr. Goodwin Watson, Professor of Education at Teachers College, Columbia University, begged the teachers of the nation to use their profession to indoctrinate children to overthrow 'conservative reactionaries' directing American government and industry. . . . (He) declared that Soviet Russia was one of the most notable international achievements of our generation."

The NEA's main objective has always been to assume national political power. It has publicly boasted of its plan to seize control of the agencies and boards that decide who is allowed to teach and what is to be taught. Now the most powerful special interest group in the U.S., the NEA's lobbying has brought about a seventeen-fold increase in federal education spending in the last twenty years. That translates into more central government control of education in America.

To make sure we're together on exactly where this powerful group stands on the many liberal vs. conservative issues of the day, here's a rundown of key ideals espoused by the NEA:

- Strongly supports hiring of homosexual teachers
- Believes union contracts with local school boards should require *all* teachers to pay dues or fees to the union
- Opposes merit pay for teachers
- Opposes voluntary prayer in schools
- Opposed tuition tax credit legislation
- Opposes the use of school facilities after school for voluntary religious meetings
- Opposes any constitutional amendment that requires a balancing of the federal budget
- Favors socialized medicine
- Spent millions of dollars in 1992 to elect Bill Clinton president and supported other liberal candidates for Congress

If you think these agenda items are simply a sideline to the NEA's central focus of encouraging excellence among its teachers, then think again. What does the NEA think about traditional teachers who obtain a teaching degree in order to inspire academic achievement and impart real knowledge to their students? Let the NEA speak for itself. In 1971, the NEA publication *Schools for the 70s and Beyond: A Call to Action,* declared, "Teachers who conform to the traditional institutional mode are out of place. They might find fulfillment as tap-dancers or guards in maximum security prisons or proprietors of reducing salons or agents of the Federal Bureau of Investigation—but they damage teaching, children, and themselves by staying in the classroom."

We're now well into our fourth decade of this prevailing attitude. As another example, then-president of the NEA George Fischer told NEA representatives during a 1971 assembly, "A good deal of work has been done to begin to bring about uniform certification controlled by the unified profession in each state. . . . With these new laws, we will finally realize our 113-year-old dream of controlling who enters, who stays, and who leaves the profession. Once this is done, we can also control the teacher training institutions."

If the NEA had its way, our nation's colleges and universities would be using cookie cutters to create American teachers. Under the NEA's uniform certification, every teacher leaving a training institution and entering the profession would be an anti-American socialist, working toward the goal of being "an agent of change." Every teacher under NEA control would want to indoctrinate—not educate—our children. Former NEA president Catherine Barrett, in the February 10, 1973, issue of *Saturday Review of Education,* makes clear the objective of this powerful organization: "Dramatic changes in the way we will raise our children in the year 2000 are indicated, particularly in terms of schooling. . . . When this happens—and it's near—the teacher can rise to his true calling. More than a dispenser of information, the teacher will be a conveyor of values, a philosopher. . . . We will be agents of change."

The teacher no longer teaches skills. He or she is now a philosopher who conveys "values." Is that why parents send their children to school? To be subjected every day to philosophical manipulation and indoctrination by the godless purveyors of humanistic "values"?

Make no mistake. The NEA will do whatever necessary to accomplish their goal, including intimidating or ostracizing teachers and parents (taxpayers—the ones paying teacher salaries, remember?) who disagree with their agenda and worldview. And by the way, the NEA has long wanted to make sure you can't grade its teachers on their work. In 1969, the *NEA Journal* published an article by Sidney Simon, who wrote, "The grading system is the most destructive, demeaning, and pointless thing in education."

Why does the NEA condemn letter grades? Because grades evidence the complete failure of our educational system under NEA's control. As long as there is a system of letter grades, the American people can determine whether their tax dollars are being used for what they were intended—the educating of children.

At their 1995 annual convention, the NEA passed resolutions that clearly show its liberal, humanistic, anti-American worldview:

> The NEA supports socialized medicine (which recognizes "domestic partners" as dependents), statehood for the District of Columbia, gun control, taxpayer benefits to illegal aliens, a national holiday honoring Caesar Chavez, ratification of the UN Treaty on the Rights of the Child. . . . The NEA even wants the purpose of Thanksgiving to be changed from thanking God to a celebration of "diversity.". . . The NEA even opposes "competency testing" for the hiring, evaluation, placement, or promotion of teachers.[16]

The NEA's extreme "religi-phobia" is demonstrated by an incident that occurred in July of 1997 at the NEA Convention. At the convention, "a choir of young black singers sang two religious songs, one of which was 'What a Mighty God We Serve.' The following day, NEA president Bob Chase apologized from the platform for the religious songs having been sung, as he emphasized they had not been cleared by the NEA. However, a lesbian caucus at the convention promoted a ninety-minute video titled 'It's Elementary: Teaching about Gay Issues in School.'"[17]

While some of the NEA's orientations may go both ways, clearly their religious inclusiveness does not.

The Outcome of Outcome-Based Education

The trickle-down of the NEA's high-ranking proclivity for things left of center has left some committed teachers drowning in a cascade of harassment. Adela Jones, a geometry teacher in Georgetown, Delaware, refused to grade on a curve, use grade inflation, or implement other trappings of Outcome-Based Education (OBE). Instead, Adela taught her classes using traditionally high standards for performance in a math class. Geometry, after all, is a college track course, and as far as she was concerned, there is one right answer to math problems. Consequently, her students should be graded on the absolute standard of right or wrong, correct or incorrect, understanding of the subject.

Predictably, because Adela's colleagues were more politically correct in their approach, Adela's classes had the highest failure rate of any teacher in the school. (And remember, no one is supposed to fail in OBE!) When administrators told Adela to bring her failure rate in line with the other teachers, she refused to play the numbers game simply to please the left-leaning administration and was fired.

Notably, Adela's students did not see her as a failure. On two different days, they walked out of school to protest her firing. They carried signs and banners proclaiming, "It was not Adela Jones' fault that I failed!" When "Dateline NBC" picked up the story, only one student went on camera to speak negatively about Adela, and even he said that, between geometry class and soccer, he could not keep up his grades.

The dismissal case went to court, where the judge learned of Adela's commitment to her students. Although often on duty from 7:00 a.m. to 7:00 p.m., she was happy to give extra instruction to any student who asked for help. In addition, she conducted a pre-test study group for those who wanted to participate. Students were even allowed to call Adela at home if they needed help in the evenings with their homework. Fortunately, the judge ordered the local school board to reinstate Adela Jones, but no wonder many excellent teachers are leaving the profession (and many who aren't leaving send their own children to private schools).

The Democratic National Committee: God Need Not Apply

While the Republican Party has its left-leaning constituents, the Democratic Party is so far liberal as to be not only anti-American but anti-God—not in word, of course, but since actions speak louder, let me give you only a few examples of what I mean.

In 2004, DNC Chairman Terry McAuliffe appointed Reverend Brenda Bartella Peterson as the senior advisor of Religious Outreach. Bartella was one of thirty-two clergy that filed a Supreme Court brief in the summer of 2004 to take the side of Michael Newdow, the atheist who sued to make it illegal for public school children to say, "under God" in the Pledge of Allegiance.

In June of 2005, DNC Chairman Howard Dean had no trouble proclaiming his disdain for Christian conservatives inside the Republican Party when he said, "They're a pretty monolithic party. It's pretty much a white conservative party." Dean later told NBC, "They have the agenda of the conservative Christians."[18]

If the Republican Party ever rejects the worldview of conservative Christians in totality, it will be to the detriment of the Republican National Committee—as it proved to be for the DNC when it radically embraced liberalism in the postwar years.

For several decades now, the Democratic Party platform and its major national candidates have embraced the same ideals as America's leading humanists. This includes many beliefs and values consistent with the *Humanist Manifestos,* such as:

- Unrestricted abortion on demand
- Partial-birth abortion
- Same-sex marriage
- Aggressive, progressive tax rates on Americans
- An inheritance tax that levies a tax on already taxed money
- De-funding of the American military
- Placing U.S. troops under UN control
- Increasing the power of the United Nations while weakening American sovereignty
- Opposing judges that believe in the sanctity of life
- Supporting judges who believe in "legislating from the bench" and opposing those who do not
- Opposing judges that believe in the myth of the separation of church and state as defined by the ACLU
- Funding school-based clinics that distribute contraceptives and provide abortion counseling
- Opposition to the posting of the Ten Commandments

You get the idea. There are *many* issues at stake. Few, however, have as far-reaching consequences as the liberals' liberal use of judicial power.

Radical Liberals Oppose Christian Judges

It only stands to reason that since the Democratic Party is filled largely with individuals who embrace a humanistic worldview, it is also a party hostile to Christianity and its adherents who unapologetically live out their Christian worldview.

In 1993, federal Judge Myron Thompson ordered the removal of the Ten Commandments from the lobby of the State of Alabama Supreme Court. Conservatives immediately went to work to stop this judicial attack on Alabama's religious liberty.

U.S. Congressman John Hostettler introduced an amendment prohibiting federal funds from being used to enforce Judge Thompson's order. Similarly, Rep. Robert Aderholt introduced (and the House twice passed) the Ten Commandments' Defense Act, allowing state and local communities—rather than federal judges—to have the final say in displays of the Ten Commandments. Senate Democrats, however, killed the bills each time.[19]

During the first and into the second term of George W. Bush, Democrats repeatedly refused to allow an up or down vote on the candidates President Bush submitted for federal judgeships. In every case, the Democrats opposed the president's nominees because of their Christian worldview—again, not in so many words, but the issues in play tell the story.

The president nominated Claude Allen for the federal Fourth Circuit Court of Appeals. Mr. Allen is a black conservative who home-schools his children. Mr. Allen had served in the Bush administration as the deputy secretary for the Department of Health and Human Services. While in that position, Mr. Allen expanded programs for youth that promote sexual abstinence until marriage. Democrats opposed Mr. Allen, stating he had a "radical record of opposition to a woman's right to choose, equal rights for gays and lesbians, and his unfounded and dangerous belief that denying students access to proper sex education will keep them safe."[20]

President Bush also appointed Janice Rogers Brown to the federal Ninth Circuit Court of Appeals, yet Democrats refused to allow an up or down vote on her confirmation for almost two years. Only after Republican leadership threatened to change the Senate rules was Judge Brown confirmed along with Judge Bill Pryor. Numerous Democrats voted against both of these judges along with a few RINO Republicans. Brown began serving on the California Supreme Court in 1996 and is known for her conservative record. Hers is an all-American success story:

> She is the daughter of a sharecropper and was born in the
> deep south during segregation; as a teen she picked cotton
> and she remembers the personal pain of the Jim Crow segre-
> gation laws; yet despite all of this, she has no bitterness; and
> her view of law has not been affected by her own personal
> experiences. In fact, she has even written an opinion against
> affirmative action (some would consider that very unusual
> for someone with her background); but she did so because
> the State [of California had passed] a ban (Prop 209) on affir-
> mative action, and she simply upheld the State law.[21]

So why would liberals oppose a black woman for the Court of Appeals, especially when there were, at the time of her appointment, only four female African Americans in the entire Court of Appeals system? Perhaps a significant part of the answer rests in a statement from her official biography that describes her as "a devoted mother and spouse, and a jurist who finds her paramount strength in prayer and the quiet study of the Bible." In fact, in a speech at a state law school, Brown declared, "Scientists and philosophers have spent the last hundred years trying to organize society as if God did not exist. . . . The[ir] project was a miserable failure."

And as if that weren't "bad enough," she wrote an opinion supporting a state parental-consent abortion law for teens. She even supports the Constitution's clause permitting the death penalty. All of this apparently is sufficient for Senate Democrats to filibuster her in an effort to prevent her from being placed in a federal court.[22]

And, of course, "white males" are not safe from the Democrats' prejudice against all things conservative, either. They opposed Bill Pryor's nomination to the federal Eleventh Circuit Court of Appeals because not only is he pro-life but he also rejects legal positivism—liberals' strategy of preference for using judges to revise the Constitution and to bring it more in line with their humanistic worldview.

During Pryor's Senate confirmation hearings, pro-abortion Democrats asked him if he stands by a comment in which he had declared the *Roe vs. Wade* decision is "the worst abomination in the history of constitutional law." Instead of evading the direct question, Mr. Pryor pointedly said, "I do." As he explained, "I believe that not only is the case unsupported by the text and structure of the Constitution, but it has led to a morally wrong result. It has led to the slaughter of millions of innocent unborn children. That's my personal belief." Pryor also asserted that in *Roe,* the Supreme Court had created "out of thin air a constitutional right to murder an unborn child" and that he would "never forget January 22, 1973 [the day the Court rendered the *Roe* decision]—the day seven members of our highest Court ripped up the Constitution."[23]

Wow! It doesn't take a political pundit to deduce that the Democrats opposed Pryor because they want to maintain laws that make it legal to kill unborn babies, but Mr. Pryor presented them with his annoying belief that every life is precious and has a God-given, constitutional right to life.

Now, even if you happen to believe what I'm about to say, the politically incorrect brashness will probably embarrass you. And there's no doubt I will send the intolerance meters of my detractors off the scale when I say this: While not every Democrat is an avowed secular or cosmic humanist, I don't know how anyone who professes to truly believe in the God of the Bible and the authority of His Word can be a Democrat. The stark difference of the Democrats' worldview is so unmistakably antithetical to biblical Christianity that I believe those who try to be both Christian and Democrat are either significantly ignorant of what it means to be one or the other, or else they are compromised to the point of delusion regarding what the two stand for. The worldview of a professing Christian and the platform positions of the Democratic Party are so opposed to one another, it is hard to conceive of how it would be possible for a truly committed and obedient follower of Jesus Christ to vote for a Democrat, let alone be an active member of the party.

American Civil Liberties (Soviet?) Union

"The most effective humanist organization for destroying the laws, morals, and traditional rights of Americans has been the ACLU. Founded in 1920, It is the legal arm of the humanist movement, established and nurtured by the Ethical Cultural Movement."[24]

I didn't make that up. David Noebel and Tim LaHaye, two of American's most perceptive observers of contemporary culture, make the case very clearly in their excellent book, *Mind Siege*. The history and practices of the ACLU strongly supports the conclusion that the organization has been a leader in undermining our constitutional liberties.

John Dewey—"father of modern education" in America, remember?—signed the *Humanist Manifesto I,* was a board member of the American Humanist Association, helped establish the League for Industrial Democracy, and helped create the American Civil Liberties Union. One of Dewey's co-founders was William Z. Foster, who had also been the head of the United States Communist Party.

But what about the ACLU founder himself, Roger Baldwin? What were his political and philosophical leanings? One hint is that on

January 20, 1920, he set up in New York City the first ACLU office—in space he shared with the Communist Party's tabloid, *New Masses.* In his book *The Family under Siege,* George Grant reports, "In 1920 he [Baldwin] also launched the Mutual Aid Society to offer financial help to leftist intellectuals, trade unionists, and the radical fringe."[25] Grant further recounts: "Baldwin also started the International Committee for Political Prisoners to provide counsel and support to anarchist and communist subversives who had been deported for their criminal activities. He helped to establish the American Fund for Public Service—with two million dollars donated by Charles Garland, a rich young revolutionary from Boston—in order to pour vast sums of money into revolutionary causes. And finally, he developed close institutional ties with the Communist movement and the Socialists International."[26]

Baldwin, Dewey, and Foster set the tone for what the ACLU would become, and today, where there is an attack on religious liberty, you can bet the ACLU is involved either directly or indirectly.

Eradicating religious freedom is only part of the ACLU agenda, though. Here is a list of "liberties" the ACLU hopes to legitimize in America:

- Legalized child pornography
- Abortion on demand
- Tax exemptions for Satanists
- Totally legalized drug use
- Mandatory sex education for all grades
- Legalized prostitution
- Legalized gambling
- Giving gays and lesbians the same legal benefits married people have
- Letting homosexuals become adoptive and foster parents
- Unconditional legal protection for flag-burners
- Greater benefits for illegal aliens and homosexuals who want to enter the U.S.

And the list of liberties the ACLU opposes? Pretty much everything conservatives support:

- Prayer in public school classrooms (as well as in locker rooms, sports arenas, graduation exercises, courtrooms, and legislative assemblies)

- Nativity scenes, crosses, and other Christian symbols on public property
- Voluntary Bible reading in public schools, even during free time and after class
- Imprinting "in God we trust" on our coins
- Access for students in Christian schools to any publicly funded services
- Accreditation for science departments at Bible-believing Christian universities
- The posting of the Ten Commandments in classrooms or courtrooms
- The words "under God" in the Pledge of Allegiance
- School officials searching students' lockers for drugs or guns
- Requiring people on welfare to work in exchange for their government aid
- Tax exemptions for Christian churches, ministries, and other charities
- Rating movies to alert parents about sex or violence
- Home-schooling
- Medical safety regulations and reporting of AIDS cases
- Public pro-life demonstrations
- Laws banning polygamy.[27]

If you still don't believe the ACLU has been one of America's most liberal and dangerous organizations from the get-go, consider the results of an investigation by the U.S. House of Representatives Special Committee on Communist Activities in the United States. On January 17, 1931, the committee report said this of the ACLU, just over ten years old at the time:

> The American Civil Liberties Union is closely affiliated with the communist movement in the United States, and fully 90 percent of its efforts are on behalf of communists who have come into conflict with the law. It claims to stand for free speech, free press, and free assembly, but it is quite apparent that the main function of the ACLU is to attempt to protect the communists in their advocacy of force and violence to overthrow the Government, replacing the American flag by a red flag and erecting a Soviet Government in place

of the republican form of government guaranteed to each state by the Federal Constitution.

Nearly four decades later, investigators from yet another source were still coming to the same conclusion about the organization. A police undercover agent, David D. Gumaer, revealed in 1969 that "206 past leading members of the ACLU had a combined record of 1,754 officially cited Communist front affiliations. . . . The present ACLU Board consists of sixty-eight members, thirty-one of whom have succeeded in amassing a total of at least 355 Communist Front Affiliations. That total does not include the citations of these individuals which appear in reports from the Senate International Security Subcommittee."[28]

Despite the clever name of the organization, "civil liberties" was not the real goal of Roger Baldwin. In fact, Baldwin was so committed to his radical liberalism that he was willing to use the power of governmental tyranny to "suppress" the masses and bring his worldview to bear: "When the power of the working class is once achieved, as it has been only in the Soviet Union, I am for maintaining it by any means whatever. No champion of a socialist society could fail to see that some suppression was necessary to achieve it."[29]

As for his atheistic, communist worldview, Baldwin, by his own admission, was not an "innocent liberal." His strategy was precise: "I joined. I don't regret being a part of the Communist tactic, which increased the effectiveness of a good cause. I knew what I was doing. I was not an innocent liberal. I wanted what the Communists wanted and I traveled the United Front road to get it."[30]

There you go, my friends. Roger Baldwin, the father of the ACLU and acclaimed liberal, admits he is a communist, and a communist by definition is an atheist and humanist. To accomplish his communist revolution in America, Baldwin's tactics are as true to communism as his underlying philosophy. It is a frighteningly effective tactic liberals in general have adopted as the means by which to achieve their goals—by using lies, deception, and lots of smoke and mirrors: "We want to look like patriots in everything we do. We want to get a lot of flags, talk a great deal about the Constitution and what our forefathers wanted to make of this country and how that we are the fellows that really stand for the spirit of our institutions."[31]

While appealing to the Constitution and waving the American flag, Baldwin and his liberal friends actually trash the Constitution, defend the right to burn the flag, and persecute genuine patriots in order to achieve their goals. Baldwin said, "I am for socialism, disarmament, and ultimately for abolishing the state itself as an instrument of violence and compulsion. I seek social ownership of property, the abolition of the propertied class, and sole control by those who produce wealth. Communism is the goal. It all sums up into one single purpose—the abolition of dog-eat-dog under which we live."[32]

The approach has been stunningly successful in many ways. For instance, despite Baldwin's hatred for the U.S. Constitution, America, God, private property, the free enterprise system, and freedom of religion, in 1981, then-President Jimmy Carter (a Democrat, in case you've forgotten) gave Baldwin the Medal of Freedom—our nation's highest civilian honor.

Fortunately, not everyone is blind to the ACLU's true intent:

Mark Campisano, former Supreme Court clerk for Justice William Brennan, has asserted, "An accounting of the ACLU's case load suggests that the organization is an ideological chameleon—that beneath the protective coloration of civil liberties, the ACLU is pursuing a very different agenda—a very liberal agenda."[33]

William Donohue has said the ACLU is the very definition of liberalism: "Social reform, in a liberal direction, is the *sine qua non* of the ACLU. Its record, far from showing a momentary wavering from impartiality, is replete with attempts to reform American society according to the wisdom of liberalism. The truth of the matter is that the ACLU has always been a highly politicized organization."[34]

In concluding this review of the ACLU, I will add that, besides fronting for communism, undermining American ideals, and crusading relentlessly against the freedoms we hold dear, the organization also shows a vile level of bad taste in the causes it celebrates. To wit, in the March 1978 issue of the *Skokie,* the ACLU rabidly defended "the right of American Nazis to march through a predominantly Jewish suburb of Chicago."[35]

So may I submit to you my suggestion for an alternate name to go with the initials ACLU? It may help you remember the organization's real agenda: American Communist and Leftist Union. And they're not alone.

Americans United for the Separation of Other Americans from Their Faith

Barry Lynn, president of AU, and his organization are opposed to many things religious but mostly things Christian—and most of all, everything evangelically Christian. Lynn has described evangelical Christians in such colorful terms as:

- radical religious fundamentalists
- bullies
- extremists who despise pro-choice advocates, working mothers, gay-rights
- smug, sneering, tyrannical, self-righteous, bigoted, hate-filled, and dangerous zealots.[36]

But of course Barry Lynn is one of the foremost preachers of tolerance. You can tell that from the way he describes Christians. After all, the liberal's definition of tolerance is to accept any belief as long as it is not rooted in Christianity.

AU was founded in 1947 under the name Protestants and Other Americans United for Separation of Church and State (POAU). Protestants were in the mix, of course, but so were groups like the American Humanist Association and the American Ethical Union, both of which deride Christianity as "superstition." Leadership included leftists Paul Blanshard, POAU's first general counsel, who claimed the church needed to "rise to the moral level of socialism," and Methodist Bishop G. Bromley Oxnam, POAU's first president. Oxnam was a former Planned Parenthood president and a fan of Stalin's Soviet Union who once chaired the Massachusetts Council of American Soviet Friendship.[37]

It should be of no surprise that ten veterans of AU's executive staff or governing boards signed onto *Humanist Manifesto II,* released in 1973.

So, as with the ACLU, let's look at a couple of examples of what AU supports. It backed the National Endowment for the Arts when the arts organization funded a crucifix dipped in urine. The AU cried censorship when the City of New York stopped funding a museum for displaying a dung-splattered painting of the Virgin Mary.

On the other hand, when the Federal Communications Commission attempted to force Christian radio stations in America to commit 50 percent of their daily programming in non-religious programs, AU supported the FCC position. Lynn went so far as to tell Focus on the Family's *Citizen* magazine that the FCC was "quite generous" to allow 50 percent Christian programming.[38]

In 1985, Lynn told the U.S. attorney general's Commission on Pornography that child pornography is protected by the First Amendment. While production of child pornography could be prevented by law, he argued its distribution could not. A few years later (1988), Lynn told the Senate Judiciary Committee that even requiring porn producers to maintain records of their performers' ages was not permissible.[39]

In addition, AU:

- opposes "In God We Trust" being printed on America's money
- opposes employing chaplains in the U.S. House of Representatives and the U.S. Senate
- opposes religious themes in public school memorials that honor slain students.

If Americans really knew what AU and Barry Lynn stood for, they would reject him as a God-hating liberal in favor of an all-powerful government that suppresses religious freedoms.

The Humanists' War against America's Heritage Occurs on Many Fronts

If for nothing else, the humanist movement can be admired for its thoroughgoing, tireless, disciplined, and stalwart battle against American values on many strategic fronts. To give you a rapid-fire sense of the sweeping battle lines of attack they follow, I've categorized below each "front" and outlined a few key examples of how the battle unfolds.

God and Freedom of Religion

Humanist Manifesto II: The separation of church and state and the separation of ideology and state are imperatives.

Humanist Manifesto II: "We find insufficient evidence for
belief in the existence of a supernatural."

NATIONAL EDUCATION ASSOCIATION

In a 1997 resolution, the NEA declared, "The Association opposes
any federal legislation or mandate that would require school districts
to schedule a moment of silence." And Resolution 26, in 2003, reads,
"The Association also opposes any federal legislation or mandate that
would require school districts to schedule a moment of silence."

AMERICAN CIVIL LIBERTIES UNION

In 1960, "the ACLU launched several legal initiatives to prohibit
Christmas decorations or the singing of carols in public schools or on
public property."[40] In the Regent's Prayer Case of 1962, "one of several
anti-prayers suits that the ACLU was involved in—lawyers argued that
a prayer recited each day in the New York public schools constituted
an unlawful 'establishment of religion.'" In 1976, the ACLU "brought
suit in New Jersey in an effort to prohibit Christmas pageants in the
public schools."[41]

In 1981, the ACLU took a case hoping "to prohibit the Gideons from
distributing Bibles to students in the public schools on the grounds
that such programs constitute a violation of the 'separation of church
and state.'"[42]

In 1986, "the ACLU was able to forbid religious invocations before
high school football games. For the first time, the lawyers successfully used 'endorsement' languages instead of the traditional 'establishment' language—the implication being that the government is
not only forbidden to establish or institutionalize religion, it is even
forbidden to endorse or condone it."[43]

In 2004, the ACLU sued the City of San Diego for renting property
to the Boy Scouts (the ACLU objects to the Boy Scouts' commitment
not to allow homosexual Scout leaders or to admit atheists).

Censorship of Creationism

Humanist Manifesto I: "Humanism believes that man is
part of nature and that he has emerged as a result of a con-
tinuous process."

NATIONAL EDUCATION ASSOCIATION

The NEA newsletter *In Brief* stated, "Radical right extremists are also attempting to impose a curriculum that mirrors their values and inculcates fundamentalist Christianity. . . . In communities all over the country, members of the religious right have attempted to impose censorship and the teaching of creationism on the public schools."[44]

"The Association . . . believes that legislation and regulations that mandate the teaching of religious doctrines, such as so-called 'creation science,' violate both student and teacher rights. The Association urges its affiliates to seek repeal of such mandates where they exist."[45]

AMERICAN CIVIL LIBERTIES UNION

The main argument of the ACLU in the Scopes Trail in 1925 was that "it is bigotry for public schools to teach only one theory of origins (creation). The ACLU launched its 'manipulated test case' strategy against the state of Tennessee's education standards, locating a small town biology teacher to act as a plaintiff and a showcase lawyer to focus national attention on the issue. Despite the fact the ACLU and its high profile defender, Clarence Darrow, lost to the state's attorney William Jennings Bryan, the publicity proved to be invaluable."[46]

In August of 2003, the ACLU filed a lawsuit seeking to force the Cobb County School (Georgia) board to remove disclaimers about evolution from high school textbooks. The stickers state that evolution is a theory not a fact and should be critically considered.[47]

In the Arkansas Creation Case of 1982, "fifty-six years after it had argued against educational exclusionism in the Scopes Trial, the ACLU reversed itself, fighting against the right to teach various views of origins in public school classrooms."[48]

Commitment to Situational Ethics and Moral Relativism

Humanist Manifesto II: "We affirm that moral values derive their source from human experience. Ethics is autonomous and situational. Ethics stem from human need and interest."

AMERICAN CIVIL LIBERTIES UNION

"The American Civil Liberties Union (ACLU) opposes criminal prohibition of drugs. Not only is prohibition a proven failure as a drug control strategy, but it subjects otherwise law-abiding citizens to arrest, prosecution and imprisonment for what they do in private."[49]

Euthanasia, Suicide, and Abortion

> *Humanist Manifesto II:* "It also includes recognition of an individual's right to die with dignity, euthanasia, and the right to suicide."
>
> *Humanist Manifesto II:* "The right to birth control, abortion . . ."

NATIONAL EDUCATION ASSOCIATION

NEA Resolution 12 in 2003 stated that the NEA supports family planning, including the right to "reproductive freedom" (a common euphemism for allowing abortion).

THE DEMOCRATIC NATIONAL COMMITTEE PLATFORM 2000

"The Party stands behind the right of every woman to choose, consistent with *Roe vs. Wade,* and regardless of ability to pay. We believe it is a fundamental constitutional liberty that individual Americans—not government—can best take responsibility for making the most difficult and intensely personal decisions regarding reproduction."

AMERICAN CIVIL LIBERTIES UNION

"The ACLU was the first national organization to argue for abortion rights before the Supreme Court, and has been the principal defender of those rights since 1973, when the Court recognized the right to choose in *Roe vs. Wade.*"[50]

In the *Doe vs. Bolton* case of 1973 "the ACLU led the legal fight in a case that—with the companion *Roe vs. Wade* ruling—eventually overturned the restrictive abortion laws in all fifty states."[51]

In the *Akron* case of 1983 "the ACLU successfully fought to overturn the right of localities to regulate the medical safety and the proper disclosure of abortion-related businesses."[52]

In 2004, the ACLU fought to have the courts force the sheriff of Phoenix, Arizona, to use taxpayer funds to transport female prisoners to and from abortion clinics.

War on Parental Authority

> *Humanist Manifesto 2000:* Although parental moral guidance is vital, parents should not simply impose their own religious outlook or moral values on their children or indoctrinate them. Children, adolescents, and young adults should have exposure to different viewpoints and enjoy encouragement to think for themselves. The view of even young children should be respected.

AMERICAN CIVIL LIBERTIES UNION

"ACLU applauds Appeals Court decision upholding minors' right to confidential abortions."[53] (In other words, the ACLU wants minor children to be able to have an abortion without their parents' knowledge.)

NATIONAL EDUCATION ASSOCIATION

The NEA, in *Today's Education 1983–84,* stated its belief that communications between certified personnel and students must be legally privileged. It urged its affiliates to aid in seeking legislation that provides this privilege and protects both educators and students.

Commitment to Hedonism and Sex Education for Children

> *Humanist Manifesto I:* "The quest for the good life is still the central task for mankind."
>
> *Humanist Manifesto II:* "We strive for the good life, here and now." "Neither do we wish to prohibit, by law or social sanction, sexual behavior between consenting adults. The many varieties of sexual exploration should not in themselves be considered 'evil.'"
>
> *Humanist Manifesto 2000:* "The opportunity for appropriate sexual education should be made available from an early age. This should include responsible behavior, family planning, and contraceptive techniques."

NATIONAL EDUCATION ASSOCIATION

"The Association urges its affiliates and members to support appropriately established sex education programs, including information on . . . birth control and family planning . . . diversity of sexual orientation."

AMERICAN CIVIL LIBERTIES UNION

In 2004 the ACLU filed a lawsuit challenging a Virginia state law that bans nude summer camps for teenagers. A nude camp was being sponsored in Virginia for students ages eleven to eighteen, and the ACLU opposed the legislation that said the students had to have a parent or guardian present.

Commitment to Redistribution of Wealth (Socialism)

> *Humanist Manifesto I:* "A socialized and cooperative economic order must be established to the end that the equitable distribution of the means of life be possible."

> *Humanist Manifesto II:* "We need to democratize the economy and judge it by its responsiveness to human needs, testing results in terms of the common good."

> *Humanist Manifesto 2000:* "We should strive to provide economic security and adequate income for everyone."

In the Sacco and Vanzetti case of 1927, the ACLU defended two notorious anarchists who had been charged with first-degree murder following a payroll robbery. With a long list of ties to the subversive socialists underground, Sacco and Vanzetti sealed the ACLU's reputation as a radical instrument of the Left for some time to come.[54]

Hatred of a Traditional America, American Sovereignty, and Commitment to the United Nations

> *Humanist Manifesto II:* "We have reached a turning point in human history where the best option is to transcend the limits of national sovereignty and to move toward the building of a world community in which all sectors of the human family can participate. We look to the development of a system of world law and a world order based upon transnational federal government."

Humanist Manifesto 2000: "We must develop an effective World Court and an International Judiciary with sufficient power to enforce its rulings." And, "The global community needs to develop a system of international law that transcends the laws of the separate nations. . . . Enhance the effectiveness of the UN by converting it from an assembly of sovereign states to an assembly of people as well. . . . If we are to solve our global problems, nation-states must transfer some of their sovereignty to a system of transnational authority. . . . Nor should any nation or group of nations be allowed to police the world or unilaterally bomb others without the concurrence of the Security Council. The world needs an effective police force to protect regions of the world from conflict and to negotiate peaceful settlements."

NATIONAL EDUCATION ASSOCIATION

In their 2003 Resolution I-2, the NEA called for an International Court of Justice: "The Association urges participation by the United States in deliberations before the court."

In the October 1947 issue of the *NEA Journal,* NEA official William Carr published an article titled "On the Waging of Peace," in which he wrote:

As you teach about the United Nations, lay the ground for a stronger United Nations by developing in your students a sense of world community. The United Nations should be transformed into a limited world government. The psychological foundations for wider loyalties must be laid. . . . Teach about the various proposals that have been made for strengthening the United Nations and the establishment of world law. Teach those attitudes which will result ultimately in the creation of a world citizenship and world government. . . . We cannot directly teach loyalty to a society that does not yet exist, but we can and should teach those skills and attitudes which will help to create a society in which world citizenship is possible.[55]

AMERICAN CIVIL LIBERTIES UNION

In the Gastonia case of 1929, "the ACLU defended seven striking workers who had been convicted of murdering a North Carolina police chief during a particularly violent confrontation. After declaring their anti-Christian and communist beliefs, the seven defendants jumped bail and fled to the Soviet Union."[56]

In the Smith Act Reversal of 1957, "the ACLU supported the defense of fourteen men convicted of conspiracy to violently overthrow the government of the United States. Lawyers argued on First Amendment free-speech grounds."[57]

Support of Homosexuality and Same-Sex Marriage

> *Humanist Manifesto 2000:* "Same-sex couples should have the same rights as heterosexual couples."

NATIONAL EDUCATION ASSOCIATION

A 1997 NEA resolution stated, "[P]rograms must increase acceptance of and sensitivity to gays and lesbians." In 1991, the NEA "received damaging national publicity when word leaked out that the convention was going to adopt an in-your-face resolution demanding that the gay rights agenda be incorporated into everything from school curricula to teacher hiring. Revolt in the ranks caused it to be withdrawn. But that was all smoke and mirrors; that convention quietly adopted at least ten separate resolutions that added up to the same objectives and this year's [1993] convention re-adopted the same resolutions."[58]

And, the NEA also is fully supportive of what are called the "multicultural" and "diversity" agendas. In two resolutions issuing from its 1999 convention it affirmed its commitment not only to "diversity"-based curricula, but urged that it be introduced in early childhood (from birth through age eight) education programs. One of the resolutions stated "that a diverse society enriches all individuals." Part of this enriching diversity, it said, is people with differences in "sexual orientation."[59]

DEMOCRATIC NATIONAL COMMITTEE PLATFORM 2000

"We continue to lead the fight to end discrimination on the basis of . . . sexual orientation. . . . We support continued efforts, like the Employment Non-Discrimination Act, to end workplace discrimination against gay men and lesbians. We support the full inclusion of gay and lesbian families in the life of the nation. This would include an equitable alignment of benefits."

AMERICAN CIVIL LIBERTIES UNION

In 1993, on the issue of gays in the military, "the ACLU took the lead in the fight to lift the historic ban on aberrant sexual proclivities in the American armed forces as well as the implementation of a liberal and preferential recruitment and promotion policy."[60]

In 2003, the ACLU celebrated its legalization of sodomy:

> We all owe an enormous debt of gratitude to the countless lawyers, academics and activists who helped bring this decision about. The ACLU is very proud of its work in helping to get rid of sodomy laws. The ACLU brought its first challenge to a sodomy law in 1963. We helped to strike down or repeal sodomy laws in California, Georgia, Kentucky, Maryland, Minnesota, Montana, Nevada, New York, Tennessee . . . you get the picture. Along with Lambda Legal we've worked for eight years to get a same-sex intimacy case to the Supreme Court. (And forgive us if we can't help but mention that the ACLU's friend-of-the-Court brief was referred to by the Supreme Court in *Lawrence* once at the oral argument and twice in the decision—a single mention of any brief is unusual enough—but three times is a hat trick!)[61]

The Massachusetts ACLU is defending the North American Man/Boy Love Association in a lawsuit by a murdered boy's parents who claim NAMBLA's Web site encourages rape and violence against children (*New York Times,* September 1, 2000). To the ACLU, NAMBLA is engaged in political advocacy. Advocacy, the ACLU preaches, however distasteful and immoral, is protected by the first amendment.[62]

Radical Environmentalism and Hatred for Private Property Rights

Humanist Manifesto 2000:
- "We need to recognize that current lifestyles in the industrialized North are unsustainable."
- "Runaway consumption is already putting unprecedented pressure on the environment."

- "... limiting fishing on the high seas that threatens the extinction of entire fish populations."
- "If present demographic trends continue, another 3 billion people will be added in the next half century. If population continues to grow as projected, it will lead to a drastic decrease in the available tillable grain lands."
- "Global warming is probably on the increase, in part as consequences of deforestation in poor countries and atmosphere carbon-dioxide emissions, especially in the affluent nations, which continue to waste natural resources."
- "The populations of others species have steadily declined, and many forms of plant and animal life are becoming extinct—perhaps the greatest extinction since the disappearance of the dinosaurs 65 million years ago."
- "We recommend the strengthening of existing UN agencies and programs most directly concerned with the environment. The United Nations Environment Programme, for example, should be given the power to enforce measures against serious ecological pollution."

Hatred of the U.S. Military and Military Funding

Humanist Manifesto II: "War is obsolete. It is an imperative to reduce the level of military expenditures and turn these savings to peaceful and people-oriented uses."

On June 14, 2005, Democrat U.S. senator Dick Durbin, of Illinois, showed his lack of respect for the U.S. military when on the floor of the Senate he compared the American military's treatment of terror detainees at Guantanamo Naval Base to torture at the hands of Nazis, Soviet gulags, and even Cambodian mass murderer Pol Pot. This comment was not made by just any U.S. senator because Durbin said this while also serving as the Democratic whip, which is the second-highest position for the minority party.

The third annual conference of the National Association for Multicultural Education (NAME) brought together multicultural educators from all fifty states. Keynote speaker Lily Wong Fillmore, a professor of language at the University of California at Berkeley, asserted that the radical curriculum reform they propose will provoke "definite clashes with the practices, beliefs and attitudes that are taught in many homes . . . . No matter what students' parents and families think about others or the environment . . . we are going to have to inculcate in our children the rules that form a credo that will work for a multicultural 21st century."[63]

The Intolerance of the Tolerance Movement

The Bible and the gospel of Jesus Christ are based upon moral absolutes and thus many individuals and organizations, as we've seen, go to great lengths to suppress the truth for which they have such hatred. But liberal influence is not confined to purely American organizations. Many take their cues from the world's greatest purveyor of liberal-think, the United Nations.

In 1995, the United Nations Educational Scientific and Cultural Organization (UNESCO) prepared the International Declaration of Principles on Tolerance that stated, "Tolerance is respect, acceptance and appreciation of the rich diversity of our world's cultures. . . . It is not only a moral duty, it is also a political and legal requirement."

According to the UN, if you were charged with being intolerant, you could be punished by law. The UN document goes on to declare:

- Intolerance is a global threat.
- Tolerance involves the rejection of dogmatism, and absolutism.
- Tolerance means that one's views are not to be imposed on others.

Note the very word *impose* is used by the United Nations. If the UN ever accomplished its goal, sharing the gospel of Jesus Christ could become illegal—a policy that many nations have already adopted.

By the way, if you think a Christian who espouses strong convictions based on moral absolutes is not treated with intolerance by liberals waving the tolerance banner, then consider this story of Tom DeLay.

In April 2002, then U.S. Majority Whip (now U.S. Senate majority leader) Tom DeLay of Texas spoke at the Worldview Weekend in Houston. I had invited Congressman DeLay to deliver a keynote address about his passion for a Christian worldview and in the process to share about his faith in Jesus Christ. (As background: Worldview Weekend is a private, for-profit corporation, and we do not allow people to videotape or record our conferences without written permission. Worldview Weekend records the keynote talks of the speakers and makes them available for sale at a later date. A private corporation, Worldview Weekend has the right to protect and profit from the intellectual property of its conferences.)

Little did I know that, when Rep. DeLay spoke, Barry Lynn's AU had a spy present who recorded our conference with a hand-held tape recorder. After delivering a remarkable speech, Mr. DeLay said he would to take questions from the audience. One gentleman stood and asked, "Here in Texas—even at Baylor—they can't even teach creationism without being kicked out. . . . Is there anything we can do, besides praying?"

Mr. DeLay responded forthrightly:

> You call your state representative, your state senator
> and say, "I want that to change. I don't like what I see. . . .
> And I want you to do something about it." They can. Texas
> A&M is a state university. The University of Texas is a state
> university. It's all run by the coordinating board, or whatever
> they call it, and they can change things. They can throw the
> P.C. out and bring God in. . . . but the immediate [solution]
> is, don't send your kids to Baylor. And don't send your kids
> to A&M. There are still some Christian schools out there—
> good, solid schools. Now they may be little, they may not
> be as prestigious as Stanford, but your kids will get a good
> solid, godly education.

After recording the Worldview Weekend without permission, AU shopped the story to various news outlets. *The Houston Chronicle* (which has a long history of attacking Mr. DeLay) lost no time in reporting this non-story, story. Within twenty-four hours the account was printed on countless Web sites, major state and national newspapers, and hundreds of local and national television news programs. Liberals were not only angry that Mr. DeLay suggested parents call their elected officials about what concerns them at taxpayer-supported colleges but that he would encourage parents to exercise the power of the free market system (which they hate) by sending their students—and money—to private colleges that operate in a manner with which they agree.

Mr. DeLay also made several other comments at our conference that outraged the liberals: "Christianity offers the only viable, reasonable, definitive answer to the questions of 'Where did I come from? Where am I going? Does life have any meaningful purpose?' Only Christianity offers a way to understand that physical and moral border. Only Christianity offers a comprehensive worldview that covers all areas of life and thought, every aspect of creation. Only Christianity offers a way to live in response to the realities that we find in this world, only Christianity."

Within days of Mr. DeLay sharing his Christian testimony and convictions he was, shall we say, smacked around. On April 24, the Houston-area *Fort Bend Star* ran a column in which the writer referred to Mr. DeLay as "our Congressvarmint, Tom, the Talibaptist."[64]

This unskilled writer could not argue with the truth spoken by Mr. DeLay, so she resorted to a further irreverent attack on Mr. DeLay: "Bless his heart, Tom just gets all carried away with that holy ghost spirit and starts handling snakes and washing feet and speaking gibberish and laying hands on folks, and stuff you just don't even want to know about."[65] The grossly unfair attacks on Mr. DeLay bothered me especially because I had invited Mr. DeLay to speak at the conference. I believed he was being persecuted for our shared faith in Jesus Christ and that I should voice my profound sadness over his treatment. To that end, I submitted an editorial to the *Houston Chronicle,* which, to the newspaper's credit, it printed. This, in part, is what I pointed out:

> Americans United for the Separation of Church and State, or AU, is a national group in Washington, D.C.—a group notorious on the Hill for its anti-religious bigotry, intolerance, and demagoguery. Americans United opposed the National Day of Reconciliation, which Hillary Clinton supported and Mr. DeLay sponsored. This group is to the left of Hillary Clinton.
>
> So Americans United sent someone surreptitiously to register as a participant at the church event for the purpose of finding a statement that could be publicized and attacked.

So they attended our ten-hour conference, found one statement they could remove from its context, and then began to market that statement to media across the country hoping to create a firestorm. This group actively sought assurances that their liberal organization would receive a positive plug in return for the "story" they were providing. Talk about a shameless public relations stunt?

Unfortunately, the *Houston Chronicle* was the paper that swallowed the bait; most others refused. Now Mr. DeLay is a "fanatic" because a politically motivated Democrat-affiliate group disingenuously attended a church conference to find a statement that it could distort into a smear campaign against Mr. DeLay.

And what was the essence of Mr. DeLay's "fanaticism"? In a question and answer period, he was asked what could be done with schools that teach things objectionable to the beliefs of both parents and students; the questioner specifically noted Baylor having demoted Dr. William Dembski because of his belief in intelligent design. Mr. DeLay broadened his response by citing examples of other large colleges that recently have begun practices to which many parents object. He indicated that the simplest solution was for parents and students to spend their hard-earned tens of thousands of dollars on a university education that does not attack their own personal values. For this you declare him to be a fanatic? Do you not believe in the free-enterprise system, free-market competition, and parents and students having a choice in their own education?

Those attending the conference never expected that while practicing their freedom of religion and freedom of speech inside a church, they would find their beliefs, and that of their guest speaker, being attacked and labeled as fanatical. The people that asked these questions now feel violated and used by a fringe, democratic group that apparently snuck into a church and distorted their questions, and the answers to those questions, in an attempt to bemoan and ridicule their deeply held religious convictions. . . .

It is unfortunate when a news source that should be the strongest advocate of free speech so objects when exercised by others holding a different view. So much for intellectual freedom and the open marketplace of ideas!

For the next few days, my e-mail box was filled with feedback from those who had read my editorial. The overwhelming majority thanked me for writing the editorial and shared their respect for Mr. DeLay. But liberals are intolerant of Christians no matter where they speak truth—whether inside or outside of the church walls. Mr. DeLay was speaking inside the auditorium of a Baptist church we had rented for our Worldview Weekend, and yet the liberals did not want to extend religious tolerance, freedom of religion, or freedom of conscious to Mr. DeLay!

So: Don't Be Fooled and Don't Apologize

I trust by now you realize what few people will admit: The modern-day liberal is a person with a truly anti-American and anti-God worldview. Their goals and intentions are rooted in a humanist worldview that desires to rob you of what countless men and women have died to preserve—a constitutional republic committed to life, liberty, the pursuit of happiness, and its affirmation of being one nation under God.

Don't be fooled and don't let down your guard. Despite their rhetoric about compassion, tolerance, and human unity, modern-day liberals are largely hateful, mean-spirited individuals who loathe everything based on absolute truth. They are offended by the truth, they hate it, and as a result, their thinking is twisted and confused.

The modern-day liberal will use intimidation and threats to terrorize anyone who gets in the way of their agenda, whether it be defeating a conservative political candidate, implementation of a radical education program, the legalization of same-sex marriage, or simply interference with your everyday life. The modern-day liberal will encourage your minor daughter to have sex, and when she gets pregnant, they will go behind your back and drag her to an abortionist. Liberals will be on the lookout for any display of religion such as a student praying or mentioning God or a public official wearing a cross or a city seal bearing a Christian symbol. Then they will rush to the phone to call the ACLU hotline. A liberal will claim to be tolerant but treat Christians like they are the reincarnation of Hitler. In short, there is little modern-day liberals will *not* do to achieve what is for them the only thing life is about: *power.*

To the modern-day secular humanist, "when you're dead, you're dead." So, power *now* is everything. Liberals wag their heads, amazed that you actually believe in God and that He reveals Himself to you through general and special revelation. To them, your belief is more an evidence of mental illness than a healthy worldview.

So, the battle lines are drawn. Unless Americans wake up and realize that the liberal humanists hate truth, the U.S. Constitution, the Bill of Rights, and Christianity, we will soon be enslaved by their worldview. It's already happening.

Chapter 4

Secular Humanism and Judicial Tyranny

Some people are bird-watchers; I have become a "court-watcher." Why? Because I believe one of the gravest threats to America is judicial tyranny. I look at lower federal court and U.S. Supreme Court rulings to see what shape our liberty and freedom are in, and right now we're in critical condition. With every court ruling that infringes on Americans' God-given rights, our nation's pulse drops, breathing slows, and death draws nearer for Lady Liberty.

But then, the death of a nation is nothing new. History is littered with once good and great peoples that have seen their day. And there is one common theme about the demise of each. Each one rejected its core principles: the values and worldview that once made them great.

I'm not willing, though, to surrender our great land to the tides of history, and I hope you're not, either. Although I'm convinced we can restore America's health, one of our once-great institutions—the United States legal system—stands in the way.

Our Courts—Not Just for Justice Anymore

America's recovery will begin only when brave men and women are willing to make sacrifices—as did our Founders—to break free from tyranny. Except this time, the tyrants we face come not from across the ocean but from across town at the local federal courthouse and from the U. S. Supreme Court in Washington, D.C. The tyranny of which I speak has grown out of a justice system that no longer simply applies the law but usurps the power of our legislators by making laws from the court bench.

"Judicial tyranny" describes what I believe is the unconstitutional, immoral, and deliberate actions of judges to reject the intentions of our nation's founding documents and the Founders' original purposes and, instead, to force on our nation their own political, philosophical, and theological worldviews. My friend and frequent Worldview Weekend speaker David Barton substantiates my contention that we are subject to judicial tyranny as he documents many appalling and arguably unconstitutional decisions in his book *Original Intent*. Consider only a few of the following freedom-robbing decisions:

- A verbal prayer offered in a school is unconstitutional, even if that prayer is voluntary and denominationally neutral (*Engel vs. Vitale,* 1962; *Abington vs. Schempp,* 1963; *Commissioner of Education vs. School Committee of Leyden,* 1971).

- Freedom of speech and press are guaranteed to students and teachers unless the topic is religious, at which times such speech becomes unconstitutional (*Stein vs. Oshinsky,* 1965; *Collines vs. Chandler Unified School Dist.,* 1981; *Bishop vs. Aronov,* 1991; *Duran vs. Nitschen,* 1991).

- It is unconstitutional for students to see the Ten Commandments because they might read, meditate upon, respect, or obey them (*Stone vs. Graham,* 1980; *Ring vs. Grand Forks Public School Dist.,* 1980; *Lanner vs. Wimmer,* 1981).

- If a student prays over his lunch, it is unconstitutional for him to pray out loud (*Reed vs. Van Hoven,* 1965).

- A school song was struck down because it promoted values such as honesty, truth, courage, and faith in the form of a "prayer" (*Doe vs. Aldine Independent School District,* 1982).

- It is unconstitutional for a war memorial to be erected in the shape of a cross (*Lowe vs. City of Eugene,* 1969).

- The Ten Commandments—despite the fact that they are the basis of civil law and are engraved in stone in the U.S. Supreme

Court building—may not be displayed at a public courthouse (*Harvey vs. Cobb County,* 1993).

- When a student addresses an assembly of his peers, he becomes a government representative, and it is unconstitutional for that student to engage in prayer (*Harris vs. Joint School District,* 1994).
- It is unconstitutional for a public cemetery to have a planter in the shape of a cross, for if someone were to view that cross, it could cause "emotional distress" and thus constitute an "injury-in-fact" (*Warsaw vs. Tehachapi,* 1990).
- It is unconstitutional for a public school graduation ceremony to contain an opening or closing prayer (*Harris vs. Joint School Board,* 1993; *Lee vs. Weisman,* 1992; *Kay vs. Douglas School District,* 1986; *Graham vs. Central Community School District,* 1985).
- It is unconstitutional for school officials to be publicly praised or recognized in an open community meeting if that meeting is sponsored by a religious group (*Jane Doe vs. Santa Fe Independent School District,* 1995).
- Displaying the Ten Commandments is permissible on government property only as part of an historical display (*McCreary County, Kentucky, vs. ACLU* and *Van Orden vs. Perry,* 2005).

A Judgment Day for Judges

As grievous as these decisions have been, there is a remedy. The judges who conferred these alarming decisions, as well as many others on the federal bench who have made equally appalling rulings, should be impeached, as provided for in the Constitution. These justices have usurped the powers of our legislators and have become unelected lawmakers—an unarguable violation of the role laid out for federal judges by the U.S. Constitution. To commit such a violation means a judge has broken his or her sworn oath to protect and defend the Constitution of the United States.

This course of action by our judiciary is no innocent drift in legal interpretation. The judges' unconstitutional moves have been calculated by a few to thrust their will upon Americans while the U.S. Congress has been asleep at the switch, seemingly unaware that the legislators' very reason for existence is being chipped away.

Benjamin Cardozo, appointed to the U.S. Supreme Court in 1932, proudly proclaimed a belief in his right to usurp powers of the U.S. Congress and to violate the check-and-balance separations of the U.S. Constitution: "I take judge-made law as one of the existing realities of life."[1]

Cardozo not only held the U.S. Constitution and U.S. Congress in contempt; he saw little purpose for people of faith—which includes most Americans—who want to apply a moral law as foundation for the legal process: "If there is any law which is back of the sovereignty of the state, and superior thereto, it is not law in such a sense as to concern the judge or lawyer, however much it concerns the statesman or the moralist."[2]

Justice Cardozo was not the first to sound this theme. In 1907, Charles Evans Hughes, who would later become chief justice of the U.S. Supreme Court, declared, "We are under a Constitution, but the Constitution is what the judges say it is."[3]

Lino Graglia, professor of constitutional law at the University of Texas School of Law, explains the crisis caused when members of the judicial branch make policy:

> Judicial usurpation of legislative power has become so common and so complete that the Supreme Court has become our most powerful and important instrument of government in terms of determining the nature and quality of American life.
>
> The result is that the central truth of constitutional law today is that it has nothing to do with the Constitution except that the words "due process" or "equal protection" are almost always used by the judges in stating their conclusions. Not to put too fine a point on it, constitutional law has become a fraud, a cover for a system of government by the majority vote of a nine-person committee of lawyers, unelected and holding office for life. The desirability of this form of government should be the central question in any realistic discussion of judicial review today.[4]

How can judges fulfill their sworn oath to defend and protect the U.S. Constitution while helping themselves to large portions of unconstitutional power and authority? How can they uphold the U.S. Constitution when they often don't even consider the Constitution when rendering decisions? Or how can federal judges claim to fulfill their sworn duty when the majority of federal judges have endeavored to replace the U.S. Constitution with a different judicial standard?

The separation of power among the three branches of our government—executive, judicial, and legislative—was designed to safeguard our nation from the very thing we now face: a runaway branch of the government. But make no mistake. The check system *is still in place*. It just isn't being used by Congress. Instead, our elected representatives go on allowing judges to enforce their new standard for law.

And exactly what is this new standard?

Moral Relativism Applied to the Law

Secular humanism and its penchant for moral relativism, along with misapplied Darwinism, has now become the postmodern foundation on which America's courts and law schools are built. Constitutional and legal scholar John Eidsmoe observes: "Twentieth-century jurisprudence is based on a Darwinian worldview. Life evolves, men evolve, society evolves, and therefore laws and the constitution's meaning evolves and changes with time."[5]

This new legal formulation is known as "legal positivism." In his book, *Christianity and the Constitution*, John Eidsmoe reviews the writings of the Critical Legal Studies movement, a group of radical lawyers, law professors, and law students. He summarizes legal positivism with the following points:

- There are no objective, God-given standards of law, or if there are, they are irrelevant to the modern legal system.
- Since God is not the author of law, the author of law must be man; in other words, law is law simply because the highest human authority, the state, has said it is law and is able to back it up by force.
- Since man and society evolve, therefore law must evolve as well.
- Judges, through their decisions, guide the evolution of law (Note again: judges "make law").

- To study law, get at the original sources of law, the decisions of judges; hence most law schools today use the "case law" method of teaching law.[6]

Another, simpler definition of legal positivism is: moral relativism applied to law. Moral relativism is the belief there is no such thing as moral absolutes—no standard of right or wrong for all people in all places at all times. At times, moral relativism is also called, simply, pragmatism. Moral relativism is closely tied to situational ethics, the belief that individuals are free to decide for themselves what is best for them to secure the most desirable outcome in any given situation.

Tracing the development of the positivistic approach to law, David Barton notes, "This philosophy of 'positivism' was introduced in the 1870s when Harvard Law School Dean Christopher Columbus Langdell (1826–1906) applied Darwin's premise of evolution to jurisprudence."[7]

Langdell's thought was advanced further by Dean Roscoe Pound and Supreme Court Justice Oliver Wendell Holmes Jr. Holmes argued there is no fixed moral foundation for law: "The felt necessities of the time, the prevalent moral and political theories . . . have a good deal more to do than the syllogism [legal reasoning process] in determining the rules by which men should be governed."[8]

Did you catch that? The "felt necessities of the time" and "prevalent moral and political theories" should be the basis of the rules by which men are governed.

Using the "felt necessities" and "prevalent theories" model, judges can allow just about anything to be legal, depending on whose feelings, morals, and political theories are chosen for reference. Guided by this dangerous thinking, we have seen countless abortions performed in America. Even the grisly partial-birth abortion procedure has passed legal muster—a practice the late Senator Daniel Patrick Moynahan called "near infanticide."

Along with millions of babies, matters of decency have also been aborted. Current U.S. Supreme Court Justice Ruth Bader Ginsburg, while serving as an attorney for the ACLU in 1977, wrote a paper, entitled "Sex Bias in the U.S. Code," for the U.S. Commission on Civil Rights. In it, she argued that the legal age for sexual activity should be lowered to twelve years old.[9] If enough judges agree the age change "is a necessity" based on the perverted "moral and political theories" of Alfred Kinsey, for instance, Americans would have to accept that it would be legal for an adult to have sex with a child of age twelve. Lest you think that too crazy to happen, bear in mind that famed sex researcher Alfred Kinsey actually promoted the idea of adults having sex with children, and there are other forces pushing in similar directions. A University of Minnesota publisher produced a book that discusses the "benefits" of children having sex with adults, and the North American Man/Boy Love Association has promoted this idea for years. These are the kinds of philosophical foundations that are now in play with relativistic judges.

If you think I'm painting with too broad a brush, consider the 2003 U.S. Supreme Court ruling in *Lawrence vs. Texas*. The Court struck down the Texas sodomy law and, via the precedent, similar laws in several other states. The effect was to make homosexual sex legal. To come to such a ruling, the justices not only ignored the Constitution and the Founders' intent, but went so far as to cite the law of another country in support of its decision!

In *Lawrence,* Justice Anthony M. Kennedy's majority opinion cited a 1967 British Parliament vote repealing laws against homosexual acts and a 1981 European Court of Human Rights decision that those laws were in violation of the European Convention on Human Rights.[10]

A New Trade Imbalance: Importing Foreign Law

There are many reasons why we condemn the use of external law when interpreting the Constitution. John Yoo, law professor at the University of California-Berkeley and visiting scholar at the American Enterprise Institute, writes in a *Law Review* article: "If foreign decisions were to become, in close cases, outcome determinative, or even were to trigger some type of defense, then they would effectively transfer federal authority outside the control of national government. The Supreme Court is in danger of setting its own social and moral agenda, ignoring the will of the American people."[11]

U.S. Supreme Court Justice Antonin Scalia did not agree with the *Lawrence* case ruling. In writing his dissent, Justice Scalia wrote, "This Court . . . should not impose foreign moods, fads, or fashions, on Americans."[12] I don't know about you, but I am incensed that the U.S. Supreme Court would ignore the original intent of the Founders, substitute some of their own intent, and then employ foreign law to justify a ruling based on their own political agenda.

Unfortunately, this is not the first time Supreme Court judges have looked outside the U.S. to find a basis for their rulings—which means there is precedent for the practice, something judges can use to their advantage. Supreme Court Justice Sandra Day O'Connor notes, "I suspect that over time we will rely increasingly, or take notice at least increasingly, on international and foreign courts in examining domestic issues."[13]

In a shocking decision in early 2005, the Court struck down a state law that had allowed a murderer under the age of eighteen to be executed for his or her crimes. This effectively banned such use of capital punishment in nineteen states. But in doing so, the judges have sentenced our Constitution to a slow death by citing foreign law as reason for the decision. In the majority opinion, Justice Kennedy wrote, "Our determination that the death penalty is disproportionate punishment for offenders under eighteen finds confirmation in the stark reality that the United States is the only country in the world that continues to give official sanction to the juvenile death penalty."[14]

Justice Kennedy also suggested that citing foreign law is an increasing trend in American jurisprudence, that the high court will more and more refer "to the laws of other countries and to international authorities as instructive for its interpretation" of the U.S. Constitution![15]

To address this problem, some members of Congress are working on legislation to guarantee such an unconstitutional process does not continue. U.S. Representative Tom Feeney of Florida and U.S. Representative Robert W. Goodlatte of Virginia were successful in getting the House Subcommittee on the Constitution to approve the "Reaffirmation of American Independence Resolution." According to Representative Feeney, the purpose of this legislation "is a salute to the framers of the Constitution and a victory for those dedicated to the protection of American sovereignty. This resolution reminds the Supreme Court that their role is interpreting U.S. law, not importing foreign law."[16]

In Article VI, the U.S. Constitution states that the Constitution is the Supreme Law of the land. So, for court justices to look outside the U.S. to base their rulings is clearly unconstitutional. "Yet lawmakers point out that at least five justices, in order to justify their decisions, have written or joined opinions citing foreign courts from Jamaica and India to Zimbabwe and the European Union."[17]

What would the Founders say about the U.S. Supreme Court looking to foreign nations to interpret American law? George Mason, "father of the Bill of Rights," addressed this issue when he wrote, "I wish America would put her trust only in God and herself and have as little to do with the politics of Europe as possible."[18]

President Thomas Jefferson said, "The comparisons of our governments with those of Europe are like a comparison of heaven and hell."[19]

Jefferson was very concerned, as were many other Founders, about the tyranny to which the judicial branch could subject America. In 1820, he expressed his apprehensions in a letter to William Charles Jarvis: "To consider the judges as the ultimate arbiters of all constitutional questions is a very dangerous doctrine indeed, and one which would place us under the despotism of an oligarch [rule by a few]. . . . The Constitution has erected no such single tribunal, knowing that to whatever hands confided, with the corruptions of time and party, its members would become despots."[20]

If there were ever a time the U.S. Congress is justified in impeaching Supreme Court justices, the ruling in *Lawrence vs. Texas* has provided the occasion. But I fear it won't happen because of the preference by many in Congress for moral relativism. Meanwhile, I believe the cultural elites laugh behind conservative backs over how easy it is to accomplish their goals, and harvest more and more control over every aspect of American life via the judicial branch of our government.

Judges Look to Judges

Ignoring the Constitution and looking to case law—including that of other countries—to justify what our laws don't permit is the motive behind the case-law philosophy. Harvard's Dean Langdell pioneered the case-law philosophy, which calls for consideration of precedents in the decisions of other judges rather than the Constitution. David Barton regards this as a strategy for subverting the intent of the Founders: "Under the case-law approach, history, precedent, and the views and beliefs of the Founders not only became irrelevant, they were even considered hindrances to the successful evolution of a society."[21]

John Dewey believed a strict adherence to the Constitution was an obstacle to the liberal, humanistic, and socialist changes he and many like him desired to accomplish: "The belief in political fixity, of the sanctity of some form of state consecrated by the efforts of our fathers and hallowed by tradition, is one of the stumbling-blocks in the way of orderly and directed change."[22]

Although judges and legal scholars now refer to judges as "making law," William Blackstone never believed judges "made law" but that they were to study the U.S. Constitution to "discover" or "apply" the law. About early leaders' high esteem of Blackstone's view, David Barton says:

> Numerous early American lawyers, legal scholars, and politicians cited Blackstone's work as a key legal source. For example, Blackstone is invoked as an authority in the writings of James Kent, James Wilson, Fisher Ames, Joseph Story, John Adams, Henry Laurens, Thomas Jefferson, John Marshall, James Madison, James Otis and more.[23] . . .

> In fact, so strong was its influence in America that Thomas Jefferson once quipped that American lawyers used Blackstone's [Commentaries] with the same dedication and reverence that Muslims used the Koran.[24]

Although introduced in the nineteenth century, legal positivism began to make real headway in our system when Earl Warren became chief justice of the U.S. Supreme Court. In the 1958 case, *Trop vs. Dulles,* Chief Justice Warren declared the Eighth Amendment of the U.S. Constitution could not have the same meaning now as it did at the time written. (The amendment reads as follows: "Excessive bail shall not be required, nor excessive fines imposed, nor cruel and unusual punishment inflicted.") In *Trop vs. Dulles,* the U.S. State Department had attempted to strip a man of his U.S. citizenship because he deserted the armed forces during World War II. But Trop's attorneys argued it was "cruel and unusual punishment" to strip him of his citizenship. Chief Justice Warren agreed, stating "the Amendment must draw its meaning from the evolving standards of decency that mark the progress of a maturing society." Legal positivism has been racing through court decisions at an ever-increasing pace since the mid-1900s. Appendix 2 offers a more in-depth look at the key rulings that reflect this trend.

The clear implication of legal positivism? Since morals and standards change over time, so does the meaning of the Constitution. Strangely, the Constitution has supposedly become much harder to understand than it once was.

A Constitution for the Common Man

Joseph Story, professor of law at Harvard and associate justice of the U.S. Supreme Court, was a leading constitutional scholar of the nineteenth century. In *Commentaries on the Constitution* (1833), he advocated interpreting the Constitution according to its plain meaning and the intent of its authors. Story emphasized that the Constitution was deliberately written so as to be understood by the common man: "I have not the ambition to be the author of any new plan of interpreting the theory of the Constitution, or of enlarging or narrowing its powers, by ingenious subtleties and learned doubts. . . . Upon subjects of government; it has always appeared to me that metaphysical refinements are out of place. A constitution of government is addressed to the common sense of the people, and never was designed for trials of logical skill, or visionary speculation."[25]

Compare Story's eloquent, yet humble, clear thinking with the aggressive positivism of Charles Hughes, New York governor and chief justice of the U.S. Supreme Court: "We are under a Constitution, but the Constitution is what the judges say it is."[26]

In 1985, to illuminate the destructiveness of this view, Edwin Meese, attorney general under then-president Ronald Reagan, delivered a speech to the American Bar Association in which he declared:

It was not long ago when constitutional interpretation was understood to move between the poles of "strict construction" and "loose construction." Today, it is argued that constitutional interpretation moves between "interpretive review" and "non-interpretive review." As one observer has pointed out, under the old system the question was how to read the Constitution; under the new approach, the question is whether to read the Constitution. . . . The result is that some judges and academics feel free (to borrow the language of the great New York jurist, Chancellor James Kent) to "roam at large in the trackless fields of their own imaginations."[27]

This Just in from the Court: Truth Is Out, Postmodernism In

In the 1992 U.S. Supreme Court ruling in *Planned Parenthood of Southeastern Pennsylvania vs. Casey, Governor of Pennsylvania,* Justices Sandra Day O'Connor, Souter, and Kennedy stated in the majority opinion, "At the heart of liberty is the right to define one's own concept of existence, of meaning of the universe and the mystery of human life."

Dr. James Dobson, president and founder of Focus on the Family, later explained the stunning and dangerous shift wrought by this ruling:

> With those words, the Court discarded its historic reliance on "a law beyond the law," or a transcendent standard. The Founding Fathers based the Constitution on the understanding that human affairs are governed by the moral law of the universe or what they termed "The Law of Nature and of Nature's God." That's why the Declaration of Independence reads, "All men are endowed by their Creator with certain unalienable Rights."

> Human dignity and freedom are precious gifts from God, rather than from government or its leaders. The Creator is also the ultimate definer of right and wrong. But after the *Casey* decision, this understanding of the moral absolutes was supplanted by "the right to define one's own concept of existence, of meaning of the universe and the mystery of human life."

It brings to mind the words of King Solomon, who wrote, "There is a way that seems right to a man, but in the end it leads to death" (Prov. 14:12 NIV).

Columnist John Leo agreed: "This 'mystery passage' [as it has become known] can be cited easily next time to justify suicide clinics, gay marriage, polygamy, inter-species marriage [such as marrying one's dog or cat] or whatever new individual right the court feels like inventing. We are moving firmly into the court's post-constitutional phase."

Similarly, Chuck Colson noted the mystery passage could mean absolutely anything to a future court, including the right to marry your toaster if you wish.

The seismic shift represented in the *Casey* decision is how we define reality. The new definition flows from a post-modern philosophy that refuses to acknowledge any absolutes—nothing right, nothing wrong, nothing moral, nothing immoral. Truth does not exist, and there are no absolutes that transcend time or situation. Everything is subject to individual interpretation.

For the U.S. Supreme Court to descend into the abyss of moral relativism is disastrous. The Constitution has been the shield and defender of basic liberties for well over 200 years, based on "The Law of Nature and of Nature's God." Now, according to Justice Kennedy and five of his colleagues, its meaning has become no more predictable than the shifting sand of personal opinion.[28]

Liberal elitists attempt to intimidate the American people by telling them they're not allowed to question the rulings of judges or have an opinion on legal rulings—particularly if they don't have a law degree. But book sense is not a substitute for common sense. As Vance Havner said, "You don't have to be listed in 'Who's Who' to know what's what." The real bottom line is that liberals don't want to be held to any standard other than their own mushy amalgamation of sound-bite thinking on issues of epic significance. They don't want to be accountable to the rule of law—they want to *be* the law.

In January 2001, U.S. Supreme Court Justice Ruth Bader Ginsburg gave a speech at the University of Melbourne Law School in Australia.

Ginsburg attacked U.S. Representative Tom DeLay, who has a long history of condemning members of the judicial branch who attempt to make law instead of interpreting it. Mr. DeLay often has spoken of the need for the U.S. Congress to reign in the runaway judiciary by using the Constitutional remedy, impeachment. Mr. DeLay believes impeachments might "intimidate" judges by holding them accountable and cautioning them not to stray from their constitutional responsibility and limitations.

Justice Ginsburg used the "you are not an expert" strategy by portraying Mr. DeLay as a dumb, blue-collar worker who was beneath her education and wisdom as she quipped that he is "not a lawyer but, I'm told, an exterminator by profession." The truth is, Tom DeLay gets in the way of Justice Ginsburg's long-standing strategy to have her way with American law. Even before joining the Court, she advocated decisions that "creatively interpreted clauses of the Constitution . . . to accommodate a modern vision" of society. She approved of "boldly dynamic interpretation, departing radically from the original understanding" of the Constitution. She also believed courts could "repair" or even "rewrite" legislation to reach desirable results.[29]

Despite invoking the "you aren't qualified" rhetoric against Mr. DeLay, what Justice Ginsburg knows, but doesn't want to acknowledge, is that the Founders wrote the Declaration of Independence, the U.S. Constitution, and the *Federalist Papers* so the average American—who at that time was a farmer—could understand their writings. Authored by Alexander Hamilton, John Jay, and James Madison, the *Federalist Papers* describe the reason and original intent behind the Declaration of Independence and U.S. Constitution, and these writings were printed in newspapers throughout the young nation. If you had lived at the time the *Federalist Papers* were first published, you would have been among a citizenry that understood, and had a great interest in, their new country's founding documents.

Americans should not be silent concerning the laws and court rulings that impact their lives. While judges may wish it, we are not slaves of the black-robed usurpers. Perhaps it is because judges are lawyers—and most lawyers are liberal—that they seem to be so readily capable of ignoring truth, distorting reality, and quickly accepting the fallacies of a postmodern worldview.

What Happens When the Moral Foundation Shifts?

The rejection of a fixed moral standard as the basis for law means there is no longer a benchmark by which a society judges good and bad behavior. After the 1962 and 1963 U.S. Supreme Court rulings that outlawed prayer and the Bible in America's public schools, cheating, stealing, rape, murder, and assault increased dramatically throughout the culture. After the 1980 U.S. Supreme Court ruling that outlawed the posting of the Ten Commandments in our nation's public schools, the increase in deviant behavior rose higher still, and that trend continues to this day.

What's more, without a fixed moral standard as the basis for law, government has no moral purpose for its existence. According to Romans 13, the God-given purpose of civil government is to protect the righteous and punish the wicked; but without a moral foundation to uphold, defend, and use as the standard by which to judge and punish evil doers, government has nothing to enforce.

The lack of a fixed moral standard as the basis for law means our rights are not God-given but only granted to us by government. These days, people are dangerously close to accepting the idea that the state grants rights to American citizens. This thinking will lead to calamity. Government is not the god who creates rights. It is merely God's minister to protect the rights God has given mankind.[30]

Absent a fixed moral standard as the basis for law, "might makes right." Thus the groundwork is laid for one of two (and possibly both) disastrous ends. Anarchy is one. And that would most likely lead to the second, which is for our nation to be subjected to the feelings, opinions, agenda, and worldview of a small group of immoral, elitist judges that rule from behind the bench or a dictator that rules from behind a gun. Attorney John Whitehead puts it this way:

> Those who do not favor taking God's law as the ultimate standard for civil morality and public justice will be forced to substitute some other criterion of good and evil for it. The civil magistrate cannot function without some ethical guidance, without some standard of good and evil. If that standard is not to be the revealed law of God (which, we must note, was addressed specifically to perennial problems

in political morality), then what will it be? In some form or expression it will have to be a law of man (or men)—the standard of self-law or autonomy. And when autonomous laws come to govern a commonwealth, the sword is certainly wielded in vain, for it represents simply the brute force of some men's will against the will of other men. "Justice" then indeed becomes a verbal cloak for whatever serves the interests of the strongmen in society (whether their strength be that of physical might or of media manipulation). Men will either choose to be governed by God or to be ruled by tyrants.[31]

The loss of a fixed moral standard means Lady Justice is no longer blind, and those that have money and influence have a greater chance of getting what they want, to the detriment and harm of the middle class and the poor. Without moral law man will not be restrained from within, so he must be restrained from without. More intrusive and larger government presence in our lives will be required.

Finally, the loss of a fixed moral standard means injustice will naturally follow, resulting in the unjust suffering and death of many. Gary DeMar outlines the destructive consequences when evolutionary thinking is applied to law and morality:

Darwinian evolution has placed law in the arena with evolving man. If man has evolved then the standards primitive man once held must change along with him. When the higher law is abandoned, another law takes its place. The humanistic doctrine of evolution allows man to create for himself the law he believes will most benefit evolving man. Law then is what men or the courts say it is. Wrongs are defined in terms of what hurts man. There is no appeal to a law-order outside man. For example, abortion is made legal because it is convenient for the mother. For some women, having a baby is "harmful" because it restricts their freedom. These women are "wrongfully" curtailed in their desire to live as they wish. Laws are then passed to alleviate the "problem." The developmental fetus is termed a "non-person" without protection from the more powerful. There is no consideration that God has defined the nature of life, or that freedom should be defined in terms of submission to the commandments of God. Nor are the necessarily destructive and suicidal long-term consequences of such legal thought and practice seriously considered.[32]

Amending the Constitution Via Cultural Change

Issues rarely, if ever, arise in which we cannot discern the original intent of the Founders and as a result apply the U.S. Constitution appropriately. Unfortunately, many have been led to believe abortion is an example of a modern-day issue not addressed in the U.S. Constitution. Thus, to rule on the question required justices to use their own independent reasoning as to what is right. Conservatives, however, do not believe the Constitution is silent about the rights of an unborn person. The Fourteenth Amendment states, "nor shall any State deprive any person of life, liberty, or property, without due process of law." Let's look at whether or not abortion should be legal under the Fourteenth Amendment.

John Eidsmoe believes it should not be legal because the Amendment is clear:

Does the term *liberty* include the right to an abortion? Does the term *person* include an unborn child and thereby guarantee the child the right to life? These questions probably never occurred to those who passed and ratified the Fourteenth Amendment in 1868; they certainly do not appear in any of the recorded debates. In determining how to apply the Fourteenth Amendment to the abortion issue, suppose that someone had asked "Does *person* include unborn children?" or "Does *liberty* include the right to abortions?" during the floor debates on the Fourteenth Amendment. What would have been the likely response, given the basic morals and values and perceptions of those involved at the time? In an effort to interpret the founding fathers' initial intent the following question could be asked, "Given the founding fathers' basic values, what would have been their view of abortion, had they known the latest scientific and technical information about the unborn child? The fact that the Fourteenth Amendment was passed and ratified in 1868 when most states had either passed or were in the process of passing laws to prohibit abortion—a fact that Justice Blackman overlooked in *Roe vs. Wade*—may help interpret and apply the signers of the Constitution intent.[33]

Obviously, the "right to abortion" is contrary to what the authors of the Fourteenth Amendment had in mind.

Naturally, there are times when changes are called for in the provisions of the Constitution, and the Founders recognized that necessity. They built into the document a very healthy, measured process for making appropriate alterations. Article V provides the formula: "The Congress, whenever two thirds of both Houses shall deem it necessary, shall propose amendments to this Constitution, or, on the application of the legislature of two-thirds of the several States, shall call a convention for proposing amendments."

Nowhere does it say judges are permitted to amend the Constitution through their decisions! Only the people—through duly elected representatives—are allowed to do so. As Samuel Adams wrote, "[T]he people alone have an incontestable, unalienable, and indefeasible right to institute government and to reform, alter, or totally change the same when their protection, safety, prosperity, and happiness require it. And the federal Constitution, according to the mode prescribed therein, has already undergone such amendments in several parts of it as from experience has been judged necessary."[34]

George Washington, in his Farewell Address, reminded the nation how critical it is to amend the Constitution only according to the process set forth in document itself: "If, in the opinion of the people, the distribution or the modification of the constitutional powers be in any particular wrong, let it be corrected by an amendment in the way which the Constitution designates. But let there be no change by usurpation; for though this, in one instance, may be the instrument of good, it is the customary weapon by which free governments are destroyed."

The "customary weapon by which free governments are destroyed"! I fear the words of our first president will prove to be prophetic. If the American people continue to allow the law to "evolve" through the decision of judges whose only yardstick is moral relativism and situational ethics, a free America will come to an end.

Chapter 5

Evolution: The Liberals' Attempt to Deny God

In 1925, the American Civil Liberties Union defended evolution in the now-famous Scopes trial. Building on the momentum started by that case, the ACLU has fought hard through the years to keep creationism from being taught in America's public schools. The ACLU, with the aid of the NEA and other liberal groups, has been tremendously successful in their censorship of facts and reality.

Since the ACLU and NEA both are liberal organizations founded and supported by well-known humanists, we should not be shocked by their contempt for the creationist worldview. Evolution, as outlined in the *Humanist Manifesto I*, *II*, and *2000*, is a major religious doctrine or tenant of secular humanism. Instead of a belief in God as the basis for their religion, humanists believe in nature or "natural science." Thus, a humanist is often said to believe in naturalism.

The humanists' point in promoting naturalistic evolution is to create an intellectually sophisticated way to deny the existence of God. I would contend, however, that believing in evolution requires more blind faith than believing in God. Dr. D. G. Lindsay agrees and describes the blind religion of evolution this way:

Evolution is a religion that attributes everything to "nature." It demands a faith that is totally blind. Since the evolutionist believes nature and its laws are the guiding force in the universe, he is totally at odds with the Christian faith and the essential miraculous aspect of creation. The miraculous events of the Bible deviate from the known laws of nature, or at least from our understanding of them. However, the evolutionist is blind to the fact that his religion, evolution, violates every known law for its own existence, making atheistic evolution more incredible (miraculous) than the Christian faith.[1]

Why Your Presupposition Matters

A humanist believes there is no God and thus that man is his own "higher power." The humanist has no choice but to reject God and believe in man and biological evolution because the alternative is to say there is a supernatural creator and intelligent designer. If there is such a creator, then He is the author of the laws of nature, and we are accountable to Him. But being accountable to anyone other than self is not acceptable to the humanist. As a result, humanists reject out of hand any and all evidence that challenges their desired reality.

The liberal, then, who chooses to have faith in evolution does so not because of compelling intellectual honesty but because the alternative requires accountability to God both in this life and the next. You can see how this would render the liberal agenda a house of cards. If the liberal acknowledges God, then abortion is murder, homosexuality is a sin, and sex outside of marriage is fornication. Most humanists refuse to admit to God's existence—regardless of the sound reasoning and evidence to the contrary—because of their commitment to self-idolatry and pride. But the Bible paints a clear picture of these people in Psalm 14:1: "The fool says in his heart, 'God does not exist.'" Only a fool could look at the historical, archaeological, prophetic, philosophical, and scientific evidence and still deny God's existence.

Scripture says, "The heavens declare the glory of God, and the sky proclaims the work of His hands" (Ps. 19:1). In this chapter, we'll look at several aspects of creation that reveal this glory of God and announce His existence.

While I admit I look at everything through the presupposition that "in the beginning, God," the humanist starts with "in the beginning, man." This means the humanist looks only at theories that don't contradict their presupposition. The *Humanist Manifesto II* states, "We find insufficient evidence for belief in the existence of a supernatural; it is either meaningless or irrelevant to the question of the survival and fulfillment of the human race. As non-theists, we begin with humans not God, nature not deity."

Anything that calls into question the original presupposition (that there is no God) is rejected, even if it means having "faith" in an idea, belief, or theory that is not mathematically possible, or even if it contradicts known scientific facts or laws of physics. As long ago as 1929, Professor D. M. S. Watson, one of the leading biologists and science writers of his day, explained that the real goal behind evolution is to reject the alternative—a belief in God. Watson notes, "Evolution [is] a theory universally accepted not because it can be proven by logically coherent evidence to be true, but because the only alternative, special creation, is clearly incredible."[2]

Professor Richard Lewontin, a geneticist and self-proclaimed Marxist, reveals why the dogmatic humanist continues to accept the lie of evolution despite its improbability and the unscientific propositions on which it is built:

> We take the side of science in spite of the patent absurdity of some of its constructs, in spite of its failure to fulfill many of its extravagant promises of health and life, in spite of the tolerance of the scientific community for unsubstantiated just-so-stories, because we have a prior commitment, a commitment to materialism. It is not that the methods and institutions of science somehow compel us to accept a material explanation of the phenomenal world, but, on the contrary, that we are forced by our a priori adherence to material causes to create an apparatus of investigation and a set of concepts that produce material explanations, no matter how counter-intuitive, no matter how mystifying to the uninitiated. Moreover, that materialism is an absolute, for we cannot allow a Divine Foot in the door.[3]

I appreciate Prof. Lewontin's candor. Few humanists are so clear-headed in understanding and articulating what they are really trying to achieve by promoting purely naturalistic explanations for everything. Evolution is not based on science, despite what most evolutionists will tell you. Dr. Robert A. Millikan, a physicist and Nobel Prize winner, was equally clear when he stated in a speech before the American Chemical Society, "The pathetic thing about it is that many scientists are trying to prove the doctrine of evolution, which no science can do."[4]

Yes, *pathetic* is a good word. It is really quite pathetic when you consider the mental gymnastics a humanist must perform to defend the presupposition that there is no intelligent designer for the universe and that spontaneous, macro-evolution is scientific. Although the humanist typically mocks as unscientific those who believe in a creator God, when the science that is the foundation of their worldview is proven to be unscientific and mathematically impossible, they choose to ignore those facts and instead create preposterous theories that not only contradict science but take more blind faith than believing in the Intelligent Designer.

Happily for some, the incredible scientific discoveries of the past few years have caused some scientists to reject the lie of evolution and explore the evidence for an "intelligent designer." The complexity of the human body and the orderliness of the universe are so overwhelming, these researchers no longer believe that everything we see and know happened by chance. Nevertheless, while no longer believing in evolution, they are not ready to say, "God is," but at least they acknowledge the necessity of an intelligent designer of some sort.

So, the issue is not that one worldview (theism) requires faith while the other (atheism) does not—both *do*. The question is: Which worldview is based on a more *rational* faith? And to that, the answer is clear. There is far greater evidence for the existence of God as Creator than for the notion that everything came about by random chance. To accept the belief that God is the Creator, you need to have faith in only one thing—an all knowing, all-powerful God. The astonishing complexity of creation is consistent with the infinitely knowledgeable, omnipotent Creator. Only such a Being could have created the universe as we know it. On the other hand, to believe in spontaneous evolution, you must have faith in billions upon billions of mathematically improbable and scientifically impossible things.

The Greater the Design the Greater the Designer

When you look at a beautiful painting, you know it had a painter. When you look at a sculpture, you know it had a sculptor. When you look at a building, you know there was an architect. That is our common experience. And when evolutionists look at the systems and patterns that govern everything from planetary orbits to life itself? They blind themselves to the obvious implications of the design and choose not to see the Designer—hardly a logical conclusion.

If we are true to the simple conventions of everyday logic, common sense suggests that the greater the design the greater the designer. And greater minds than mine say the same thing. Historian and philosopher of science Stephen Meyer has said, "We have not yet encountered any good in principle reason to exclude design from science."[5]

William Paley, who went to Cambridge in 1759 to study mathematics and later taught there for nine years, argued that there must be only one Designer, since there is manifest in nature a uniformity of divine purpose in all parts of the world.[6]

The "teleological argument" for God begins by acknowledging the apparent design of the world from which it argues to the Designer beyond the world. Paley articulated the traditional form of this argument in his watchmaker analogy: (1) Every watch has a watchmaker; (2) the world is more complex than a watch; (3) hence, the world must have had a world maker.[7] Said George Gallup, world-famed researcher and statistician, "I could prove God statistically! Take the human body alone. The chance that all the functions of the individual would just happen is a statistical monstrosity!"[8]

With that in mind, let's look at only a few examples of order and complexity in everyday things that we take for granted:
- The brain weighs just over three pounds but can do what many tons of electrical equipment cannot. It contains up to 15 billion neurons, each a living unit within itself. More than 100 thousand billion (10^{14}) electrical connections are present—which is more than all the electrical connections in all the electrical appliances in the world.[9]
- The human heart is a ten-ounce pump that can operate without

maintenance or lubrication for about seventy-five years—an engineering marvel.[10]

- In the fraction of a second it takes you to read one word on this page, the marrow in your bones produces more than 100,000 red blood cells.[11]
- The human eye contains 130,000 light sensitive rods and cones that generate photochemical reactions that convert light into electrical impulses. One billion such impulses are transmitted to the brain every second. The eye can make more than 100,000 different motions and, when confronted with darkness, can increase its ability to see 100,000 times. It comes complete with automatic aiming, automatic focusing, and automatic maintenance during one's sleep.[12]
- The ear is as much an acoustic marvel as the eye is an optic one. The inner ear is like a keyboard with 15,000 keys—that's the number of different tones that can be distinguished. Not only does the ear perform the function of hearing; it controls our equilibrium as well.[13]
- Each one of us came from a single fertilized cell. In the nucleus of that dot of material was DNA—the genetic programming for every facet of the yet-undeveloped adult—organs, nerves, hair, skin color, and even personality traits. These were programmed into those incredibly tiny specks of matter called chromosomes. According to Ashley Montague in his book, *Human Heredity,* the space occupied by all this data is inconceivably small. If the DNA blueprints for every one of the six billion human beings on earth were gathered together, they would fit into the space of an aspirin tablet.[14] Not only that, the total DNA storage capacity of a single amoeba can contain the information in a thousand sets of encyclopedias.[15] DNA is the equivalent of a program, and everyone knows a program had to have a programmer. Bill Gates has said, "DNA is like a computer program, but far, far more advanced than any software we've ever created."[16]

Every adult carries about 100 billion miles of DNA strands—a distance greater than the diameter of the solar system. Each cell has four to six feet of the DNA ladder—and every adult human has 100 trillion cells.[17] In *Darwin's Black Box: The Biochemical Challenge to Evolution,* Michael Behe, a biochemist who argues that many biological systems are "irreducibly complex" at the molecular level, wrote, "If any one part were missing because the needed part had not yet evolved, the entire system would not work. Many irreducibly complex systems support life and if the missing part kept the life supporting system from functioning, that would be a fatal blow for many structures or creatures."

Michael Behe has forcefully argued that there are several examples of cellular functions that could not have been formed gradually by any natural process, including "cilium, vision, blood clotting, or any complex biochemical process."[18]

"Other examples of irreducible complexity abound, including aspects of DNA reduplication, electron transport, telomere synthesis, photosynthesis, transcription regulation, and more."[19] From these facts, Behe makes a bold conclusion: "The result of these cumulative efforts to investigate the cell—to investigate life at the molecular level—is a loud, clear, piercing cry of 'design!' The result is so unambiguous and so significant that it must be ranked as one of the greatest achievements in the history of science.[20]

- It would be fair to say that a single cell is the most complex structure known to man.[21] Some cells are so small that a million of them could occupy a space no larger than the head of a pin. The cell has turned out to be a micro-universe, containing trillions of molecules. These molecules are the building blocks for countless structures, performing chains of complex biochemical reactions with precision.

One biologist has made the following statement regarding the complexity of a cell: "Even if we knew all there is to know about how a cell works, we would still be baffled. How nerve cells create emotions, thoughts, behavior, memory, and other perceptions cannot yet, if indeed ever, be described in the language of molecular biology."[22]

D. G. Lindsay adds:

A single cell exhibits the same degree of complexity as a city with all of its systems of operation, communication and government. Within each tiny cell are power plants that generate energy; factories that produce foods essential for life; complex transportation systems that guide specific chemicals from one location to another; barricades that control the import and export of materials across the cell. Every minute structure within a cell has a specific function. Without the full complement of all these systems, the cell cannot function. In fact, even the slightest malfunction within the cell can bring about the immediate termination of its existence. How unbelievable that such awesome complexity could have arisen by chance![23]

The power within an atom is so incomprehensible that the energy stored within the atoms of only one railroad ticket is enough to power a diesel train around the world several times.[24] D. G. Lindsay describes the relation between the complexity of the atom and the Creator:

> What is the binding force of an atom? Scientists have discovered this binding force and its properties have been worked out mathematically, but they do not know what it is or how it got there. Recently they have found two new forces within the atom called the pi-mesons. They believe the pi-mesons may be the energy holding things together. It is totally invisible; it can't be seen, felt, tasted or weighed. But it is there! What is this nuclear glue?

> Though man can continue to observe and research the atom, discovering how it works and of what it is comprised, the question still remains: Who is the creator and the controller of these incredible forces? Did it all come about by unintelligent chance or was there intelligence involved? If so, whose? . . . In him (Christ) *all things hold together* (Col. 1:17 NIV). The Son is the radiance of God's glory and the exact representation of his being, *sustaining all things* by his powerful word (Heb. 1:3 NIV).[25]

Evidence of Design for Non-biophysicists

Humanists have spread evolutionary thinking across many areas of human development, including linguistics. It stands to reason, though, that if languages evolved the earliest languages should be the simplest. To the contrary, though, language studies reveal that more ancient languages are actually more complex than many modern languages—for example: Latin (200 BC), Greek (800 BC) and Vedic Sanskrit (pre-1,000 BC). The best evidence indicates that languages devolve. They actually become simpler rather than more complex.[26]

The study of verbal communication also offers intriguing evidence against evolution. Studies of the thirty-six documented cases of children raised without human contact (feral children) show that speech appears to be learned only from other humans. Apparently, humans do not learn to speak automatically. This suggests that the first humans must have been specially endowed with an ability to talk. There is no evidence speech has evolved.[27]

Something from Nothing

An evolutionist has to believe in the mathematical improbability that *something* has come from *nothing*. The argument goes that, given enough time, anything can happen. There is no logical reason to make that assumption, however. Nothing in our experience or any scientific inquiry suggests there can exist any effect without an associated cause. No amount of time factored into the equation can be shown to change that. Famed astronomer Sir Fred Hoyle once set about to determine the probability that something—anything whatsoever—could come about completely at random. His conclusion is best expressed by an entertaining and mind-boggling analogy. He "compares it to lining up 10^{50} (ten with fifty zeros after it) blind people, giving each one a scrambled Rubik's Cube, and finding that they all solve the cube at the same moment."[28] Just so you'll be sure to grasp the magnitude of Hoyle's statement: Note that the number 1 billion has only *nine* zeros after it—Hoyle's number has *fifty!*

And Hoyle isn't alone in his musings. Dr. Walter T. Brown offers this assessment: "The simplest conceivable form of life should have at least 600 different protein molecules. The mathematical probability that just one molecule could form by the chance arrangement of the proper sequence of amino acids is far less than 1 in 10^{450} (The magnitude of the number 10^{450} can begin to be appreciated by realizing that the visible universe is about 10^{28} inches in diameter)."[29]

To put these numbers in perspective, it is instructive to note that, according to mathematics—Borel's Single Law of Chance, to be specific—when the odds of any event occurring are less than 1 in 10^{50}, it is considered to be "impossible."[30]

Even some who are not specifically creationists question Darwinian evolution. Molecular biologist Michael Denton explains the complexity of a cell and the absolute zero probability that it could come into being without an intelligent designer:

Perhaps in no other area of modern biology is the challenge posed by the extreme complexity and ingenuity of biological adaptations more apparent than in the fascinating new molecular world of the cell. . . . To grasp the reality of life as it has been revealed by molecular biology, we must magnify a cell a thousand million times until it is twenty kilometers in diameter and resembles a giant airship large enough to cover a great city like London or New York. What we would then see would be an object of unparalleled complexity and adaptive design. On the surface of the cell we would see millions of openings, like the port holes of a vast space ship, opening and closing to allow a continual stream of materials to flow in and out. If we were to enter one of these openings we would find ourselves in a world of supreme technology and bewildering complexity. Is it really credible that random processes could have constructed a reality, the smallest element of which—a functional protein or gene—is complex beyond our own creative capacities, a reality which is the very antithesis of chance, which excels in every sense anything produced by the intelligence of man? Alongside the level of ingenuity and complexity exhibited by the molecular machinery of life, even our most advanced artifacts appear clumsy. . . . It would be an illusion to think that what we are aware of at present is any more than a fraction of the full extent of biological design. In practically every field of fundamental biological research ever-increasing levels of design and complexity are being revealed at an ever-accelerating rate.[31]

The mathematical impossibility of the universe simply "occurring" reveals just how silly it is for anyone to believe in Darwinian evolution. Nevertheless, naturalistic evolutionists would have us believe everything happened by random spontaneity—life chanced to come about from non-life; matter came into existence from nothing.

Right.

Sidestepping Cause and Effect

Evolutionists believe that something which had a beginning—i.e., the cosmos—had no cause. Hmm. But what about that basic, universally accepted principle of physics known as "the law of cause and effect"? It's the inconvenient reality that everything which has a beginning has to have a cause. If a baseball zings past your head, you know it did not just spontaneously begin moving along that trajectory by itself. The baseball and its motion had a cause—someone either picked up the ball and threw it or slapped it your way with a bat.

The world works that way, but there's reason to believe God doesn't. He did not need a cause because He had no beginning. He always was (see John 1:1). Of course, a critic may say, "Well, you claim God has always been here, but perhaps it's actually the world that has always existed, and there is no God." In this debate, though, science is once again our ally. The world is not eternal, as we will see in our next point.

The Bothersome Fundamental Laws of the Universe That Just Don't Help the Evolutionists' Case

To make the theory "work," evolutionists have to explain away tested and known laws of science. The laws of thermodynamics—the most fundamental laws of the physical sciences—confirm that the universe had a beginning. Let's look at each in turn.

The First Law of Thermodynamics, also referred to as the Law of Energy Conservation, states that the total amount of energy in the universe remains constant. Although energy can change form, it is never created or destroyed. Natural processes cannot make more energy. Therefore something or someone independent of the universe had to create energy to begin with.

The Second Law of Thermodynamics is also called the Law of Energy Decay or Law of Entropy. It states that the amount of energy available for useful work is running down or being depleted. In other words, like a watch you wind up, the universe is running down. This implies there had to be a point at which it was wound up. The world has not always "just been here," or it would have ceased to exist long ago due to entropy. And, from an evolutionary standpoint, there's another inopportune reality to the Second Law: Since the universe started, it has been going from a state of order to a state of disorder. Oh my. Now that does create an evolutionary pickle. Evolution tells us things get more orderly as we go along, not less. Unfortunately, no one has yet explained how we can have it both ways. But then, that's because, quite simply, we can't. That evolutionists believe a primordial soup impulsively delivered life into being and that life became increasingly organized—enough to randomly generate DNA, the human eye, ears, and your brain—is so radically inconsistent with the Second Law of Thermodynamics as to be absurd.

The Big Bang to the Rescue. Not.

In the 1960s, when naturalistic scientists faced the challenges of the First and Second Laws of Thermodynamics, the Big Bang theory was born. It says, in simple terms, that the universe began with a colossal explosion. Then, as the matter generated by the explosion spread apart, things began to come together very nicely to form the universe as we know it. So to clarify: order and precision resulted from an explosion.

If nothing else, the evolutionists' Big Bang theory clearly denotes a moment at which the universe began. This is a positive notion for those who believe in an intelligent designer. Now we have moved the ball down the field and caused evolutionists to change their strategy. From claiming the earth has always existed, they've postulated a *beginning* at the big bang. But, a beginning. Now why does that sound familiar? Oh yes, a beginning must have a cause, right?

The Big Bang theory opens up another whole can of worms for the evolutionist: like, what (*Who?*) made the big Bang happen? Sadly for the evolutionist, this theory that they'd like to think holds so much promise for atheism still seems to lead us back to a big Someone out there. Yes, even in Big Bang World, it's still true: matter doesn't come from non-matter. The gases needed to create the bang could not just magically appear. Cause and effect assures us that simply doesn't happen. Big bang gases had to have been created. Even the evolutionist seems to need a "who" to create the matter that mixed together and banged.

There's also that pesky reality of what is consistent with what we observe around us. One obvious question about the big bang is: When was the last time you saw or heard of an explosion that resulted in precision and order? Explosions tend to have the opposite effect.

Another reason to wonder about the Big Bang theory is:

the big bang had to have exploded with just the right degree of vigor for our present universe to have formed. If it had occurred with too little velocity, the universe would have collapsed back in on itself shortly after the big bang because of gravitational forces; if it had occurred with too much velocity, the matter would have streaked away so fast that it would have been impossible for galaxies and solar systems to subsequently form. To state it another way, the force of gravity must be fine-tuned to allow the universe to expand at precisely the right rate (accurate to within 1 part in 10^{60}).[32]

Whether Bang or not, a great deal of evidence now supports the option that the universe had a beginning. Robert Jastrow, founder and former director of NASA's Goddard Institute for Space Studies, has summarized the evidence in his book *God and the Astronomers,* saying, "Now three lines of evidence—the motions of the galaxies, the laws of thermodynamics, and the life story of the stars—pointed to one conclusion: all indicated that the Universe had a beginning."[33] If we are speaking of a beginning of the universe—a movement from no matter to matter—then we are clearly in the realm of unrepeatable events covered by origin science.[34]

Let's face it, evolutionists have their backs against the wall—and not because we used the Bible to put them there. I realize Bible verses wouldn't convince them anyway, but the point is that they're not necessary. Science, which is the thing humanists come closest to worshiping, put them there. I confess I think that's a delightful irony. For years, Christians were mocked for believing in a God that created the world, yet now evolutionists are stumbling all over their concepts, changing positions, fearing what fatal blow to the theory they'll have to dodge as new scientific discoveries cause more insurmountable problems. The question really is, how many fatal blows will it take?

Few premiere scientists still believe in Darwin's evolution. Soon only the stupid will accept the theory—which is really funny because a few years ago it was the evolutionist who claimed that only stupid folks would believe in creation. Henry Margenau observed, "If you take the top notch scientists, you find very few atheists among them."[35]

God is the author of all science, and evolutionists can read the signs and admit His existence now or later. Either way, they will eventually come to know that He is.

A Matter of Mind

Corliss Lamont, author of *The Philosophy of Humanism,* says humanism "considers all forms of the supernatural as myth."[36] Lamont goes on to proclaim that "the cosmos, in the individualized form of human beings giving rein to their imagination, created the gods."[37] What this necessarily implies is that matter—benign, unthinking *stuff*—came before and gave rise to minds capable of "creating the gods." Think about this for a minute. What the atheist/evolutionist is saying is that mere substances created smart things that ponder the universe—non-intelligence created intelligence. An evolutionist must believe intelligence grows out of non-intelligence because matter preceded mind. Again, does that stack up against what is observable about the world? Hardly. We always see intelligence as the generator of order—of things—not the other way around.

Is it really plausible that out of a primordial soup, a random process of impossibility erupted from the slime and happened to create eyes, ears, and brains? Spontaneous generation says one system can evolve into another, increasing along the way in information needed to become a more complex structure, but Dr. Walter Brown describes why spontaneous generation is absurd:

> All isolated systems contain a fixed amount of information. No isolated, non-trivial system has ever been observed to spontaneously increase its information content. Natural processes without exception destroy information. Only outside intelligence can increase the information content of an isolated system. Since all scientific observations are consistent with this generalization, it could be called "The Law of Intelligence." This law has three corollaries or consequences: (a) Macroevolution cannot occur, (b) Outside intelligence was involved in the creation of the universe and the creation of all forms of life, (c) A "big bang" cannot precede life.[38]

Intelligence coming from non-intelligence is just one more of the many unscientific, mathematically impossible things in which an evolutionist has to have faith. Christians, on the other hand, believe the mind proceeded matter—the mind of God created matter.

Fossil, Fossil, Who's Got the (Transitional) Fossil?

Remember that Wendy's commercial "Where's the beef?" Well, to the evolutionist I say, "Where's the transitional fossil?"

Charles Darwin expected countless transitional fossils would eventually be found. Although he was somewhat puzzled by the lack of transitional fossils even in his day, few enough dinosaur remains had been uncovered that Darwin could readily assume future discoveries would unearth what he was expecting. But nearly 150 years and thousands of fossil digs later, not one credible transitional fossil has been found. Not a single bone substantiates the idea that one species has ever mutated into another. Transitional forms do not exist. Darwin himself posed the central question that is more embarrassing to evolutionists today than ever: "Why is not every geological formation and every stratum full of such intermediate links? Geology assuredly does not reveal any such finely graduated organic chain; and this is the most obvious and serious objection which can be urged against the theory."[39]

Dr. Colin Patterson, an evolutionist with the British Museum of Natural History, wrote a book but did not include a single picture of a transitional fossil. When someone wrote him to ask why this was the case, Dr. Patterson responded:

> I fully agree with your comments on the lack of direct illustration of evolutionary transitions in my book. If I knew of any, fossil or living, I would certainly have included them. You suggest that an artist should be used to visualize such transformations, but where would he get the information from? I could not, honestly, provide it, and if I were to leave it to artistic license, would that not mislead the reader? . . . As a paleontologist myself, I am much occupied with the philosophical problems of identifying ancestral forms in the fossil record. You say that I should at least "show a photo of the fossil from which each type of organism was derived." I will lay it on the line—there is not one such fossil for which one could make a watertight argument.[40]

Stephen Jay Gould is perhaps one of the most well-known evolutionists, and he, too, recognizes the problem: "The absence of fossil evidence for intermediary stages between major transitions in organic design, indeed our inability, even in our imagination, to construct functional intermediates in many cases, has been a persistent and nagging problem for gradualistic accounts of evolution."[41] Gould also states, "I regard the failure to find a clear 'vector of progress' in life's history as the most puzzling fact of the fossil record."[42]

But what about those ape-men bones that were found and used to draw pictures of man changing from ape to man? After all, they were in our school textbooks. Dr. Walter Brown in his book, *In the Beginning,* writes:

> It is now universally acknowledged that Piltdown man was a hoax, and yet it was in textbooks for over forty years.
>
> The only evidence for Nebraska man turned out to be a pig's tooth.
>
> Prior to 1978, the evidence for Ramapithecus consisted of a mere handful of teeth and jaw fragments. It is now known that these fragments were pieced together incorrectly

by Louis Leakey in a form resembling part of the human jaw. Ramapithecus was just an ape.

Eugene Dubois acknowledged forty years ago when he discovered Java "man" that it was probably just a large gibbon. Dubois also admitted that he had withheld parts of four other high bones of apes, found in the same area, that supported that conclusion.

The fossils of Perking man are considered by many experts to be the remains of apes that were systematically decapitated and exploited for food by true man. Furthermore, Skull 1470, discovered by Richard Leakey, is more humanlike and yet older than Homo erectus (Java man and Peking man) and the Australopithecines. Since man cannot be older than his ancestors, something is obviously wrong.

The first confirmed limb bones of Homo habilis have recently been discovered. They show that this animal clearly had apelike proportions and should never have been classified as manlike (Homo).

Detailed computer studies of the Australopithecines have shown that they are not intermediate between man and living apes. The Australopithecines, which were made famous by Louis and Mary Leakey, are actually quite distinct from both men and the living apes. One Australopithecine fossil, referred to as Lucy, was initially presented as evidence that the Australopithecines walked upright in a human manner. However, studies of Lucy's entire anatomy, not just her knee joints, now show that this is highly improbable. She probably swung from trees. The Australopithecines are a type of extinct ape.

For about 100 years the world was led to believe that Neanderthal man was stooped and apelike. Recent studies show that this erroneous belief was based upon some Neanderthal men who were crippled with arthritis and rickets. Neanderthal man, Heidelberg man, and Cro-Magnon man were completely human. Artists' depictions of them, especially of their fleshly portions, are often quite imaginative and are not supported by the evidence.

Furthermore, the techniques used to date these fossils are highly questionable.[43]

It is galling to note that when these various "discoveries" were unearthed, the liberal media considered it big news. Yet, when the discoveries were shown to prove nothing about transitional evolution, the same media outlets either did not mention the new findings or did so on the "back page in small print."

So if the fossil record does not show transitional forms, then what does it reveal? According to Oswald Spengler, "We find perfectly stable and unaltered forms preserving through long ages, forms that have not developed themselves on the fitness principle, but appear suddenly and at once in their definitive shape; that do not thereafter evolve towards better adaptation, but become rarer and finally disappear."[44]

Other Glimpses of the Obvious

The fossil record doesn't substantiate evolution, and neither do several other not-too-difficult observations. Again, invoking what we see around us, there has never been an example of macroevolution observed in any species. And with good reason. Macroevolution requires that organisms mutate, and there's a problem with mutations. Have you ever heard of a good mutation?

In *How Now Shall We Live?*, Charles Colson and Nancy Pearcey observe, "Since breeding does nothing more than shuffle existing genes, the only way to drive evolution to the new levels of complexity is to introduce new genetic material. And the only natural source of new genetic materials in nature is mutations. In today's new neo-Darwinism, the central mechanism for evolution is random mutation and natural selection."[45]

Only an evolutionist attempting to justify a worldview that rejects God would be desperate enough to propose that mutations are a positive thing. The odds are astronomically against enough good mutations occurring to outweigh the bad ones so that a species can successfully transition from one type into another. Mutations are not a good thing. They are almost always fatal to the mutated organism. Yet, once again, let's not confuse evolutionists with the facts.

Evolutionists press on. Scientists have spent years subjecting fruit flies and the like to mutations, attempting to change a fruit fly into something else. What they've managed to do is change eye color, wing size, and a few other characteristics—and to kill a few tens of thousands by mutating them into unviable fruit flies. But the persistent little things always seem to remain fruit flies. Don't you just hate it when that happens?

Consider this startlingly revealing statement by a former chief science advisor with BBC Television: "It is a striking, but not much mentioned fact that, though geneticists have been breeding fruit flies for sixty years or more in labs all round the world—flies which produce a new generation every eleven days—they have never yet seen the emergence of a new species or even a new enzyme."[46]

In *Not by Chance,* biophysicist Dr. Lee Spetner, who taught information and communication at John Hopkins University, wrote:

In this chapter I'll bring several examples of evolution [i.e., instances alleged to be examples of evolution], particularly mutations and show that information is not increased. . . . But in all reading I've done in the life-sciences literature, I've never found a mutation that added information. All point mutations that have been studied on the molecular level turn out to reduce the genetic information and not to increase it. The NDT [neo-Darwinian theory] is supposed to explain how the information of life has built up by evolution. The essential biological differences between a human and a bacterium is in the information they contain. All other biological differences follow from that. The human genome has much more information than does the bacterial genome. Information cannot be built up by mutations that lose it. A business can't make money by loosing it a little at a time.[47]

Remember, according to Darwin himself, mutations are absolutely necessary for his evolutionary process to work. Additional testimony by experts further damages the possibility that mutations would do what Darwin claimed in order for you and me to evolve.

James F. Crow, while professor of genetics at the University of Wisconsin, wrote, "Even if we didn't have a great deal of data on this point, we could still be quite sure on theoretical grounds that mutants would usually be detrimental. For a mutation is a random change of a highly organized, reasonably smoothly functioning living body. A random change in the highly integrated system of chemical processes which constitute life is almost certain to impair it—just as a random interchange of connections in a television set is not likely to improve the picture."[48] Geneticist Richard B. Goldschmidt also notes, "If life really depends on each gene being as unique as it appears to be, then it is too unique to come into being by chance mutations."[49]

In conclusion, I challenge you to commit to memory two or three of the incredible things we've discussed that an evolutionist has to believe to think evolution is for real. Then the next time you talk to an evolutionist or someone thinking of accepting the evolution lie, ask why they are willing to believe in billions upon billions of mathematically impossible happenings that contradict known and tested laws of science when the alternative is a well-reasoned faith in one all-knowing, all-powerful, intelligent designer known as God.

Remember. The real goal of evolution is not to gain knowledge about how the world came to be. The primary purpose is to explain away the existence of God because of foolish pride and the humanistic desire to be "as god." Atheists just don't want to admit that Someone could be so powerful and unimaginably intelligent as to put together the cosmos as we know it. It's too . . . well . . . humbling.

Chapter 6

Taking the Dilemma
Out of Moral Dilemmas

Liberals, we see, try to take the miracle out of creation and continue to fail. But when it comes to sidestepping that irritating Moral Law, their track record is, I fear, considerably better. Let's look at how they're doing, and what we can do about it.

Gambling, the state lottery, abortion, school-based health clinics, capital punishment, government welfare programs, doctor-assisted suicide, and euthanasia are all issues that raise moral dilemmas with which many people wrestle. Yet, are these concerns really so complicated?

Many Christians turn to the back of their Bibles and flip through their concordances to see if they can find Scripture verses about abortion, gambling, euthanasia, and so forth, but to little avail. The Bible does not mention these moral dilemmas by name. It does, however, give us clear principles and standards that allow us to maintain a firm biblical worldview on most moral dilemmas of our day.

Because the Bible is a reflection of God's character, the more we study Scripture, the more likely we are to know how God would have us think and live in accord with His perfect nature. Let's make some applications to what we see happening around us. I suspect one of the issues about which God is most displeased is the American liberals' love affair with abortion rights.

Abortion and High School Counselors

Attorney John Eldredge reveals only one of the many tragic stories about young girls victimized by school counselors and abortion doctors:

Abortion has been one of the most emotionally charged issues in America since it was legalized in 1973. While it may be legal, not everything that is legal is moral, and abortion is clearly immoral. We have a tendency to forget that the statistics we read in our newspapers and the reports we hear on the nightly news represent the lives of real people.

Numbers like 1.6 million abortions every year can be overwhelming. For many of us, figures like these are too much to comprehend. Perhaps we can relate to one woman and one child whose life is in question.

Rachel was 17 when she learned she was pregnant. Her high school counselor recommended she have an abortion and arranged for state funding and recommended a particular abortion clinic. No other alternatives were discussed. Rachel was afraid to tell her parents that she had become pregnant. Unaware of any alternatives, she consented to the abortion.

Several days later she developed flu-like symptoms in her chest. She went to her family doctor, but she did not tell him about the abortion because she did not think the symptoms were related. Sometime later, Rachel became so sick her father took her to a local hospital. The next morning she was found in a comatose condition.

Subsequently, it was discovered that she had developed bacterial endocarditis—a condition directly attributable to a post-abortion surgical infection. The bacterial endocarditis had caused blood clots to develop and become lodged in the vascular system of her brain, causing a stroke. When Rachel recovered from her coma, she was left permanently wheelchair-bound. Why was it not required by law that her parents know before the procedure ever happened?

Rachel's story is not uncommon, although the consequences for her were particularly extreme. Consider also
the millions of women and girls who undergo deep physical
and emotional distress as a result of abortion. Add to that
all of the butchered children who if allowed to live would
have been starting kindergarten this year, or playing on the
varsity team, or going off to college, but were never given a
chance.[1]

Pro-abortion liberals (i.e., most liberals) justify the killing of
babies with lame excuses such as:

- A fetus is not a human being.
- A woman has the right to do whatever she wants with her own
  body.
- Abortion is the best way to handle an unwanted pregnancy.

Let's address these pro-abortion arguments one at a time, and we
will see the fallacy of the futile, self-serving thinking involved.

Is It a Human Being?

Liberals have argued abortion is morally acceptable because the
fetus is not a live human being at the early stages of development. If
this were the case—which it is not—why then do liberals justify full-
term abortion when an ultrasound clearly shows the baby is human
and not a dog or cat? A four-year-old knows that humans have humans,
dogs have dogs, cats have cats, and birds have birds. To claim that the
fetus is not human goes against common sense and science.

The fetus is clearly a human fetus and is clearly alive. Kerby
Anderson describes the medical and scientific evidence that the fetus
is a live human being:

Death used to be defined by the cessation of heartbeat.
A stopped heart was a clear sign of death. If the cessation of
heartbeat could define death, could the onset of a heartbeat
define life? The heart is formed by the eighteenth day in the
womb. If heartbeat were used to define life, then nearly all
abortions would be outlawed. Physicians now use a more
rigorous criterion for death: brain-wave activity. A flat EEG

(electroencephalograph) is one of the most important criteria used to determine death. If the cessation of brain-wave activity can define death, could the onset of brain-wave activity define life? Individual brain waves are detected in the fetus in about forty to forty-three days. Using brain-wave activity to define life would outlaw at least a majority of abortions.[2]

Other milestones of fetal development are equally telling:

- *At three weeks* the backbone, spinal column, and nervous system are forming. The kidneys, liver, and intestines are taking shape.

- *At five weeks* the neural tube enlarges into three parts, soon to become a complex brain. The spine and spinal cord grows faster than the rest of the body and gives the appearance of a tail.

- *At seven weeks* facial features are visible, including a mouth and tongue. The eyes have a retina and lens. The major muscle system is developed, and the unborn child practices moving. The child has its own blood type, distinct from the mother, and blood cells are now produced by the liver instead of the yolk sac.

- *In the eighth week,* brain waves can be measured, fingers are visible, and toes will develop in the next few days.

- *In the tenth week,* the heart is almost completely developed and very much resembles that of a newborn baby. An opening in the atrium of the heart and the presence of a bypass valve direct much of the blood away from the lungs since the child's blood is oxygenated through the placenta. Twenty tiny baby teeth are forming in the gums.

- *In the twelfth week,* the vocal chords are complete, and the child sometimes cries silently. The brain is fully formed, and the child may even suck his thumb. Eyelids now cover the eyes but will remain shut until the seventh month to protect the delicate optical nerve fibers.[3]

This is the development of the baby in just its first twelve weeks of life—the first trimester!

Pro-abortion advocates argue that the baby feels no pain. While all medical evidence and science shows that the baby indeed does feel pain, liberals have fought federal legislation that requires giving the unborn baby an anesthetic so it will not suffer. Humanist liberals seem strangely unconcerned about even the possibility that unborn children might feel pain as doctors systematically dismember them through horrific abortion procedures such as:

- *Dilation and Curettage.* The physician dilates the cervix with a series of instruments to allow the insertion of a curette—a loop shaped knife—into the womb. The instrument is used to scrape the placenta from the uterus and then cut the baby apart. The pieces are then pulled through the cervix. The tiny body must then be reassembled by an attending nurse to make sure no parts remain in the womb to cause infection.[4]
- *Suction Aspiration.* [This procedure] is used in 80 percent of the abortions up to the twelfth week of pregnancy. The mouth of the cervix is dilated. A hollow tube with a knife-edged tip is inserted into the womb. A suction force twenty-eight times stronger than a vacuum cleaner literally tears the developing baby and the placenta to pieces. These pieces are sucked into a container.[5]
- *Saline Injection.* Also known as salt poisoning. A strong salt solution is injected through the mother's abdominal wall into the amniotic fluid surrounding the baby. The baby then breathes and swallows the solution causing internal poisoning and burning. In a few hours the unborn child dies from salt poisoning, dehydration, and hemorrhaging. The mother goes into labor and delivers a dead (or dying) baby.[6]
- *Prostaglandin.* Involves the use of prostaglandin hormones, which are injected into the womb or released in a vaginal suppository. This causes the uterus to contract and deliver the child prematurely. A saline solution is sometimes injected first, killing the baby before birth, in order to make the procedure less distressful for the mother and the medical staff.[7]
- *Dilation and Evacuation.* Commonly called a D&E, this procedure is used after the twelfth week of pregnancy. The doctor dilates the mother's cervix and uses forceps to reach into the

uterus. He grasps the arms and legs, dismembers the body, and crushes the skull to remove it. The placenta and smaller pieces are removed by suction and sharp cutting.[8]

- *Hysterotomy.* Similar to a Caesarean section, this is done in the last three months of pregnancy. The procedure involves opening the womb surgically and removing the baby. The purpose of this procedure, unlike that of a C-section, is to end the infant's life.[9]
- *Dilation and Extraction.* Also known as "partial-birth abortion." The physician dilates the cervix and pulls the baby's body out, except for the head. Leaving the head inside, the doctor inserts scissors in the skull of the baby and sucks out the brains. The head collapses and the baby is brought out to die.[10]

Can a Woman Do Anything She Wants with Her Body?

According to liberals, a woman has a right to do whatever she wants with her own body, but is that really true? Is it legal, for instance, for a woman to commit suicide? No, it is not. Women are regularly arrested and taken to jail or a mental hospital for attempting to kill themselves. Yet under the reasoning of the liberals, these women are being denied the right to do what they want with their own bodies, including killing it.

Is it legal for a woman to shoot her veins up with illegal drugs or use her nose to snort cocaine? No, it is not. But again, using the liberals' reasoning, women who are prosecuted for using illegal drugs are being denied their right to do what they want with their bodies.

Is it legal for a woman to sell her body as a prostitute? No again. Aren't these women being denied the right to do what they want with their own bodies?

You see, the argument that a woman has a right to do whatever she wants with her body—and thus to kill her unborn child—does not hold up. The laws of America do not give a woman an unrestrained right to do whatever she wants with herself. So why should she have the right to kill her unborn child? The answer, of course, is that she shouldn't, but even asking the question begs yet another critical question: Is the baby part of the woman's body? Here again, the answer is clearly no. The baby is a separate human being who will eventually be capable of living completely apart from the mother. Having an abortion is not the same has having your appendix taken out. The appendix is part of the mother's body. It was there when she was born, and the appendix is not a being of any sort that can live separate from the mother.

Scientific data weighs in heavily against the argument that the baby is part of the mother's body. As occasional Worldview Weekend speaker Kerby Anderson points out in his book, *Moral Dilemmas,* the baby is a unique person with its own DNA code and fingerprint:

> At conception the embryo is genetically distinct from the mother. To say that the developing baby is no different from the mother's appendix is scientifically inaccurate. A developing embryo is genetically different from the mother. A developing embryo is also genetically different from the sperm and egg that created it. A human being has forty-six chromosomes (sometimes forty-seven chromosomes). A sperm and an egg each have twenty-three chromosomes. A trained geneticist can distinguish between the DNA of an embryo and the DNA of a sperm and egg. But that geneticist cannot distinguish between DNA of a developing embryo and the DNA of a full-grown human being.[11]

The biblical worldview tells us abortion is murder, and we are clearly told in the Ten Commandments, "Thou shall not murder." In Exodus 21:22–25, we read there was punishment for causing harm or death to an unborn child, and our contemporary laws remain consistent with this scriptural admonition. When a person kills a pregnant woman, he or she is charged with a double homicide. How can you have a double homicide unless there are two individual lives?

Genesis 1:26–27; 5:1; 9:6; Psalm 139; 1 Corinthians 11:7; and James 3:9 reveal that every human is created in the image of God, and Psalm 51:5 tells us that the baby even has a sin nature. The Greek word for "baby," by the way, is the same word when referring to a baby inside or outside of the woman, revealing the fact that God views the unborn baby and just-born infant equally. Clearly, America has strayed from a biblical worldview, and this is no more clearly seen than through the slaughter of more than 40 million babies since 1973.

My friend, Sean McDowell, told me about a man in Wisconsin who was sent to prison for twelve years for killing cats. Yet, Amy Grossberg received only two and a half years in prison and her boyfriend Brian Peterson only two years for throwing their newborn baby in a dumpster after delivering it in a hotel room.

Ideas do have consequences, and because of the 1973 U.S. Supreme Court ruling on *Roe vs. Wade* that legalized abortion, a culture of death has been allowed to grow and flourish in America. Abortion has led to euthanasia and infanticide (I consider partial-birth abortion to be infanticide).

Dr. Peter Singer, professor of ethics at Princeton University, is an outspoken promoter of abortion, euthanasia, and the outright murder of a baby if the parents, after its birth, simply do not want the child. Students at the university organized a group called Princeton Students against the Hiring of Peter Singer and issued a statement in which they point out why Singer should not be hired as Princeton's professor of ethics. Quoting from Dr. Singer's own books such as *Practical Ethics* (2nd ed.) and *Should the Baby Live?*, they state:

We the undersigned protest the hiring of Dr. Peter Singer as the Ira DeCamp Professor of Bioethics at Princeton University's Center for Human Values. We protest his hiring because Dr. Singer denies the intrinsic moral worth of an entire class of human beings—newborn children—and promotes policies that would deprive many infants with disabilities of their basic human right to legal protection against homicide.

In his book *Practical Ethics*, Dr. Singer states that no infant has as strong a claim to life as a rational, self-conscious human being. Dr. Singer's criteria for distinguishing newborn infants from "normal human beings" (including more mature infants) thus hinge on subjectively imposed conditions such as "rationality, autonomy, and self-consciousness." This lesser claim to life is also applied to those older children or adults whose mental age is and has always been that of an infant.

His assertion of the appropriateness of killing some humans based on the decision of others, concerning the "quality" of their lives, should strike fear into everyone who cherishes equality and honors human life. Furthermore, Dr. Singer defines certain disabled persons as individuals who are living "a life not worth living." His views permit the killing of certain newborn infants with disabilities up to 28 days after birth. Dr. Singer states that "killing a disabled infant is not morally equivalent to killing a person. Very often, it is not wrong at all." Dr. Singer's message threatens individuals with disabilities and contributes to the erosion of the public's regard for the fundamental human rights of disabled people.

Finally, Dr. Singer suggests that the regulated killing of babies with spina bifida be permitted. He would extend to parents the authority to "replace" a Down's syndrome or hemophiliac infant (i.e., kill the child and conceive another) if adequate family or societal resources were not forthcoming. Although Dr. Singer concentrates on disabled infants, the ethical arguments and metaphors that he provisionally adopts leave open the potential empowerment of parents to kill a non-disabled newborn whose "replacement" would ameliorate their prospects for a happy life.

The hiring of Dr. Peter Singer to a professorial chair in ethics at a university as prestigious as Princeton will certainly, though perhaps unintentionally, legitimate his claims. Thus legitimated, Dr. Singer will use the platform afforded by Princeton to continue to argue for the killing of certain disabled babies, and his teachings may help cast the practice of infanticide in a more respectable light; further, his teaching may encourage the propagation of infanticide. The hiring of Dr. Peter Singer is a blatant violation of Princeton University's policy of respect for people with disabilities. . . .

Dr. Singer's view that many disabled babies may rightly be killed demeans and threatens those with handicaps. His ideology reinforces the false notion that many disabled persons' lives are less worth living and are inherently inferior to the lives of others. Despite his assurances that he rejects discrimination against the adult disability population, it is demeaning to suggest to them that their parents would have been justified in killing them as newborns. If Princeton University is committed to upholding the principles of non-discrimination, it must rescind its decision to hire Dr. Peter Singer.[12]

Opening Pandora's Box

The Princeton students were exactly right about the legitimizing influence of placing someone like Singer in a prestigious position. Through this and other such actions, ideas that once would have been recognized as despicable, have gained respectability little by little.

Because abortion was legalized, America now debates the moral ity and legality of euthanasia and doctor-assisted suicide. Kerby Anderson explains the ever-widening risk for Americans brought about by the opening of this Pandora's Box:

Ever since the Supreme Court ruled in *Roe vs. Wade* that the life of unborn babies could be terminated for reasons of convenience, there has been an erosion of the doctrine of the sanctity of life, even though the Supreme Court has been reluctant to legalize euthanasia. . . . This progression was inevitable. Once society begins to devalue the life of an unborn child, it is but a small step to being willing to do the same with a child who has been born. Abortion slides naturally into infanticide and eventually into euthanasia. In the past few years doctors have allowed a number of so-called Baby Does to die (either by failing to perform life-saving operations or else by not feeding the infants). The progression from this toward euthanasia is inevitable. Once society becomes accustomed to using a "quality of life" standard for infants, it will more willingly accept the same standard for the elderly.[13]

Euthanasia and Doctor-assisted Suicide

Because "euthanasia" is used in different ways, it is crucial to define the term in order to discuss adequately the ethical issues involved. Some people argue that certain forms of euthanasia are consistent with a biblical worldview, and it is important to know why. In his book, *Moral Dilemmas*, Kerby Anderson offers great insight on various references to euthanasia:

Voluntary, passive euthanasia: This form of euthanasia assumes that medical personnel, at the patient's request, will merely allow nature to take its course. In the past, passive euthanasia meant that the physician did nothing to hasten death but did provide care, comfort, and counsel to dying patients. This is not truly euthanasia in the modern sense.[14]

Voluntary, active euthanasia: This means that the physician, by request, hastens death by taking some active means (e.g., lethal injection). This raises the controversial issue of whether non-medical personnel such as a spouse or friend would be permitted to end the suffering of another.[15]

Involuntary, passive euthanasia: This assumes that the patient has not expressed a willingness to die or cannot do so. The medical personnel do not go to any extraordinary measures to save the patient and often withhold food (by removing nasogastric tubes), antibiotics, or life-support systems (respirators).[16]

Involuntary, active euthanasia: This category begins to blur into homicide. In this case the physician does something active to hasten death, regardless of the patient's wishes, for humanitarian reasons, economic considerations, or genetic justifications.[17]

As you can see from the definitions of euthanasia, the passive forms of euthanasia are not of concern in most cases because nothing is being done to hasten the end of life. In such situations, medical personnel keep the terminal patient comfortable and pain-free while allowing nature to take its course with regard to the death itself.

It is the active forms of euthanasia—whether voluntary or involuntary—that are of great concern. Active, involuntary euthanasia can include "mercy killings" in which a family member or doctor takes the life of a terminally ill patient or a patient that has "no quality of life." In the past few years there have been several cases where a wife or husband have shot and killed a sleeping spouse that was either terminal or was greatly disabled due to Alzheimer's or Parkinson's diseases. In such cases, the spouses have been prosecuted for murder, as they should.

In other forms of active, involuntary euthanasia, family members talk a doctor into using drugs to euthanize a patient, or the doctor simply does so on his own without the family's knowledge or consent.

As researcher R. Finigsen reports: "The Dutch experience is instructive. A survey of Dutch physicians was made in 1990 by the Remmelink Committee. They found that 1,030 patients were killed without their consent. Of these, 140 were fully mentally competent and 110 were only slightly mentally impaired. The report also found that another 14,175 (1,701 of them were mentally competent) were denied medical treatment without their consent and died."[18]

In *Ethics for a Brave New World*, Dr. J. S. Feinberg offers a brief history of how a U.S. Supreme Court decision laid the groundwork for active euthanasia:

Several events in recent years have really captured the attention of Americans, polarized views on the euthanasia question and galvanized many to action. One is Dr. Kevorkian's suicide machine, and another is the book *Final Exit*. But undoubtedly the right-to-die case of Nancy Cruzan has been the most significant factor in raising people's awareness and "temperature" on this issue. Because of its importance, we briefly sketch the details of this case.

On January 11, 1983, twenty-five-year-old Nancy Cruzan was in an automobile accident in the Ozarks in southwestern Missouri. Paramedics arrived and restarted her breathing, but she had been without oxygen for so long that she never regained consciousness. On February 5, 1983, doctors implanted a feeding tube in Nancy's stomach. Apart from this apparatus, she was not on life-support systems.

Over the next years Nancy did not die, but she did not improve. She seemed to be in what is called a permanent vegetative state. As a result, in October 1987, Nancy's parents went to court to get permission to remove the feeding tube and let her die as they believed she would want.

On July 27, 1988, the Jasper County (Missouri) Judge granted them permission to remove the tube. However, the case was appealed to the Missouri Supreme Court, and on November 16, 1988, the court in a 4-3 decision overturned the lower court ruling, claiming there was no legal authority to grant the Cruzans' request.

The Cruzans appealed the case to the U.S. Supreme Court. It was the first time the Supreme Court had ruled on a right-to-die case. In a 5-4 decision on June 25, 1990, the Court ruled to deny the Cruzans' request. However, the decision was not based on a belief that food and water could not be removed because they are basics of patient care and are not medicine. Nor was it based on a belief that patients do not have a right to choose to die. Instead, the ruling came because there was no "clear and convincing evidence" that Nancy would have wanted to stop artificial nutrition.

Had she signed a living will to that effect or granted power of attorney to her family to make decisions on her healthcare, the petition would have been granted. But she had done neither, and once comatose she obviously couldn't. Though the Cruzans' request was rejected, the Supreme Court in essence affirmed a patient's right to die under certain circumstances so long as there is a living will specifying those situations or a power of attorney granting decision-making power to a surrogate.

On August 30, 1990, the Cruzans went back to the Missouri judge and asked for another hearing, claiming they had new evidence that their daughter had once told three people she would rather die than live in a persistent vegetative state. In light of the Supreme Court's ruling that clear evidence of her desire to die was necessary to remove the tube, and in view of the new testimony to that effect, on December 14, 1990, the judge ruled that Cruzan's parents could remove her feeding tube. Shortly thereafter, that was done, and Nancy Cruzan finally died.[19]

The non-decision decision by the U.S. Supreme Court opened the floodgate for cases like that of Terri Schiavo. In 1990, Terri Schiavo, a twenty-seven-year-old Florida woman suffered a heart attack and lost oxygen to her brain that left her greatly disabled and without the ability to speak. Terri's husband fought to have her feeding tube removed and to starve her to death despite the fact her parents did not want their daughter to be a victim of active euthanasia. Terri's parents even agreed to take complete responsibility for Terri's care and medical expenses. The October 28, 2003, *St. Petersburg Times* published a story by Curtis Krueger that revealed Terri's awareness:

Terri Schiavo smiles. She laughs, cries, and moans. Her eyes appear to follow a balloon around the room. When a cotton swab slips into her mouth, she grimaces. Those images, from video clips on television and a Web site created by Schiavo's family, have helped fuel the national debate over whether to remove the feeding tube that has kept the brain-damaged Pinellas County woman alive.

The multi-year legal battled resulted in the Florida legislature passing Terri's Law in 2004 that would allow Governor Jeb Bush to intervene, which he did, ordering Terri's feeding tube to be re-connected so Terri would not starve to death.

On September 23, 2004, the Florida Supreme Court ruled Terri's Law was unconstitutional based on a separation of powers concern. It seems the judges are far more concerned about a separation of powers issue than the murder of Terri Schiavo.

The Terri Schiavo case is a great example of the dangers of active euthanasia. Terri's family is fighting for her life and believes that she would not want to be killed. Terri's husband believes Terri would want to be killed. The solution to this problem is to choose to follow the Hippocratic Oath which is "to do no harm."[20]

Obviously, doctor-assisted suicide is active euthanasia. In Terri's case, there were two versions of the question. One is: What would Terri want? If she could choose death and her preference was granted, it would be a case of *voluntary*, active euthanasia. The other question is: Should another person (i.e., Terry's husband) be permitted to decide she should die? If so, this would be *involuntary*, active euthanasia. Tragically, we will never know Terri's wishes. On March 18, 2005, by court order, Terri's feeding tube was disconnected. Without the food and water it supplied, this full-grown but helpless American citizen starved to death under the watchful eyes of her physicians.

Writing about Terri's death, David Limbaugh explained the implications for America:

> What this boils down to is that our courts (and far too many in society) are so acclimated to our Culture of Death that they are erring on the side of death. Despite enormous doubts about Terri's condition, her intentions and even her initial injury, the courts are determining that in the end, none of this matters because anyone in Terri's diminished state (no matter what it specifically is) is better off dead. It's essentially a court-ordered murder based on the court's subjective assessment of the victims' quality of life—an assessment tainted by its diminished reverence for human life.
>
> The decision to kill Terri Schiavo is not in defense of Terri's intentions, about which there is way too much doubt, but to godlessness, humanism and death. It is to quench society's lust for death.
>
> This case marks a turning point in the Culture War, where society is making a giant leap toward the dark side, embracing the lie over truth and death over life. In our relentless quest to become like gods, we are crossing another sacred line, and it is hard to imagine how we might return.[21]

The consequences of legalizing active euthanasia will impact every American because of the frightful danger that doctor-assisted suicide could be forced onto those that don't want to be killed. As

Limbaugh notes, this takes our culture of death to a far deeper level of potentially appalling personal disasters. Kerby Anderson also offers this compelling observation:

> First, physician-assisted suicide would change the nature of the medical profession itself. Physicians would be cast in the role of killers rather than healers. The Hippocratic Oath was written to place the medical profession on the foundation of healing, not killing. For twenty-four hundred years patients have had the assurance that doctors have taken an oath to heal them, not kill them. This would change with legalized euthanasia.
>
> Second, medical care would be affected. Physicians would begin to ration healthcare so that elderly and severely disabled patients would not be receiving the same quality of care as everyone else.
>
> Legalizing euthanasia would result in less care for the dying, rather than better care. Legalizing physician-assisted suicide would open the door to anyone wanting the "right" to kill themselves. Soon this would apply not only to voluntary euthanasia but also to involuntary euthanasia as various court precedents began to broaden the application of the right to die to other groups in society, like the disabled or the clinically depressed.[22]

While you will not find the word *euthanasia* in the Bible, the relevant biblical principles are evident for those who want to have a biblical worldview on this issue. Many verses regarding abortion, for instance, can be applied to euthanasia. In addition, there are Scripture verses that relate specifically to the taking of the life of an adult. In the story of the death of Saul in 2 Samuel 1:1—16, for example:

> After the death of Saul, David returned from defeating the Amalekites and stayed at Ziklag two days. On the third day, a man with torn clothes and dust on his head came from Saul's camp. When he came to David, he fell to the ground and paid homage. David asked him, "Where have you come from?"
>
> He replied to him, "I've escaped from the Israelite camp."
>
> "What was the outcome? Tell me," David asked him.

"The troops fled from the battle," he answered. "Many of the troops have fallen and are dead. Also, Saul and his son Jonathan are dead."

David asked the young man who had brought him the report, "How do you know Saul and his son Jonathan are dead?"

"I happened to be on Mount Gilboa," he replied, "and there was Saul, leaning on his spear. At that very moment the chariots and the cavalry were closing in on him. When he turned around and saw me, he called out to me, so I answered: I'm at your service. He asked me, 'Who are you?' I told him: I'm an Amalekite. Then he begged me, 'Stand over me and kill me, for I'm mortally wounded, but my life still lingers.' So I stood over him and killed him because I knew that after he had fallen he couldn't survive. I took the crown that was on his head and the armband that was on his arm, and I've brought them here to my lord."

Then David took hold of his clothes and tore them, and all the men with him did the same. They mourned, wept, and fasted until the evening for those who died by the sword— for Saul, his son Jonathan, and the Lord's people and the house of Israel.

David inquired of the young man who had brought him the report, "Where are you from?"

"I'm the son of a foreigner," he said. "I'm an Amalekite."

David questioned him, "How is it that you were not afraid to lift your hand to destroy the Lords' anointed?" Then David summoned one of this servants and said, "Come here and kill him!" The servant struck him, and he died. For David had said to the Amalekite, "Your blood is on your own head because your own mouth testified against you by saying, 'I killed the Lord's anointed.'"

Here we see the issue of euthanasia and capital punishment in the same verses. Saul was injured on the battlefield and requested that the young man kill him. Instead of a doctor doing the killing, a soldier performed the active euthanasia. When the young man told King David what he had done, David rebuked him, told him he had committed murder, and ordered that the young man be executed.

As the king, David was head of the government and, as such, had the biblical right and authority to use capital punishment on those who committed capital crimes. That is what happened when David ordered the death of the young man who murdered Saul. David didn't view the young man's act of voluntary active euthanasia as acceptable. Psalm 139:16 tells us that our days are ordained by God, meaning He is in charge of when we are born and when we die.

A further biblical indication of the sanctity of life is the general prohibition against life-taking. Killing is condemned both in the Old Testament (Exod. 20:13) and New (Matt. 5:21; 19:18; Mark 10:19; Luke 18:20; Rom. 13:9). While there are exceptions to the rule (e.g., killing in self-defense, capital punishment, just war), the deliberate, intentional taking of innocent life is not one of them. In most cases, euthanasia is the deliberate taking of innocent life, and biblical teaching renders those cases morally unacceptable.[23]

While abortion and euthanasia are crucial life-and death issues, some moral issues do not involve killing but nevertheless have a sweeping impact on our culture. Even as we sink deeper into a culture of death, we are also mired in a culture of greed.

Everyone Wants to Be a Millionaire

Although many forms of gambling remain illegal throughout the United States, where it is practiced—whether through legally-operated casinos or state-sponsored lotteries—the cultural fallout is immense. This shouldn't come as a surprise because the Bible has much to say about the problems caused by this "sport."

More than 1,700 verses in Scripture have to do with finances, and many American pastors have been vigilant in preaching about gambling—particularly state-based gambling when it is on their state ballot. While this is a good thing, the tide against which these faithful preachers are swimming is overwhelming in many ways. One of the most difficult aspects of addressing the gambling issue is that, of all the moral issues we might discuss, this one looks the most like a wolf in sheep's clothing. Outwardly, gambling appears to be harmless entertainment—possibly even a great way to come up with a little extra money. Underneath, though, the vicious reality is anything but benign. Let's look first at some scriptural reasons why this is so.

Romans 13:1–4 tells us the purpose of civil government is to protect the righteous and punish the wicked:

> Everyone must submit to the governing authorities, for there is no authority except from God, and those that exist are instituted by God. So then, the one who resists the authority is opposing God's command, and those who oppose it will bring judgment on themselves. For rulers are not a terror to good conduct, but to bad. Do you want to be unafraid of the authority? Do good and you will have its approval. For government is God's servant to you for good. But if you do wrong, be afraid, because it does not carry the sword for no reason. For government is God's servant, an avenger that brings wrath on the one who does wrong.

This passage makes it clear that government officials are ministers of God. States that sponsor gambling are sponsoring a vice that God says to avoid. Why? Because gambling encourages laziness, greed, coveting, and it takes advantage of the poor—all of which God opposes. The civil government cannot follow its God-given purpose and protect the righteous when it is establishing habits that promote unrighteousness or wrong living.

While I am encouraged by pastors who do preach from the Bible why the church should oppose gambling, many pastors believe such matters should not be addressed by the church because they are "political issues." Not only do I think they are wrong to think so, but I believe their attitude is largely responsible for America's moral decline. Such pastors have betrayed their flocks as well as the teaching and proclamation of the whole counsel of God.

Hotel casinos, riverboat casinos, lottery tickets, pull-tabs at the local bar, online gambling, horse tracks, and neighborhood poker games have all become a great American pastime. But before we look at a Christian worldview response to gambling, let's consider the following facts about gambling in America:

- Legalized gambling siphons off a great deal of money from the economy. More is wagered on gambling than is spent on elementary and secondary education ($286 billion versus $213 billion in 1990). Historian John Ezel concludes, in his book *Fortune's Merry Wheel*, "If history teaches us anything, a study of over 1,300 legal lotteries held in the United States proves . . . they cost more than they brought in if their total impact on society is reckoned."[24]

- In one year, more than $550 billion is spent in legalized gambling. Every day, $88 million are spent on lotteries alone—more money than is spent on food.
- Ten million Americans have a gambling addiction. Six percent of all adolescents are addicted to gambling. Three-fourths of high school students are involved in some form of gambling. When gamblers come to the point of seeking help, their debts usually range between $18,000 and $50,000.
- When legalized gambling enters a new area, there is a 100-500 percent increase in cases of compulsive gambling, and at least two-thirds of compulsive gamblers turn to crime to finance their addiction.
- A Colorado city realized a six-fold increase in child protection cases the year after a casino arrived.
- Domestic violence and child abuse dramatically increase, and 20 percent of compulsive gamblers attempt suicide.
- *U.S. News & World Report* confirmed: "Crime rates are higher in places with gambling, 1,092 incidents per 10,000 population in 1994, compared with 593 per 10,000 for the entire nation."
- In a testimony before a U.S. Congressional committee on small businesses, the statement was made that for every one dollar a state receives from gambling revenue, it costs that state at least three dollars in increased services such as criminal justice and welfare.
- About half of the college students surveyed in the United States and Canada said they had gambled at a casino during the previous year.
- In New Jersey "gambling is festering in every high school and college," said Edward Looney, director of the New Jersey Council on Compulsive Gambling. "It's absolutely epidemic. Just about any college in the country has students who gamble at racetracks and casinos."[25]

- As a veteran judge for some twenty-five years in the municipal courts of Chicago and the circuit court of Cook County, Illinois, Jacob M. Brande lays his finger on fifteen specific causes of juvenile delinquency, one of which is gambling.[26]

Despite the devastating impact of gambling on Americans, many lawmakers continue to support legislation that allows for the proliferation of gambling. Understanding the economic liability and seeing the issue through the lens of a Christian worldview, some conservative lawmakers, however, do oppose the expansion of gambling. Gambling is wrong from a Christian worldview for the reasons I outline below.

State-sponsored Robbery

State-sponsored and state-approved gambling is wrong because the marketing and advertising of gaming is inherently deceptive. The next time you see a TV commercial or hear a radio spot promoting a state lottery, note well the sales pitch. It won't tell the truth. Do these commercials, for instance, tell you (or even imply!) that your chances of winning are so remote that you have a better chance of being struck by lightning than winning or that a woman has a better chance of bearing triplets than of "hitting it big"? Do lottery commercials mention the devastating consequences gambling has proven to have on marriages and children? Not hardly. The commercials promise you a great time, lots of fun, happiness, and imply that you might even get rich. Bear in mind, too, this is the message coming from your own government, the institution legally and morally bound to look out for your best interests. The ads spout nothing but outright deception—which the Bible vehemently warns against. Here are a few examples of just how vehemently:

- *Leviticus 6:2, 5*—"When someone sins and offends the LORD by deceiving his neighbor in regard to a deposit, a security, or a robbery; or defrauds his neighbor, . . . [h]e must make full restitution."
- *Proverbs 6:19* lists, as two of six things the Lord hates: "a lying witness who gives false testimony, and one who stirs up trouble among brothers."
- *Proverbs 11:18*—"The wicked man earns an empty wage."

States, of course, are not the only guilty parties. I wonder if the Indian tribes and businessmen who make their living from gambling have ever read these verses. Indeed, state-sponsored or other legal gambling spreads strife among families, and gambling businesses always use deception to get people to buy that lottery ticket or go to the casino.

The Bible also is rife with warnings against taking advantage of the poor. Yet, numerous national studies show that the ones who pay the dearest price for the vice of gambling are low-income families:

> Lotteries "are more aggressive than most other forms of gambling, since individuals in lower income brackets spend proportionally more money on them than do persons with higher income," according to the National Policy on Gambling.
>
> In Georgia, those who make less than $25,000 a year spend three times as much on lottery tickets than those who make $75,000 or more per year. On the national average, lottery gamblers with household incomes under $10,000 bet nearly three times as much on the lottery as those with incomes of more than $50,000.[27]

Economics professor and lottery expert Robert Goodman says that after three to five years, many people stop playing the lottery because they can no longer afford it.[28]

For the poor, this imbalance of spending is not simply a matter of shifting priorities among a household's discretionary income. Here, we are talking about households that have no discretionary income. What is lost through gambling is lost from providing the basic necessities, clearly an affront to 1 Timothy 5:8: "Now if anyone does not provide for his own relatives, and especially for his household, he has denied the faith and is worse than an unbeliever." Many low-income people take money that should be used for milk, food, housing, healthcare, and clothes and squander it on their state lottery.

Again, in 2 Corinthians 12:14, Paul points out that "children are not obligated to save up for their parents, but parents for their children." Gambling, however, takes away from the resources parents should be using to care and provide for their children. And there's more:

- *Proverbs 14:21*—"whoever shows kindness to the poor will be happy."
- *Proverbs 14:31*—"The one who oppresses the poor insults their Maker, but one who is kind to the needy honors Him."
- *Proverbs 22:16*—"Oppressing the poor to enrich oneself, and giving to the rich—both lead only to poverty."

State-sponsored gambling clearly oppresses the poor. And that's very bad economic news indeed. To make matters worse, gambling of all kinds also incites the worst of motives in people:

- *Exodus 20:17* says we are not to covet that which belongs to others. But when people play the lottery or gamble, they are coveting or desiring that which is not rightfully theirs and that which they have not earned through legitimate work or investing. As Christians we are to "put our hand to the plow" and earn money through the sweat of our brow, not by being involved in get-rich schemes, ill-gotten gains, or greedy ambition.
- *Proverbs 12:11* promises, "The one who works his land will have plenty of food, but whoever chases fantasies lacks sense." While most people today are not farmers, the biblical principle is clear that we are to pursue an honest occupation to earn money to support our families.
- *Proverbs 28:20* warns, "A faithful man will have many blessings, but one in a hurry to get rich will not go unpunished."
- *2 Thessalonians 3:10–12* admonishes: "In fact, when we were with you, this is what we commanded you: 'If anyone isn't willing to work, he should not eat.' For we hear that there are some among you who walk irresponsibly, not working at all, but interfering with the work [of others]. Now we command and exhort such people, by the Lord Jesus Christ, that quietly working, they may eat their own bread."
- *Ephesians 4:28* notes, "The thief must no longer steal. Instead, he must do honest work with his own hands, so that he has something to share with anyone in need."

Gambling simply does not fit a biblical worldview. Whether it distorts the truth (and it does) or degrades life for the poor (and it does), gambling violates biblical principles. In particular, government support of gambling represents a clear abdication of the government's responsibility to treat citizens justly. Unfortunately, there are other dire issues in which contemporary American government is also in danger of abdicating its duty.

Capital Punishment and Military Action

Capital punishment is a moral issue of our day on which many Christians are divided. Similarly, some well-intended Christians are pacifists and do not feel God would want them to participate in the military where, if called to serve in a war, they might have to kill another person (thankfully, the U.S. government acknowledges this fact and allows for conscientious objectors to avoid military service). On both of these issues, there is legitimate room for disagreement among believers, but, nevertheless, some biblical principles are clear.

While not every Christian has to agree that capital punishment is permissible, it is a fact that God does give authority to governments to administer justice through the practice of capital punishment for capital crimes. According to the book of Genesis, God Himself used capital punishment by causing a worldwide flood to destroy the wicked. Later, God used fire from heaven to destroy Sodom and Gomorrah for their crimes against Him. And in Exodus, God used the Red Sea to crush the army of Pharaoh. He caused the ground to open up and swallow some of the children of Israel as they camped at the base of Mt. Sinai, engaging in immorality and idolatry. And as to the *government's* authority to mete out justice, Genesis 9:6 says, "Whoever sheds man's blood, his blood will be shed by man, for God made man in His image."

Although it is wrong to kill an innocent man or woman because every person is created in the image of God, there are clear references to capital punishment in both the Old and New Testaments. So you can see that capital punishment—"the death penalty"—is still applicable today. You'll recall in Romans 13:1–4, the government is authorized to enforce "good conduct." Paul refers to the sword to make clear that the government has the God-given right to distribute justice, including capital punishment. In the case of war, the government is also using the power of the sword to bring justice to those who have committed capital crimes and to defend Americans.

When President Bush sent troops into Afghanistan and other areas to capture or kill the terrorists responsible for the deaths of more than three thousand Americans on September 11, 2001, he was biblically justified. The president of the United States has the biblical and constitutional authority to use our military to defend America, to kill those who seek to kill us, and to avenge those who have killed innocent people. When President Bush characterizes the war on terror as "a just war," it is consistent with a biblical perspective.

So, sometimes we "get it right," and sometimes we don't. At present, we're doing pretty well on the "just war" front, but we're still struggling in a significant home-front issue.

Marriage Doesn't Go Both Ways

Homosexual and lesbian activists are trying to redefine marriage so as to include same-sex couples. Author and family expert Bob Knight explains why marriage cannot be redefined, only destroyed:

> The term "marriage" refers specifically to the joining of two people of the opposite sex. When that is lost, "marriage" becomes meaningless. You can no more leave an entire sex out of marriage and call it "marriage" than you can leave chocolate out of a "chocolate brownie" recipe. It becomes something else. Giving non-marital relationships the same status as marriage does not expand the definition of marriage; it destroys it. For example, if you declare that, because it has similar properties, wine should be labeled identically to grape juice, you have destroyed the definitions of both "wine" and "grape juice." The consumer would not know what he is getting.[29]

Legalization of same-sex marriage would be legally and culturally devastating not only for the institution of marriage, but for families. Tony Perkins, president of the Family Research Counsel, delivered a speech before twenty thousand people in Seattle, Washington. Here is a small sampling of his great discourse:

Let me tell you another reason the policy of same-sex "marriage" will affect you. If you have not discovered this yet, you will. For those pushing the homosexual agenda, tolerance is not a two-way street. It is a one-way street: "their way."

Just north of us in Canada, a measure currently in parliament, C-250, is about to become law. Known as the "chill bill," the law is targeted at churches and would ban publicly expressed opposition to same-sex "marriage" or any other political goal of homosexual groups. The quoting of Scripture will soon be hate speech.

Already in Sweden sermons are explicitly covered by an anti-hate speech law passed to protect homosexuals. In England, the "Gender Recognition Bill," which was passed by the House of Lords last month allows people to declare their gender and makes it illegal for a clergyman to refuse to conduct a marriage between two people of the same sex if they say they are not of the same sex.[30]

In an article in *The Weekly Standard*, Stanley Kurtz points out: "Marriage in Scandinavia is in deep decline, with children shouldering the burden of rising rates of family dissolution. And the mainspring of the decline—an increasingly sharp separation between marriage and parenthood—can be linked to gay marriage."[31]

And Peter Sprigg delivered these remarks on March 29, 2004, at the World Congress of Families III in Mexico City:

And so, as one part of our broad-based efforts to support the traditional family, we oppose what is sometimes called "the gay agenda." It is an agenda that demands the full acceptance of the practice of homosexuality: morally, socially, legally, religiously, politically, and financially. Indeed, it calls for not only acceptance, but affirmation and celebration of this behavior as normal. It even demands that homosexuality be seen as desirable for those who desire it. This is "the gay agenda"—and we are against it.

This agenda has already made remarkable progress. Homosexual activists knew that their behavior would never be accepted as "normal" if doctors considered it a form of mental illness. Therefore, in 1973 they forced a resolution through the American Psychiatric Association to remove homosexuality from the Diagnostic and Statistical Manual of Mental Disorders. It is important for everyone to realize that the 1973 decision was *not* the result of new clinical research or scientific evidence. It was, rather, a *political* decision made in response to a vicious campaign of harassment and intimidation by homosexual activists.

Indeed, studies actually continue to show that homosexuals experience high rates of mental illness. For example, the Netherlands Mental Health Survey and Incidence Study, reported in the *Archives of General Psychiatry* in 2001, found that "people with same-sex sexual behavior are at greater risk for psychiatric disorders."[32]

The fact that this is true even in one of the most "gay-friendly" nations on earth—indeed, the first nation to grant same-sex civil marriage—undermines the argument that such mental illnesses are merely a reaction to society's alleged "discrimination."

Peter Sprigg continued to click off the devastating impact legalizing same-sex marriage will have on families in America:

The final harm done by same-sex marriage would undoubtedly be a slide down the proverbial "slippery slope." Advocates of same-sex marriage seek to remove the potential for procreation from the definition of marriage, making gender irrelevant in the choice of a spouse, and re-defining marriage only in terms of a loving and committed relationship. If that happens, then it is hard to see how other restrictions upon one's choice of marriage partner can be sustained. These include the traditional restrictions against marrying a child, a close blood relative, or a person who is already married.

While pedophile or incestuous marriages may be further off, polygamous marriages have much stronger precedents in history and culture than do even homosexual ones. Lawsuits have already been filed in American courts—with the support of the American Civil Liberties Union—demanding recognition of plural marriages. And—I am not making this up. News reports in recent weeks have carried stories of an Indian girl being married to a dog, and a French woman who was legally permitted (with the approval of the president of France) to marry her boyfriend—who is already dead.

Lesbian activist Paula Ettelbrick, currently the executive director of the International Gay and Lesbian Human Rights Commission, has said that homosexuality "means pushing the parameters of sex, sexuality, and family, and in the process transforming the very fabric of society." In fact, homosexuality and homosexual civil marriage would rip the fabric of society in ways that may be difficult, if not impossible, to mend.[33]

The Marriage Smoke Screen

Numerous studies reveal the average homosexual has hundreds of sexual relationships. Given this fact, it stands to reason that homosexuals are not interested so much in getting married and having one life partner as they are in using the marriage issue to further a liberal, anti-family, anti-Christian political and worldview agenda. Consider the following facts:

- The number of registered same-sex unions in Sweden is reported to be about 1,500 (for a total of 3,000 individuals) out of the estimated homosexual and lesbian population of 140,000.[34] This indicates that only about 2 percent of Swedish homosexuals and lesbians choose to enter into legally recognized unions. Put another way, about 98 percent of Swedish homosexuals and lesbians do not officially register as same-sex couples.[35]

- A news report by the Gay Financial Network predicted that "some 10,000 gay couples could be married" in the first year following the legalization of gay "marriage" in the Netherlands. In reality, far fewer chose to solemnize their relationships. The Office of Legislative Research released a report in October 2002 stating: "The Dutch Ministry of Economic Affairs reports that 3,383 of the 121,776 marriages licensed between April 1, 2001, and June 30, 2002, involved people of the same sex."[36]

The Dutch study of partnered homosexuals, which was published in the journal *AIDS*, found that men with a steady partner also had an average of eight other sexual partners per year.[37]

A. P. Bell and M. S. Weinberg, in their classic study of male and female homosexuality, found that 43 percent of white male homosexuals had sex with 500 or more partners, and 28 percent had 1,000 or more sex partners.[38] In their study of the sexual profiles of 2,583 older homosexuals published in the *Journal of Sex Research*, Paul Van de Ven and others found that "the modal range for number of sexual partners ever [of homosexuals] was 101-500." In addition, 10.2 percent to 15.7 percent had between 501 and 1,000 partners. A further 10.2 percent to 15.7 percent reported having had more than 1,000 lifetime sexual partners.[39] A survey conducted by the homosexual magazine *Genre* found that 24 percent of the respondents said they had had more than 100 sexual partners in their lifetime. The magazine noted that several respondents suggested including a category of those who had more than 1,000 sexual partners.[40]

Radical homosexual and lesbian activists are not interested in marriage but an agenda. Listen to what homosexual activist Michelangelo Signorile has said concerning the desire of homosexuals to get married and live in a monogamous relationship: "For these men the term 'monogamy' simply doesn't necessarily mean sexual exclusivity. . . . The term 'open relationship' has for a great many gay men come to have one specific definition: A relationship in which the partners have sex on the outside often, put away their resentment and jealousy, and discuss their outside sex with each other, or share sex partners."[41]

Former homosexual William Aaron explains why homosexuals are not interested in monogamy: "In the gay life, fidelity is almost impossible. Since part of the compulsion of homosexuality seems to be a need on the part of the homophile to 'absorb' masculinity from his sexual partners, he must be constantly on the lookout for [new partners]. Consequently the most successful homophile 'marriages' are those where there is an arrangement between the two to have affairs on the side while maintaining the semblance of permanence in their living arrangement."[42]

To further blow away the marriage smoke screen, my friend Bob Knight explains why having a narrow, legal definition of marriage is not discriminatory:

Marriage laws are not discriminatory. Marriage is open to all adults, subject to age and blood relation limitations. As with any acquired status, the applicant must meet minimal requirements, which in terms of marriage, means finding an opposite-sex spouse. Same-sex partners do not qualify. To put it another way, clerks will not issue dog licenses to cats, and it is not out of "bigotry" toward cats. Comparing current laws limiting marriage to a man and a woman with the laws in some states that once limited inter-racial marriage is irrelevant and misleading. The very soul of marriage–the joining of the two sexes—was never at issue when the Supreme Court struck down laws against inter-racial marriage.

Requiring citizens to sanction or subsidize homosexual relationships violates the freedom of conscience of millions of Christians, Jews, Muslims and other people who believe marriage is the union of the two sexes.

Civil marriage is a public act. Homosexuals are free to have a "union" ceremony with each other privately, but they are not free to demand that such a relationship be solemnized and subsidized under the law.

Homosexual activists say they need legal status so they can visit their partners in hospitals, etc. But hospitals leave visitation up to the patient, except in very rare instances. This "issue" is a smoke screen to cover the fact that, using legal instruments such as power of attorney, drafting a will, etc., homosexuals can share property, designate heirs, dictate hospital visitors and give authority for medical decisions. What they should not obtain is identical recognition and support for a relationship that is not equally essential to society's survival.[43]

Bob goes on to describe the legal and social fallout of redefining marriage to include same-sex couples. If same-sex relationships acquire marital-type status in the law, several things will occur:

- Businesses that decline to recognize non-marital relationships will increasingly be punished through loss of contracts and even legal action. This is already occurring in San Francisco and in Canada.
- Other groups, such as bisexuals and polygamists, will demand the right to redefine marriage to suit their own proclivities. Once the standard of one-man, one-woman marriage is broken, there is no logical stopping point.
- As society rewards homosexual behavior, more young people will be encouraged to experiment and more will be discouraged from overcoming homosexual desires.
- Popular understanding of what marriage is and what it requires will undergo change. Homosexual relationships, which usually lack both permanence and fidelity, are unlikely to change to fit the traditional model of lifelong, faithful marriage. Instead, society's expectations of marriage will change in response to the homosexual model, thus leading to a further weakening of the institution of marriage. Some homosexual activists have acknowledged that they intend to use marriage mainly as a way to radically shift society's entire conception of sexual morality.[44]

Same Sex Marriage Is Not a Civil Rights Issue

Few things are more offensive to my black friends than liberals and homosexual and lesbian activists claiming that the right for people of the same sex to marry is a civil rights issue. Dr. Timothy J. Dailey describes why same-sex marriage is not a civil rights issue:

Defining marriage as the union of a man and a woman would not deny homosexuals the basic civil rights accorded other citizens. Nowhere in the Bill of Rights or in any legislation proceeding from it are homosexuals excluded from the rights enjoyed by all citizens—including the right to marry.

However, no citizen has the unrestricted right to marry whoever they want. A parent cannot marry their child (even if he or she is of age), two or more spouses, or the husband or wife of another person. Such restrictions are based upon the accumulated wisdom not only of Western civilization but also of societies and cultures around the world for millennia.[45]

While there are many reasons same-sex marriage should not be legalized, I believe the main reason is because our Founders told us that under the form of government they set up, we are not to make laws that contradict the laws of nature and nature's God. Homosexuality and lesbianism are against the laws of God and nature, and God calls homosexuality an abomination. He established marriage in the Garden of Eden when He said, "This is why a man leaves his father and mother and bonds with his wife, and they become one flesh" (Gen. 2:24).

Chapter 7

The Unstated State Religion

We've already discussed the reality that humanism, by many defi-nitions, is a religion. Because that is the case, then we need to acknowledge that the battle raging in America between radical liber-als and traditional conservatives is a battle between two opposing religious worldviews. It also follows that the intent of humanists is to replace America's Christian worldview founding and heritage with that of their religion, humanism.

Humanistic liberals will not admit that, but the facts remain. And because there are some well-meaning liberals, it is possible many liberals don't even realize their philosophy, ideology, and worldview has been built on a humanistic foundation.

Radical Liberals and the God of Their Imagination

Having said that, I can hear some liberals screaming indignantly, "I believe in God!" To which I respond, "You may believe in God, but that is all you have, a belief. Unless a person has a love for and com-mitment to God, then believing in God does little good. The Bible says even the demons believe. It is a love for God that causes people to serve and obey Him. In fact, the Bible is clear that if you claim to love God but don't keep His commandments, then you really don't love God. In the end, on judgment day, simply believing that the God of the Bible does exist will not be good enough."

A saving belief is one that produces repentance from sin and a commitment to reading, studying, and following God's Word. It's a belief that transforms actions, thoughts, and goals.

The radical liberals consider God to be an outgrowth of imagination. Radical liberals may believe in a deity but not in the God of the Bible. It is a god they have created as surely as if they had sculpted an idol of clay or wood. Such a god merely serves their own desires, wishes, and purposes. In reality, their god is their commitment to a system and worldview of values that makes people the center and measure of all things. Mankind is really their god, and humanism is their religion.

America—and in some cases even the church—is filled with those who claim to be Christians but embrace radically liberal ideas and beliefs. Many such beliefs are 100 percent contrary to the teachings of Jesus Christ. For people to call themselves Christians and liberals is an oxymoron when you realize the definition of a modern-day liberal. Yet, people like pastor and author Tony Campolo and others claim to be Christians while proclaiming extreme, Far-Left philosophies that embrace socialism, radical environmentalism, and even open the door to homosexuality. While I certainly cannot judge the motives of their hearts, I can be a "fruit tester" to see if there is any spiritual fruit produced in their lives that is consistent with the biblical signs of a true Christian.

Humanism Is a Religion

Although earlier in this book we touched upon the tenets of religious humanism, it's important to take a more in-depth look at how religious humanism actually is if we are to fully appreciate its infiltration into our lives. So let's begin this important discussion by defining the term *religion.*

Random House Unabridged Dictionary of the English Language defines *religion* as "a set of beliefs." *Webster's New World Dictionary* defines *religion* as "a system of belief."[1] The word *belief* is defined as opinions and "thoughts upon which people base their actions.[2] Since an individual's worldview is the foundation of their values, and their values form the basis for their actions, it is clear that humanism is a religious worldview. It supplies the belief system on which believers in that system base their actions.

Unfortunately, most Americans do not realize humanism is a religion promoted in America's public schools with taxpayer funds. While this is going on, the ACLU and others, as we have noted, file lawsuit upon lawsuit. They target students who pray over their lunch, mention God or Jesus Christ in their graduation speeches, sing Christmas carols, have Christmas parties, observe Thanksgiving, and on and on. While the ACLU and their ilk fight to remove the religion of Christianity from our schools, colleges, courtrooms, city halls, city seals, or the city square, their dirty little secret is they really don't want a religion-free zone. They want to replace the Judeo-Christian faith and acknowledgment of God's place in our history with their religion of secular humanism. If Americans in large enough numbers would come to understand the facts I document in this chapter, the fight would no longer be misconstrued by the opposition and liberal media.

Dr. David Noebel and Dr. Tim LaHaye, in their 2003 *New York Times* best-seller *Mind Siege,* wrote, "The truth is, humanism is unmistakably and demonstrably a religion. One need merely visit the second edition of *A World Religions Reader* to note the prominence given to secular humanism as one of the World's religions. Indeed, in a list of the World's religions: Hinduism, Buddhism, Shintoism, Judaism, Christianity, Islam, and Sikhism, secular humanism is at the top."[3]

Some argue that humanism—unlike Christianity—does not force a specific set of religious positions and beliefs on people. Dr. Noebel counters: "Humanists preach a faith every bit as dogmatic as Christianity. Moral relativism is foundational for Secular Humanist ethics; spontaneous generation and evolution are basic to their biology; naturalism is foundational to their philosophy; and atheism is their theological perspective."[4]

Not All Humanisms Are Alike

You might recall the 1986 song "We are the World." It became the anthem of the New Age movement. Written by Michael "Jack-o" Jackson and Lionel Richie, and sung by a host of stars, it was the theme song for "Live Aid," which was viewed by 1.5 billion people. Michael Jackson said the song was "divinely inspired," but it would not be the divine influence as Christians understand it. One line from the song, for example, says, "Just as Jesus turned the stones into bread." Excuse me? If the New Agers would bother to check in with the Bible, they would know that Satan tempted Jesus to turn the stones into bread, but Jesus refused. Harry Belafonte, a well-known entertainer, admitted the purpose of the song: "We Are the World" was not so much to feed the starving people of Ethiopia, but "it was to create a sense of globalism and unity and oneness in the children."

Another name for the New Age—a decidedly religious movement—is cosmic humanism. New Age leader and author Marilyn Ferguson has said, "LSD gave a whole generation a religious experience."[5] This deceptive religious worldview is an apostasy (apostasy means to have a form of godliness but to deny God). Cosmic humanism not only denies God but proclaims that man is God.

Humanism had its beginning in the Garden of Eden when Satan, taking the form of a serpent, deceived Adam and Eve into believing that if they would eat from the Tree of the Knowledge of Good and Evil they would be like God. Early on, mankind bought into the lie of humanism.

Although all forms of humanism regard mankind as the master of all, the New Age movement differs from secular humanism in some significant ways. In his book *The Battle for Truth,* David Noebel explains how the New Age movement differs from secular humanism and is thus called cosmic humanism:

> Cosmic humanism (the New Age movement) differs from Christianity and the secular worldviews in that it embraces neither theism nor atheism. Cosmic humanism begins by denying the preeminence of any purported special revelation over any other. That is, cosmic humanists believe that the Bible is no more the Word of God than is the Koran, or the words of Confucius. David Spangler, who has been described as the "Emerson of the New Age" says, "We can take all the Scriptures, and all the teachings, and all the tablets, and all the laws, and all the marshmallows and have a jolly good bonfire and marshmallow roast, because that is all they are worth."[6]

Dr. Noebel further explains that cosmic humanism ends up believing there is a God but that everything is God—you, me, the trees, stars, the moon, and so forth. God is an amalgamation of life forces. Or something like that.

The New National Religion?

A number of surveys reveal that Americans, knowingly or unknowingly, embrace New Age religion. In fact, several studies reveal that the majority of Americans agree with New Age philosophies while claiming to believe in the God of the Bible. Although they claim a worldview that has a form of godliness, the reality is more and more Americans are embracing various philosophies that deny the God of the Bible as well as the authority of Scripture. In fact, most Americans, including those who regularly attend church, are biblically illiterate and believe the Bible says things that it doesn't.

The Barna Group has conducted numerous national studies that clearly show the influence of the New Age movement on the beliefs of Americans. One 2004 survey revealed some striking beliefs:

- "More than half of all adults (54 percent) believe that if a person is generally good, or does enough good things for others during their life, they will earn a place in Heaven."[7]
- Three out of five adults (60 percent) say that the devil, or Satan, is not a living being but is a symbol of evil.[8]
- More than two out of every five adults (44 percent) believe that when Jesus Christ lived on earth He committed sins.[9]
- 4 percent believe everyone is God.
- 7 percent believe God is the total realization of personal, human potential.
- 4 percent believe there are many gods, each with different power and authority.
- 9 percent believe God is a state of higher consciousness that a person may reach.
- 3 percent believe there is no such thing as God.[10]

Other surveys confirm Americans are embracing new-age theology. A 2001 Barna survey revealed that a majority (61 percent) agree the Holy Spirit is a symbol of God's presence or power but is not a living entity.[11] Another study showed that, in a typical month, one out of three adults (36 percent) reads their horoscope.[12] And a 2004 survey explained what unchurched people believe:

- 65 percent say Satan is not a living being but only a symbol of evil.[13]

- 57 percent of adults state that a good person can earn his or her way into heaven, compared to 64 percent who believed so in 2000.[14]
- 51 percent assert that when Jesus Christ lived on earth He committed sins.[15]

In regards to Bible knowledge among Americans, Barna found that:

- 12 percent of adults believe the name of Noah's wife was Joan of Arc (the Bible does not give her name).[16]
- The majority of adults (56 percent) are convinced the Bible proclaims that the single, most important task in life is taking care of one's family.[17]
- Three-quarters of Americans (75 percent) believe the Bible teaches that God helps those who help themselves.[18]

Even among those who claim to be a "born-again Christian" or "evangelical," many say they don't believe in a literal Satan, hell, Holy Spirit, or in absolute moral truth for all people, places, and time. The Bible declares that a man cannot serve two masters or be so unstable in his thinking and still claim to be a true follower of Jesus Christ. The disparity between what many say they are and what they actually believe is evidence that New Age religion has even taken hold of self-professing Christians. As Americans become more and more ignorant of the Bible, the number that accept New Age philosophies—even while claiming to be "born again" or "evangelical" Christians—will no doubt increase in number.

The Not-So-New New Age

Why is the New Age movement growing in popularity? Because it allows a person to claim spirituality while being accountable to no standards and potentially living "like the devil." The New Age movement justifies and encourages the American culture's growing acceptance and practice of paganism as expressed through rampant pornography, abortion on demand, euthanasia, doctor-assisted suicide, hedonism, occult practices, promotion of same-sex relationships, multiculturalism, political correctness, and condom distribution in schools. All of this adds up to a pagan worldview that is encouraged through cosmic humanism.

Reincarnation, crystals, spirit and Master Guides, god-consciences, good and bad karma, global consciences, harmonic convergence, pantheism, and *Mother Earth* are all words you have likely heard. These are all aspects of the New Age worldview, cleverly packaged and integrated into pop culture through films, television, music, best-selling books, and public school curriculum. While there are New Age churches you can attend, even some "traditional" churches teach New Age doctrines and don't realize it.

The New Age movement claims to be new, but it certainly is not. As I pointed out, New Age philosophy has been around since Satan in the Garden of Eden deceived Adam and Eve into believing they could be "as God." Even today, Satan, the mastermind behind the New Age movement, works to deceive both Christians and non-Christians.

The movement does, indeed, have a global plan. Several popular New Age authors of the 1800s told followers to keep "the plan" a secret until 1975.[19] Although certain aspects of the plan became evident before 1975, since then many millions have rushed to embrace the movement's beliefs, plans, goals, and personalities. Modern adoption of the tenets of New Age thinking can be seen in the famous 1960s musical *Hair.* The theme song, "The Age of Aquarius" (also known as the Age of New Beginnings), expresses exactly what New Agers strive for as they struggle to bring about a one-world government, one-world religion, and one-world economic structure.

While we can examine the general beliefs of the New Age movement, it is important to remember that a New Ager's beliefs are limited only to what each individual follower desires to believe and practice. Most New Age humanists pick and choose their beliefs by the standard that "if it feels good and works for me, it is all right." Therefore, the beliefs of a New Age humanist vary from person to person. Nevertheless, it is possible to discern the basic or foundational beliefs of cosmic humanism.

The front cover of the December 7, 1987, issue of *Time* magazine featured a picture of Shirley McClain, one of the best-known cosmic humanists. The magazine's exposé on the New Age movement reported that:

- The New Age is a combination of spirituality and superstition, fad and farce.
- The main goal of the New Age is to define yourself.

- A basic New Age belief is that you can be whatever you want to be.
- The New Age proclaims that man is co-creator of the Universe.

The Court Confirms: Humanism Is a Religion

In 1961, the Supreme Court handed down the *Torcaso vs. Watkins* decision regarding a Maryland notary public who was initially disqualified from office because he would not declare a belief in God. The Court, however, ruled in his favor. It argued that "theistic religions [religions that believe in one God] could not be favored by the Court over non-theistic religions. In a footnote it clarified what it meant by non-theistic religions."[20] In the footnote, Justice Hugo L. Black wrote, "Among religions in this country which do not teach what would generally be considered a belief in the existence of God are Buddhism, Taoism, Ethical Culture, Secular Humanism, and others."[21]

Slam dunk! The Court's footnote acknowledging humanism as a religion laid the groundwork for multiple lawsuits that have allowed conservatives to stop the federal funding of humanism in our schools, right?

Wrong.

Dr. David Noebel, a regular keynote speaker at the Worldview Weekends, bemoans the Court's double standard. Decisions often give the religion of humanism a free pass while stripping away the religious freedoms of more and more Christians under a misinterpretation of the First Amendment. Dr. Noebel notes:

Unfortunately, the Court has not been consistent in applying this understanding to its present interpretation of the First Amendment. If the no-establishment clause of the First Amendment really means that there should be a "wall of separation" between church and state, why are only theistic religions disestablished? If Secular Humanism is a religion—something the U.S. Supreme Court has claimed, and something countless Humanists proclaim—why is it allowed access to our public schools when there is to be no established religion?[22]

Having It Both Ways

Now that humanists clearly have the upper hand in public education, they recognize what is at stake and are scrambling to shore up their advantage. Dr. Noebel notes, "Paul Kurtz, author of *Humanist Manifesto II* and editor of *Free Inquiry*, one of the most popular humanist magazines, attempted in his book *Eupraxophy: Living without Religion*, to prove that Secular Humanism is *not* a religion."

So why does Kurtz want to argue that humanism is not a religion when the *Humanist Manifesto I* and countless humanist authors, professors, and ministers say that humanism is a religion? Kurtz himself gives the answer: "For if humanism, even naturalistic and secular humanism is a religion, then we would be faced with a violation of the First Amendment to the United States Constitution, which states that 'Congress shall make no law representing the establishment of religion or the free exercise thereof.'"[23]

The dirty little secret of humanists is that they know humanism is a religion, but they will deny it when it puts at risk the federal tax dollars Congress appropriates to fund humanist-leaning textbooks and programs in America. Not only that, many members of the U.S. Congress know exactly what is going on. Most American citizens, though, are simply unaware and continue through the allocation of their tax dollars to establish a religion: the religion of humanism.

In 1986, Paul C. Vitz, a professor of psychology at New York University, was commissioned by the United States government to examine the state of education in America. Vitz's findings document that indeed a group of secularists and liberals had been effective in pushing their religion into American textbooks by eliminating Christianity, God, and the impact of both on America, its people, its laws, success, and enduring freedoms. In his report, Vitz wrote, "[A] very widespread secular and liberal mindset appears to be responsible. This mindset pervades the leadership in the world of education and a secular and liberal bias is its inevitable consequence."[24]

He goes on to write, "Most disturbing was the constant omission of reference to the large role that religion has always played in American life. This fact has been seen as a fundamental feature of American society by foreign observers since de Tocqueville."[25]

And by the way, not only has the U.S. Supreme Court acknowledged humanism as a religion, but the Internal Revenue Service has recognized it as a religion for years. Numerous humanist organizations, including the American Humanist Association, have a "religious" tax exemption.

Humanists take full advantage of "having it both ways." In the July 8, 2000, *Dallas Morning News* article entitled "Atheists Need Fellowship, Too," Selwyn Crawford wrote, "The North Texas Church for Free Thought—nicknamed the 'church for the unchurched'—has become a model for other atheist congregations, sparking interest in similar ventures around Texas, the nation, and the world."

But What Do Humanists Say for Themselves?

While Paul Kurtz argues humanism is not a religion because of his fear of losing access to the public schools, his colleagues continue to stack up evidence that proves humanism is a religion. The *Humanist Manifesto I* describes humanism as a religion, again and again: "The time has come for widespread recognition of the radical changes in religious beliefs. . . . In every field of human activity, the vital movement is now the direction of a candid and explicit humanism. In order that religious humanism may be better understood we, the undersigned, desire to make certain affirmations which we believe the facts of our contemporary life demonstrate."[26]

Notice the manifesto refers to their belief system as "religious humanism." Curtis W. Reese, a signatory of *Humanist Manifesto I*, comments, "Within the liberal churches of America there is a religious movement which has come to be known as humanism."[27] And in his book, *Humanist Religion*, Reese writes, "When a man commits himself to a great cause, we say that this cause becomes his religion."[28]

Ray Wood Sellars, author of *Humanist Manifesto I*, claims, "Humanity has struck its tents and is again on the march toward a religious faith, which I dare to believe will provide us with a religion greater than Christianity."[29] Sellars continues, "The religion of humanism will be a growth due to, and resting on, the cooperative spiritual life to the making of which will go a multitude of minds and hearts."[30] Humanist though he may be, Ray Sellars was also something of a prophet when he referred to his belief system as "the humanistic religion into which Christianity will gradually be transformed."[31]

Many churches and Christians have merged a humanist world-view with Christianity. Scripture also foretells this apostasy within the church. The falling away from traditionally held biblical truths will lay the foundation for an apostate church to accept false teachings of the last days about which the Bible has much to say.

Many facets of humanism can be traced back to the modern movement's "early days." Despite the fact that he was a mainline church pastor for more than ten years, Charles Francis Potter became a Unitarian pastor—and a signer of *Humanist Manifesto I*. In his book, *Humanism: A New Religion,* Potter writes, "Humanism is a new religion altogether."[32] Interestingly, Potter not only introduces the very question we are asking, but he answers it for us. "Is humanism a religion? It is both a religion and a philosophy of culture."[33]

Or consider the thinking of John H. Dietrich, a Unitarian minister and a signatory of *Humanist Manifesto.* He wrote a booklet called *Humanism*, in which he notes, "There has grown up within the liberal churches of America a very definite movement known as Humanism, which is seeking to ground religion in human living rather than in some supernatural existence, by interpreting the good life in terms of human values and by directing man's religious aspirations toward the enhancement of human life."[34]

Harvard Divinity School professor Harvey Cox recognizes secular humanism as "a new closed world view which functions very much like a new religion . . . where it pretends not to be a world view but nonetheless seeks to impose its ideology through the organs of the state."[35]

The documentation from speeches, books, booklets, and papers written by the world's leading humanists—from America and around the world—could fill volumes. The proof is there for those who dare to face the reality that America has rejected the wishes of our Founding Fathers and allowed Congress to fund, and the Courts to defend, a religion with which the majority of Americans neither identify nor agree.

There is no such thing as being religiously neutral. The NEA, ACLU, DNC, and every other anti-God organization in America is not religion neutral.

There is even a magazine published for those who practice "religious socialism." The magazine's Web site notes: *"Religious Socialism is the quarterly publication of the Religion of Socialism Commission of DSA. It is the only periodical dedicated to people of faith and socialism in North America. . . . It is open to people of all faiths whose socialism is in some way inspired by their spiritual identity."* The Religion of Socialism Commission "has held conferences and seminars dealing with what we feel is an intrinsic connection between religious beliefs and the fight for social justice."

Finally, the *Humanist Manifesto I* acknowledges that everything is a religious issue: "The distinction between the sacred and the secular can no longer be maintained."

I rest my case. The humanists know that all issues are religious issues.

A Religious Issue in Every Pot

A few years ago I had a phone conversation with a man who was the acting president of a well-known religious organization. This man told me he believed abortion was a moral and political issue but not a spiritual issue. I was so amazed at this comment that I repeated what he said and asked him if I had heard him correctly. He confirmed that I had. Fortunately, due to other comments made publicly in the same vain, this gentleman was not confirmed by his peers as the official president of this association.

This gentleman's belief that abortion is not a spiritual issue but a moral and political position, though, is sadly consistent with what many in today's evangelical churches believe. Sometimes my greatest struggle is not with those who admit their liberal beliefs but with those who, consciously or not, sidestep taking a position on issues because they are supposedly not spiritual issues.

As conservatives seek to reclaim America and defend and protect the freedoms given to us by God, it is imperative that we understand we are fighting a religious and spiritual worldview battle regardless of what the liberals claim. In our courts, the schools, state houses, and the U.S. Congress, every issue is religious. And more often than not, when liberals and conservatives debate them, the bottom line is a battle between a secular humanist worldview and a Christian worldview.

Can You Legislate Morality?

Liberals claim they never "legislate morality," and when conservatives try to do so they are violating the "separation of church and state." I dare say "You can't legislate morality" is one of the most-quoted phrases of liberals when they oppose a piece of legislation but have a weak argument against its passage. Unfortunately, many Christians have bought this silly line of reasoning without thinking about it. The reality is that liberals have gotten very good at legislating *their* morality.

All laws impose someone's morality. Those of us who desire to see partial birth abortion outlawed are attempting to bring our biblical morality and worldview to bear on the issue. Those who oppose banning the procedure desire to maintain a morality based on their humanistic, relativistic worldview. The truth is, our laws legislate morality every day. The question is not whether morality can be legislated but, rather, whose morality will be legislated?

Laws against murder, rape, stealing, child pornography, or kidnapping are all laws that legislate morality. Such laws call for people not to do these hurtful things. But what about those who argue, "Just because you legislate morality doesn't mean people will obey the law"? Their statement is true, of course, but just because not everyone obeys the law does not mean we should eliminate the laws against murder. If perfect obedience were the measure of the rightness of law, we would have no laws at all. Everyone would just do what is right in his or her own eyes. Nonetheless, statistics show that the overwhelming majority of people in America obey laws even when they are not being watched. Most voluntarily pay their taxes, register for the selective service at age eighteen, and drive the speed limit.

Sometimes there's another argument forthcoming: "You cannot change the heart with legislation." To that I say, the changing of a person's heart is not the foremost goal of legislating morality. When a lusty guy sees an attractive woman walking to her car in a dark, secluded parking lot and has immoral thoughts about her but chooses not to rape her because he might get caught and go to prison, it is immaterial whether or not the law has changed his heart. As long as the law caused that individual to control his immoral impulses for fear of retribution, then the law has done its job.

Even so, there is historical evidence that, over time, laws *can* change people's hearts. Take slavery, for instance. At the time our nation outlawed slavery, many people disagreed with that law and thought they should be allowed to enslave other individuals based on the color of their skin. Today, however, you would be hard-pressed to find someone in American who genuinely thinks slavery is morally acceptable. Over time, the law has caused most people to think of slavery as immoral. Today, Americans obey anti-slavery laws not for fear of retribution but out of a heart's desire to respect their fellow-man's right to freedom—regardless of their skin color.

Unfortunately, such a process can also work against improvements in morality. In 1960, very few Americans would have agreed that abortion, the killing of an unborn child, is morally acceptable. It was certainly something most pregnant mothers would not do, and neither the father nor mother of a pregnant girl would encourage her to get an abortion. Even the unmarried father of an unborn baby was less likely to encourage his girlfriend to murder the child they had conceived together. But because the U.S. Supreme Court—the highest judicial authority in our land—has ruled that abortion is legal, many Americans have come to consider abortion morally acceptable. The U.S. Supreme Court position on the issue has had a powerful—and negative—impact on the morals of millions. This is because most people equate what the law says with what is right and moral. What a disaster when the government encourages immorality! These two examples show the power of government to accomplish either good or evil.

In his outstanding book, *Why You Can't Stay Silent,* Tom Minnery of Focus on the Family writes:

> When people say, "You can't legislate morality," they probably mean there is a limit to how effective laws are in bringing people to act rightly. That's true, but we still need laws against murder or any other serious violation of God's standards. Admittedly, we can't force anyone to acknowledge God or willingly obey Him, but like it or not, they either have to accept God's ideas about what's right and wrong or pay

the consequences. We've just said that biblical morality—no lying, cheating, stealing, murdering, etcetera—is good for society, and we should be pleased that our forefathers had enough sense to translate these godly principles into law. Those principles work well for everybody because they reflect what is true about human nature.[36]

Why did the Founders decide that America's laws were to be based on God's laws? Because they not only understood that God's way is the best way, regardless of culture or religion; they also knew God's moral law is written on the hearts of all people. In *Original Intent,* David Barton writes, "The Founders believed the Bible to be the perfect example of moral legislation and the source of what they called, 'the moral law.' For nearly 150 years, the courts agreed and relied on this moral law as the basis for our civil laws."[37]

Scripture offers numerous verses that call us to promote righteousness, which is exactly what "legislating morality" does:

- *Matthew 5:6*—"Blessed are those who hunger and thirst for righteousness, because they will be filled."
- *Proverbs 14:34*—"Righteousness exalts a nation, but sin is a disgrace to any people."
- *Proverbs 11:11*—"A city is built up by the blessing of the upright, but it is torn down by the mouth of the wicked."
- *Proverbs 29:2*—"When the righteous flourish, the people rejoice, but when the wicked rule, people groan."

Yes, we can—and *should*—legislate morality. Most importantly, Christians must be involved in the process if we desire to promote righteousness and be salt and light in a dark world. After all, if God, the Ultimate Law-giver, created government, shouldn't His people use the legislative process to promote His morality? The purveyors of religion-without-God have already been doing that. It's time we shift the momentum back toward the real truth and nothing but the truth.

Chapter 8

Why Humanism (Modern-day Liberalism) Is a Lie and Christianity (True Conservatism) Is the Truth

The bottom line to our discussion is very straightforward· If Christianity is false then humanism is true. On the other hand, if Christianity is true, then humanism is false—which also means either liberalism is based on truth or conservatism is. While it is logically possible that two opposing religious worldviews could *both* be wrong (i.e., Christianity and humanism might both be wrong), it is an absolute certainty that they cannot both be true. Because it's difficult to imagine an alternative to those two worldviews, then we're left with assuming that one of them—but *only* one—is true. So the question becomes, which one is it?

If we can prove one worldview to be true, then we know the opposing view is false. Thus, to conclude our discussion of the liberal/conservative split in America, I will provide only a small portion of the evidence that Christianity (the base of conservatism) is true and that humanism (the base of liberalism) is a lie.

Former Skeptics Surprised by Truth

Two nationally-known authors, who have spoken on numerous occasions for Worldview Weekend seminars, once set out to disprove Christianity and yet found it to be true. Dr. Frank Harber studied nine of the world's major religions, trying to find out which one, if any, had a corner on the truth. At the end of his intellectually rigorous investigation, Dr. Harber concluded that Christianity is the one. Today, Dr. Harber holds a Ph.D. from Southwestern Seminary, which he earned faster than anyone in that institution's history. He is also one of America's premiere defenders of the Christian faith as an author, conference speaker, pastor of a church of more than four thousand, and host of a daily radio broadcast heard on more than 550 stations.

Josh McDowell has spoken several times for Worldview Weekend and is likely the most well-known skeptic-turned-defender of Christianity. As a student at Kellogg College in Michigan, McDowell was challenged by some Christian students to examine the claims of Christ. Although he set out to prove Christianity false, he found that Christ's claim to be God was supported historically, archaeologically, and prophetically. Since then, Josh McDowell's books have sold millions of copies, and he has spoken to millions of people in churches and college campuses throughout America and the world.

How did these two men conclude Christianity is true? They determined that its essential doctrines can be confirmed. With that in mind, let's look at just a few of these tenets of the faith and the evidence for their validity.

How Do We Know the Bible Is True?

Folks in the "religious right" are often derided as "Bible-thumpers," but that is simply a tactic the Left uses to minimize the validity of a conservative mind-set without addressing the real issues involved. There's a reason the Bible is crucial to thoughtful conservatives: It is the basis for the Christian worldview and, hence, for much of Western civilization—and American society in particular.

All right. So the Bible is our base. But can we show that it is a solid one? The answer to that is, "Absolutely!" Those who deride the "thumpers" would do well to take note of how intellectually sound and verifiably accurate the source actually is.

For centuries, atheists have been trying to prove Christianity is false, and the preferred way to do that has been to show the Bible is not a trustworthy document. Despite exhaustive examination, investigation, and attack by determined skeptics, however, the Bible has been consistently proven to be an absolutely truthful document. Christians credit that to its supernatural nature.

In one nineteenth-century investigation into the veracity of Scripture, the Institute of Paris issued eighty-two errors that it believed could discredit Christianity. Since that time, though, all eighty-two difficulties have been cleared away with new discoveries.[1]

Even *Time* magazine has published articles about the continuing discoveries that prove the Bible true. For instance, in the December 18, 1995, issue entitled "Are the Bible's Stories True?," Michael D. Lemonick tells of two tiny but significant silver scrolls found in a Jerusalem tomb: "They were dated around 600 B.C., shortly before the destruction of Solomon's Temple and the Israelites' exile in Babylon. When scientists carefully unrolled the scrolls at the Israel Museum, they found a benediction from the Book of Numbers etched into their surface. The discovery made it clear that parts of the Old Testament were being copied long before some skeptics had believed they were even written."[2]

By any standards, the Bible is a remarkable document. It was written over the course of many years by dozens of men from diverse walks of life—men in different countries and educated at various levels. Yet, despite all these differences, the Bible presents a consistent message from beginning to end. Why? Christians believe it is because the authors wrote the Bible as they were led by God. This amazing consistency is evidence the Bible is of a supernatural nature. Biblical scholar F. F. Bruce concludes:

> The Bible, at first sight, appears to be a collection of literature—mainly Jewish. If we inquire into the circumstances under which the various biblical documents were written, we find that they were written at intervals over a space of nearly 1400 years.
>
> The writers wrote in various lands, from Italy in the west to Mesopotamia and possibly Persia in the east. The writers themselves were a heterogeneous number of people, not only separated from each other by hundreds of years and hundreds of miles, but belonging to the most diverse walks of life. In their ranks we have kings, herdsmen, soldiers,

legislators, fishermen, statesmen, courtiers, priests and prophets, a tent-making rabbi, and a Gentile physician, not to speak of others of whom we know nothing apart from the writings they have left us.

The writings themselves belong to a great variety of literary types. They include history, law (civil, criminal, ethical, ritual, sanitary), religious poetry, didactic treatise, lyric poetry, parable and allegory, biography, personal correspondence, personal memoirs and diaries, in addition to the distinctively biblical types of prophecy and apocalyptic.

For all that, the Bible is not simply an anthology; there is a unity that binds the whole together. An anthology is compiled by an anthologist, but no anthologist compiled the Bible.[3]

As fascinating as the consistency of its message is, perhaps the most compelling evidence of the Bible's supernatural origin is the accuracy with which its many, many prophecies are fulfilled. Later, we will look at the most historically significant prophecies—those concerning the birth, life, and death of Jesus Christ, given hundreds of years before His birth—that came true with pinpoint accuracy. But just for starters, note the relevant issues the Bible predicted thousands of years ago:

- Evolution accepted instead of Creation—"They willfully ignore this: long ago the heavens and the earth existed out of water and through water by the word of God. Through these the world of that time perished when it was flooded by water." (2 Pet. 3:5–6)
- Technological explosion that includes a tremendous increase in knowledge, velocity of transportation, and worldwide communications—"But you, Daniel, keep these words secret and seal the book until the time of the end. Many will roam about, and knowledge will increase." (Dan. 12:4)
- "The chariots dash madly through the streets; they rush around in the plazas. They look like torches; they dart back and forth like lightning." (Nah. 2:4)
- For other examples, see Matthew 24:30; Amos 8:11–13; and Revelation 11:7.

There has certainly been an astonishing increase in knowledge. In the last fifty years, there has been more scientific progress than in the previous five thousand years. And get this: 90 percent of all scientists who ever lived are alive today.

Then, too, think of the unbelievable advances in transportation. Before 1830, man traveled by horse, foot, or sailboat. From 1830 to 1890, steam engines were introduced, which gave us trains and ships. From 1890 to today, we have seen the creation of automobiles, airplanes, jets, and spacecrafts capable of traveling to the moon. We have even landed unmanned spacecrafts on the planet Mars.

If there were no other support, the nation of Israel by itself is evidence of the supernatural nature of God's Word. The Bible foretold that Israel would once again be a nation and—after more than two thousand years—in 1948 that came to pass just as predicted in Ezekiel 36 and 37. Later, in Ezekiel 45:12 we are even told that the form of money to be used in this re-established Israel would be the shekel. That, too, has happened. Ezekiel 37:21 explains that the Jewish people would return from "out of the nations where they have gone" to their homeland. In Zephaniah 3:9, the Bible foretells the official language of the re-established Israel will be Hebrew. And today, the daily newspapers in Israel are printed in Hebrew.

In Ezekiel 36:26–35 and Isaiah 27:6 the Bible prophesies that the desert of Israel will be as a garden. Today, an Israeli farmer produces four to six times what an average farmer in America produces. Israel exports fruit and flowers to other countries in incredible numbers—producing all this in a desert!

In Ezekiel 37:10, the Bible tells us Israel will field a great army. Military history of the last fifty years confirms that Israel's army, air force, and intelligence agency are forces to be reckoned with.

Passing It Down and Getting It Right

Most children have played the "telephone game." You know the way it works. You sit in a circle and tell your neighbor a secret. Your neighbor then whispers it to his or her neighbor. That neighbor whispers to the next neighbor and so on until the message makes it back to the first person. When the secret has made it around the circle, the one who started it tells the group both the original secret and the final message they received. The first and last secrets are rarely the same, and that's the point of the game—to laugh over how much the message changes. Sometimes, the secret has been altered by deleting a few words that dilute the meaning. In other cases, words have been substituted that completely change the content of the original message.

Skeptics and critics of the Bible claim that duplication of the Bible from generation to generation has likewise caused it to fall victim to the "telephone game" of history. Therefore, the Bible cannot be trusted. Archaeological discoveries, however, have proven again and again that the Bible is the all-time, number-one most validated writing of antiquity.

There are few, if any, skeptics about the works of Caesar, Aristotle, or Plato. Yet the writings by these men are not nearly so validated by reliable historic manuscripts as the New Testament. For example, the time span from the original manuscript to oldest existing manuscripts of Caesar, Aristotle, or Plato range from 1,000 to 1,400 years. The time span from the original writing of the New Testament to oldest existing partial manuscripts or fragments of the New Testament, though, is only about fifty years. The oldest existing complete manuscript of the New Testament is a copy made just 225 years from the time the New Testament was originally written. Besides that, there are more manuscripts to back up the New Testament than any other work of antiquity. It is supported by 24,286 historical copies.[4] The second-most verified work of antiquity is Homer's *Illiad*, but it boasts only 643 manuscripts. By comparison, we only have ten to back up Caesar's *Gallic Wars* and only three manuscripts for Plato. Josh McDowell puts this wealth of resources for the Bible in perspective: "If you destroyed all the Bibles and biblical manuscripts, one could reconstruct all but eleven verses of the entire New Testament from quotations found in other materials written within 150 to 200 years after the time of Jesus Christ."[5]

A. T. Robertson suggests that biblical textual criticism has determined there are questions about only a "thousandth part of the entire text."[6] This would make the reconstructed text of the New Testament 99.9 percent free from substantial or consequential error. Hence, as B. B. Warfield observed, "The great mass of the New Testament, in other words, has been transmitted to us with no, or next to no variations."[7]

So exactly how do these experts recognize when antique documents are valid? In looking at documents of antiquity to determine their authenticity and accuracy, experts apply three different tests—bibliographical, internal, and external. Let's take a closer look at each of these tests to see how well the Bible passes each one.

The Bibliographical Test

Because we do not have the original documents, scholars must determine how reliable and accurate the copies are that we do have and what the time interval is between the original and the existing copy or copies.[8] To clarify our terms: a *manuscript* is a handwritten literary composition in contrast to a printed copy, and an *original manuscript* is the first one produced, usually referred to as an *autograph*.

There are no known autographs of the New Testament. In fact, none are needed because of the abundance of manuscript copies.[9] The total of Greek manuscripts alone is 5,686, and there are also more than 10,000 New Testament manuscripts in Latin.[10] Plenty to work with to make sure we have the "real thing."

In another attack strategy, some critics have argued the Bible was written after the predicted events occurred, suggesting that prophecies were "faked" because they were written after the supposedly predicted events had already occurred. Such criticism, though, does not stand up to scrutiny. In the John Rylands Library in Manchester, England, for instance, resides what is known as the John Rylands Fragment. This papyrus contains five verses from the Gospel of John (18:31–33, 37–38). It was found in Egypt and is dated between A.D. 117 and 138. The great philologist (a person who studies written texts to establish their authenticity) Adolf Deissmann argued that it may have been even earlier.[11] This discovery destroyed the idea that the New Testament was written during the second century—time for myths to grow around the truth.[12]

A frequent Worldview Weekend speaker and one of the most prolific defenders of the Bible is Dr. Norm Geisler, president of Southern Evangelical Seminary and the author of more than fifty books. Geisler notes:

> An honest comparison of three observations: (1) the number of manuscripts, (2) the time span between the original and

the earliest copy, and (3) the accuracy of the New Testament, all bear witness that the New Testament is the most historically accurate and reliable document from all of antiquity. If one cannot trust the New Testament at this point, then one must reject all of ancient history, which rests on much weaker evidence. So definite is the evidence for the New Testament that no less a scholar than the late Sir Frederic Kenyon could write,[13] "The interval then between the dates of original composition and the earliest extant evidence becomes so small as to be in fact negligible, and the last foundation for any doubt that the Scriptures have come down to us substantially as they were written has now been removed. Both the authenticity and the general integrity of the books of the New Testament may be regarded as finally established."[14]

The Bible overwhelmingly passes the bibliographical test.

The Internal Test

The internal test is about looking for contradictions within the document. While skeptics and critics like to point to some eight hundred "contradictions" in the Bible, a studied look at each one proves none to be genuinely contradictory at all. For instance, one of the Gospels recounts that, after betraying Jesus, the disciple Judas hung himself. In another Gospel, it says Judas fell off a cliff and his bowels broke open and his guts spilled into the field. Are these two accounts in conflict? No, they are not. It is possible for both to be true.

In Jerusalem, the traditional site of Judas' suicide is a cliff that overhangs a field. As a result, it is easy to see that, after hanging himself, there are several possibilities as to what happened to Judas' body:

- It rotted and fell apart, landing in the field below the cliff.
- Someone came along, cut it down, and his body dropped from the cliff into the field.
- The rope or limb eventually broke, and the body fell into the field.

Here's another example. The books of Matthew and Mark note that when the women went to the tomb of Jesus on resurrection morning, there was an angel there. In Luke and John, it says there were two angels at the tomb. Are these contradictory statements? No! It is likely that one of the women spoke of the one angel she saw, while the other woman spoke of the two angels she saw. It is also likely that one gospel writer was focusing only on the one angel that *spoke*, while the other gospel writer added to the facts by mentioning that at least one of the women saw two angels.

This is not an unusual way to find an event being reported. Let's take an example from everyday life. Actor Kirk Cameron has spoken at several Worldview Weekends. If two newspaper reporters show up to cover the Worldview Weekend and take notes for writing an article about the conference, you could have two accounts that each mention different facts about the weekend. Yet they would not contradict each other. If one reporter writes that Kirk Cameron was on the stage speaking and goes on to give a summary of Kirk's remarks but does not mention that I was sitting in a chair off to the side of the stage, is that a false report? Of course not. If the other reporter writes that Kirk Cameron was on the stage speaking and says Brannon Howse was sitting in a chair on stage to the left of Kirk, does that reporter's story contradict the first reporter's story? No again. Are these two articles by two different reporters contradictory? Certainly not. To the contrary, the very fact that they differ in some of the details actually substantiates the stories. One reporter simply chose to give more detail than the other. Only if one reporter claims that Kirk Cameron was speaking and that he was the only one on the stage while the other reporter's story says Kirk Cameron was speaking and Brannon Howse was sitting in a chair on the stage to Kirk's left, would you have two contradictory articles.

The gospel records that there was an angel at the tomb on resurrection morning, but it does not say "there was only one angel at the tomb." Thus the gospel accounts that mention one angel at the tomb and the gospel accounts that mention two angels at the tomb do not contradict each other.

Remember, these are only two examples of more than eight hundred such "contradictions" the skeptics and critics point out to discredit the Bible. Each of the supposed discrepancies can be readily explained by understanding the proper way to interpret and study the events reported in Scripture.

To add a final confirmation to our discussion of the internal test, let me introduce you to Dr. Gleason Archer, an expert on the Bible and biblical criticism. Before you read what he has to say about the trustworthiness of the Bible, take a look at Dr. Archer's resume:

As an undergraduate at Harvard, I was fascinated by apologetics and biblical evidences; so I labored to obtain knowledge of the languages and cultures that have any bearing on biblical scholarship. As a classics major in college, I received training in Latin and Greek, also in French and German. At seminary I majored in Hebrew, Aramaic, and Arabic; and in post-graduate years I became involved in Syriac and Akkadian, to the extent of teaching elective courses in each of these subjects. Earlier, during my final two years of high school, I had acquired a special interest in Middle Kingdom Egyptian studies, which was furthered as I later taught courses in this field. At the Oriental Institute in Chicago, I did specialized study in Eighteenth Dynasty historical records and also studied Coptic and Sumerian. Combined with this work in ancient languages was a full course of training at law school, after which I was admitted to the Massachusetts Bar in 1939. This gave me a thorough grounding in the field of legal evidences.[15]

Dr. Archer is more than qualified to speak about the accuracy of the Scriptures. In the foreword to his *Encyclopedia of Bible Difficulties,* Dr. Archer offers this testimony about the internal consistency of the Bible:

As I have dealt with one apparent discrepancy after another and have studied the alleged contradictions between the biblical record and the evidence of linguistics, archaeology, or science, my confidence in the trustworthiness of Scripture has been repeatedly verified and strengthened by the discovery that almost every problem in Scripture that has ever been discovered by man, from ancient times until now, has been dealt with in a completely satisfactory manner by the biblical text itself—or else by objective archaeological information. The deductions that may be validly drawn from ancient Egyptian, Sumerian, or Akkadian documents all harmonize with the biblical records; and no properly trained evangelical scholar has anything to fear from the hostile arguments and challenges of humanistic rationalists or detractors of any and every persuasion.[16]

The Bible overwhelmingly passes the internal test.

The External Test

The external test asks, what is outside the text? What pieces of literature or other data, apart from the one being studied, confirm the accuracy of the inner testimony of the document?

Numerous external sources, such as non-Christian historians and archaeological discoveries, corroborate the Bible. In *The New Evidence that Demands a Verdict*, Josh McDowell writes that Jewish historian Josephus "makes many statements that verify, either generally or in specific detail, the historical nature of both the Old and New Testaments of the Bible."[17]

For instance, Josephus documented Daniel's incredible predictions of the empires that would come and go. The prophet predicted years in advance the destruction of Babylon by the Medes and Persians and the establishment of the Mede-Persian Empire.

Daniel also predicted the rise of the kingdom of Greece, and that upon the death of Alexander the Great, the Greek empire would be divided among four generals. Daniel's prophecies are further indication of the supernatural nature of God's Word. Josephus documents that Daniel made these predictions years in advance of their being fulfilled. Josephus documents the existence of James the brother of Jesus and John the Baptist. He even gives a brief description of Jesus.

The external evidence for the life of Jesus Christ is so substantial, in fact, that even without the Four Gospels and using only non-Christian sources, we can confirm the Gospel accounts. According to Dr. Norm Geisler, these non-Christian sources "come largely from Greek, Roman, Jewish, and Samaritan sources of the first century":

> In brief they inform us that: (1) Jesus was from Nazareth; (2) he lived a wise and virtuous life; (3) he was crucified in Palestine under Pontius Pilate during the reign of Tiberius Caesar at Passover time, being considered the Jewish King;

(4) he was believed by his disciples to have been raised from the dead three days later; (5) his enemies acknowledged that he performed unusual feats they called "sorcery"; (6) his small band of disciples multiplied rapidly, spreading even as far as Rome; (7) his disciples denied polytheism, lived moral lives, and worshiped Christ as Divine. This picture confirms the view of Christ presented in the New Testament Gospels.[18]

The evidence for the authenticity and veracity of the Bible fills thousands of books that can be readily obtained by those who truly want proof that the Bible as we know it today is a completely reliable version of the original. The teachings of Scripture simply cannot be undermined with the argument that the Bible may not be an accurate document. It passes with flying colors all scholarly tests for antique documents.

Still, there is even more evidence.

Archaeological Confirmation

Not a single archaeological discovery has ever proven anything about the Bible to be false. To the contrary, discoveries continue to bear out the accuracy of the Bible as archaeologists unearth cities mentioned in the Bible, for example, with the names of leaders and rulers etched in stone as well as other artifacts. As one archaeologist commented, "Archaeologists used to dig to disprove the Bible; now archaeologists read the Bible to find out where to dig."

Millar Burrows of Yale confirms that archaeologists continue to discover what the Bible says they should, where they should:

The Bible is supported by archaeological evidence again and again. On the whole, there can be no question that the results of excavation have increased the respect of scholars for the Bible as a collection of historical documents. The confirmation is both general and specific. The fact that the record can be so often explained or illustrated by archaeological history as only a genuine product of ancient life could do. In addition to this general authentication, however, we find the record verified repeatedly at specific points. Names of places and persons turn up at the right places and in the right periods.[19]

It is clear skeptics cannot argue that archaeological discoveries disprove the Bible. Sir Frederic Kenyon wrote, "It is therefore legitimate to say that, in respect of that part of the Old Testament against which the disintegrating criticism of the last half of the nineteenth century was chiefly directed, the evidence of archaeology has been to re-establish its value by rendering it more intelligible through a fuller knowledge of its background and setting. Archaeology has not yet said its last word: but the results already achieved confirm what faith would suggest, that the Bible can do nothing but gain from an increase of knowledge."[20]

For example, the excavation of Gezer in 1969 ran across a massive layer of ash that covered most of the mound. Sifting through the material yielded pieces of Hebrew, Egyptian, and Philistine artifacts. Apparently, all three cultures had been there at the same time. This puzzled researchers greatly until they realized that the Bible told them exactly what they had found: "Pharaoh king of Egypt had attacked and captured Gezer. He then burned it down, killed the Canaanites who lived in the city, and gave it as a dowry to his daughter, Solomon's wife (1 Kings 9:16)."[21]

There have been more than 25,000 archaeological discoveries in connection with the Old Testament, and not one contradicts the Bible. Archaeologist William F. Albright has declared, "The excessive skepticism shown toward the Bible by important historical schools of the eighteenth and nineteenth centuries, certain phases of which still appear periodically, has been progressively discredited. Discovery after discovery has established the accuracy of innumerable details, and has brought increased recognition to the value of the Bible as a source of history."[22]

The same can be said of the New Testament. Some critics, for example, have argued that the book of Luke is inaccurate, but Professor F. F. Bruce points out, "Where Luke has been suspected of inaccuracy, and accuracy has been vindicated by some inscription evidence, it may be legitimate to say that archaeology has confirmed the New Testament record."[23]

Similarly, Yale archaeologist Millar Burrows reports, "On the whole, archaeological work has unquestionably strengthened confidence in the reliability of the Scriptural record. More than one archaeologist has found his respect for the Bible increased by the experience of excavation in Palestine."[24]

Sir William Ramsey is one scholar who originally believed the book of Acts, written by Luke, was not accurate. However, after thirty years of study, he changed his mind and declared, "Luke is a historian of the first rank; not merely are his statements of fact trustworthy, . . . this author should be placed along with the very greatest of historians."[25]

As with the Old Testament, archaeological discoveries bear witness to the places described in the New Testament. This includes:

- The pavement of John 19:13
- The pool of Bethesda
- Jacob's well
- The pool of Siloam
- The ancient cities of Bethlehem, Nazareth, Cana, Capernaum, and Chorazin
- The residence of Pilate in Jerusalem.[26]

So, the Bible also sails through the external test.

But How Do We Know Jesus Is God?

So we now know without a doubt that the Bible accurately reflects the events and people it describes. Nevertheless, a skeptic could legitimately still challenge a Bible thumper on this point: The Bible may tell the story as it happened, but how do you know the people whose lives and word were recorded were telling the truth? And among all biblical figures, no character makes a better target than Jesus Himself.

Every time you write a check, you acknowledge that Jesus Christ walked on earth. Every time you take a test and write your name and date at the top of the page, you acknowledge that Jesus Christ lived. It is a historical fact that Jesus of Nazareth was a real person. No credible historian can impugn the evidence that Jesus Christ *was*. But what evidence is there that Jesus Christ was God come to earth in the form of a man?

The deity of Jesus Christ is crucial to proving Christianity true because unless Jesus was God He is a dead Savior, and a dead Savior

can hardly save others if He cannot save Himself. So how do we know
Jesus was God?

Someone who claims to be God could surely prove He was God,
right?

Jesus gave more than enough signs to show who He really was.
The things Jesus did revealed that He was and is a supernatural
being. Only God could predict the location of His birth, the details
of His life, betrayal, death, burial, and resurrection. Only if Jesus
Christ is God could He have performed miracles, predicted the future
through prophecies with complete accuracy, defeated death, and
guaranteed forgiveness of sins and eternal life to those who repent
and follow Him. Dr. Tim LaHaye, who has spoken for the Worldview
Weekend, writes:

> Scholars agree there are at least 109 distinct prophecies
> that the Messiah had to fulfill. For all of them to be fulfilled
> by one individual requires a man so unusual and a life so
> unique as to eliminate all pretenders and indeed all men
> who have ever lived—except one! Quite possibly a scheme
> could have been hatched to make Jesus' life seem prophetic
> by creating these "prophecies" after He had passed from the
> scene. Modern scholars have established that such a scheme
> is simply not possible.

The very latest the Old Testament could have been written was
some two to three hundred years before Jesus' birth, for that is when
the Septuagint (a Greek translation of the Hebrew Scriptures) was
written. Most scholars of antiquities admit that the Hebrew original
must have existed at least 50 to 150 years before the Septuagint
was produced. That means that all 109 prophecies of Jesus' life and
death had to be written at least 250 to 400 years prior to His birth!
Consequently, these prophecies are more than adequate witnesses to
His unique person and identity.[27]

LaHaye goes on to say, "Consider the mathematics involved in the
fulfillment of these prophecies. The probability that just 20 of these
109 prophecies could be fulfilled in one man by chance is less than
one in one quadrillion, one hundred and twenty-five trillion. Most
people cannot even imagine such a number. If they did, it would look
something like this: 1 in 1,125,000,000,000,000."[28]

In addition, Norman Geisler contends, "Even the most liberal critic of the Old Testament admits to the completion of the prophetic books by some four hundred years before Christ and the book of Daniel by about 165 B.C."[29]

In his book, *Unshakable Foundations*, Dr. Geisler lists a small sampling of some of the prophecies fulfilled in Jesus Christ:

1. The Christ (Messiah) will be born of a woman (Gen. 3:15).
2. He will be born of a virgin (Isa. 7:14).
3. He will be of the seed of Abraham (Gen. 12:1–3; 22:18).
4. He will be of the tribe of Judah (Gen. 49:10; Luke 3:23, 33).
5. He will be of the House of David (2 Sam. 7:12; Matt. 1:1).
6. His birthplace will be Bethlehem (Mic. 5:2; Matt. 2:1).
7. He will be anointed by the Holy Spirit (Isa. 11:2; Matt. 3:16–17).
8. He will be heralded by a messenger of God (Isa. 40:3; Matt. 3:1–2).
9. He will perform miracles (Isa. 35:5–6; Matt. 9:35).
10. He will cleanse the temple (Mal. 3:1; Matt. 21:12).
11. He will be rejected by His own people (Ps. 118:22; 1 Pet. 2:7).
12. He will die some 483 years after 444 B.C. (Dan. 9:24).
13. He will die a humiliating death (Ps. 22; Isa. 53; Matt. 27), involving:
    A. Rejection by Israel (Isa. 53:3; John 1:10–11; 7:5, 48).
    B. Silence before His accusers (Isa. 53:7; Matt. 27:12–19).
    C. Humiliation—being mocked (Ps. 22:16; John 20:25).
    D. Piercing of His hands and feet (Ps. 22:16; John 20:25).
    E. Being crucified with thieves (Isa. 53:12; Luke 23:33).
    F. Praying for His persecutors (Isa. 53:12; Luke 23:34).
    G. Piercing of His side (Zech. 12:10; John 19:34).
    H. Burial in a rich man's tomb (Isa. 53:9; Matt. 27:57–60).
    I. Casting lots for His garments (Ps. 22:18; John 19:23–24).
14. He will rise from the dead (Ps. 16:10; Mark 16:6; Acts 2:31).
15. He will ascend into heaven (Ps. 68:18; Acts 1:9).
16. He will sit at the right hand of God (Ps. 110:1; Heb. 1:3).[30]

For those who think perhaps a psychic could have made such accurate predictions of the future, they simply do not know the facts:

One test of a prophet was whether they ever uttered predictions that did not come to pass (Deuteronomy

18:22). Those whose prophecies failed were stoned (18:20); a practice that no doubt gave pause to any who were not absolutely sure their messages were from God. Amid hundreds of prophecies, biblical prophets are not known to have made a single error. A study of psychics in 1975 and observed until 1981 showed that of the seventy-two predictions, only six were fulfilled in any way. Two of these were vague and two others were hardly surprising—the U.S. and Russia would remain leading powers and there would be no world wars. The people's Almanac (1976) did a study of predictions of twenty-five top psychics. The results: of the total seventy-two predictions, sixty-six (92 percent) were totally wrong (Kole 69). An accuracy rate around 8 percent could easily be explained by chance and general knowledge of circumstances. In 1993 the psychics missed every major unexpected news story, including Michael Jordan's retirement, the Midwest flooding, and the Israel-PLO peace treaty. Among their false prophecies were that the Queen of England would become a nun, and Kathie Lee Gifford would replace Jay Leno as host of "The Tonight Show."[31]

You get the picture. The prophets certainly did. What remains, though, is to confront the most often derided—and most central—fact of Christianity.

Evidence for the Resurrection

The strongest evidence for the truth claims of Jesus Christ is His resurrection from the dead. In Matthew 12, the Pharisees ask Jesus to give them a sign that everything He says is true. Jesus replies by saying, "no sign will be given to it except the sign of the prophet Jonah. For as Jonah was in the belly of the great fish three days and three nights, so the Son of Man will be in the heart of the earth three days and three nights" (vv. 39–40).

Jesus foretold His own death, which anyone could do if he were willing to arrange his own death, but Jesus also foretold His resurrection. Then He actually did rise from the dead.

Skeptics and critics have tried to explain away the resurrection by offering a variety of alternate explanations. One such scenario alleges that the women and disciples went to the wrong tomb. Think about this for a minute. How could it be the wrong tomb if the women and the disciples found the burial clothes lying there? Tim LaHaye writes, "The grave clothes of Jesus were still there and in perfect order, lying undisturbed as if enclosing a mummy—yet no body was inside! Everything was still intact. He Himself was gone, but somehow He had left behind His grave clothes. John knew instantly that the only thing that could cause such a miracle was the transformation of Jesus' dead body into a new, resurrected body that was no longer subject to time and space."[32]

And by the way, did the Roman soldiers and Roman authorities also forget where the tomb was? The tomb was closed with a Roman seal that had been broken. This provides another clue that it was the correct tomb. If the women and the disciples had been at the wrong tomb, the Jewish authorities and Romans would have stopped the spread of the resurrection story simply by pointing the women and the disciples to the correct tomb, where they would have found the still-dead body of Jesus.

And consider this: The tomb that was borrowed for the body of Jesus had been provided by a rich man named Joseph of Arimathea. The Bible says the tomb was brand new. Do you think that Joseph, after spending the money to have someone carve out a small cavern in stone, would just forget the location of this new tomb?

Worldview and apologetic expert Dr. Tim LaHaye entombs the absurd excuse that the women and disciples were at the wrong place: "It would have been impossible to challenge people to worship a 'resurrected' Savior if His body were still in the tomb! His disciples might have managed the deception for a time if they had moved to a city several hundred miles away from where the events in question took place. But that is not what they did. Immediately they began preaching right there in Jerusalem that He rose from the dead. And they used the empty tomb as 'exhibit A,' their first piece of evidence."[33]

But maybe someone stole the body. Critics have long claimed that the disciples stole the body to give the appearance that Jesus had risen from the dead. This raises the question: How could the disciples have moved a stone away from the tomb without waking up the guards, assuming they were sleeping? Disturbing a tomb could get you the death penalty, and the punishment for a guard falling asleep at his post was also death. Don't you think the fear of death would have kept at least one of the guards awake, if not all of them? Do you think the disciples would risk being killed for raiding the tomb just to pull off a fake resurrection? Remember, the disciples were a band of depressed and defeated men who had just witnessed Jesus' very public crucifixion. They did not expect Jesus to rise from the dead. It is not plausible that demoralized, scared men would risk being killed themselves for a dead Jesus.

Not only that, to move the stone would have required more than eleven men. Remember, Judas had betrayed Jesus and hung himself, leaving only eleven disciples. Even if these had wanted to perpetrate a hoax, where would they have found others willing to assist in rolling away the stone at the risk of death? Josh McDowell made a compelling discovery as part of his research: "In the Mark 16:4 portion of the Bezae manuscript in the Cambridge Library in England, a parenthetical statement was found that adds, 'And when He was laid there, he (Joseph) put against the tomb a stone which 20 men could not roll away.'"[34]

The Bible states clearly that the stone was moved by an angel from heaven and not by the disciples or the women. Note, too, that the enemies of Jesus never acknowledged that the body of Jesus was missing. In fact, they sought to hatch a plan to explain what the overwhelming evidence, which they saw first hand, revealed—Jesus had risen from the dead. Matthew 28:11–15 recounts: "As they were on their way, some of the guard came into the city and reported to the chief priests everything that had happened. After the priests had assembled with the elders and agreed on a plan, they gave the soldiers a large sum of money and told them, 'Say this, "His disciples came during the night and stole Him while we were sleeping." If this reaches the governor's ears, we will deal with him and keep you out of trouble.' So they took the money and did as they were instructed. And this story has been spread among Jewish people to this day."

If the authorities really believed that the disciples had stolen the body of Jesus, they would have had them killed (the punishment for disturbing a grave, remember?). If the body of Jesus was still in the tomb and the disciples were lying about the resurrection of Jesus, the authorities would have put the body of Jesus on display to end the resurrection story. And if the authorities had taken the body of Jesus to a new and secret location they would have produced it. Finally, if the body of Jesus was stolen, why were the grave clothes still in the tomb in the orderly condition one would expect if Jesus had left the graves clothes supernaturally and without unwrapping Himself? They wouldn't be.

But wait—the skeptics have more. What if Jesus didn't really die?

The Swoon Theory

The swoon theory is the belief that Jesus did not die from being crucified. He simply passed out and was taken down from the cross, unconscious, and the cool air in the tomb revived him.

Pardon me, but this is one of the stupidest theories ever.

Anyone that knows anything about Roman crucifixion is aware that Roman executioners were very good at their job (anyone who doubts this might want to see Mel Gibson's disturbingly realistic film, *The Passion*). In some cases, the guards would break the legs of any victims that would not die fast enough. With legs broken, they could not push themselves up in order to breathe, so the condemned person would finally die from suffocation. When the guards came to break Jesus' legs, He was already dead. To verify this, one soldier pierced the side of Jesus, and blood and water poured out.

Numerous medical experts agree that the description of Jesus' crucifixion points to the unmistakable medical evidence that Jesus was dead when taken down from the cross. In an article in *The Journal of the American Medical Association*, W. D. Edwards, W. J. Gabel, and F. E. Hosmer conclude:

> Jesus of Nazareth underwent Jewish and Roman trials,
> was flogged and was sentenced to death by crucifixion. The
> scourging produced deep stripe-like lacerations and appre-
> ciable blood loss and it probably set the stage for hypovo-
> lemic shock as evidenced by the fact that Jesus was too

weakened to carry the crossbar (patibulum) to Golgotha. At the site of crucifixion his wrists were nailed to the patibulum and after the patibulum was lifted onto the upright post (stipes) his feet were nailed to the stipes.

The major pathophysiologic effect of crucifixion was an interference with normal respirations. Accordingly death resulted primarily from hypovolemic shock and exhaustion asphyxia. Jesus' death was ensured by the thrust of a soldier's spear into his side. Modern medical interpretation of the historical evidence indicates that Jesus was dead when taken down from the cross. (*JAMA* 1986; 255:1455–63)

The article also notes: "Clearly, the weight of historical and medical evidence indicates that Jesus was dead before the wound to his side was inflicted and supports the traditional view that the spear, thrust between his right ribs, probably perforated not only the right lung but also the pericardium and heart and thereby ensured his death. Accordingly, interpretations based on the assumption that Jesus did not die on the cross appear to be at odds with modern medical knowledge."

Besides, is it plausible that if Jesus did not die and was revived by the cool air in the tomb that He was able to roll away a stone from the tomb's opening—a stone that took more than twenty healthy men to put into place? If others moved the stone and Jesus walked out, it is equally implausible that the disciples would have been energized and inspired by this half-dead man. Would such a weak and near-death Jesus have caused the disciples to snap out of their fear and depression and run about declaring a strong and mighty Savior? Even nineteenth-century skeptic David Strauss wondered the same thing:

It is impossible that one who had just come forth from the grave half dead, who crept about weak and ill, who stood in need of medical treatment, of bandaging, strengthening, and tender care, and who at last succumbed to suffering, could ever have given to the disciples that impression that He was a conqueror over death and the grave—that He was the Prince of Life—which lay at the bottom of their future ministry. Such a resuscitation could only have weakened

the impression which He had made upon them in life and in death—or at the most could have given it an elegiac voice—but could by no possibility change their sorrow into enthusiasm, or elevated their reverence into worship.[35]
No, Jesus didn't faint on the cross to pass for dead.

The Hallucination Theory

The hallucination theory is the belief that everyone who reported seeing Jesus was hallucinating. According to the Bible, there were more than five hundred eyewitnesses that saw the resurrected Jesus and yet the skeptics suggest all five hundred-plus had the same hallucination—many of them at the exact same moment. Medical evidence suggests, to the contrary, that hallucinations are highly individual experiences and not duplicated from one person to another. Furthermore, Jesus appeared to the disciples many times over the course of forty days, and He ate meals with them. After Jesus ascended into heaven (while His disciples watched), none of them continued to speak of seeing Jesus. So in order to accept the hallucination theory, someone would have to believe—against all reason—that the hallucinations of the disciples were identical and started and stopped at the same time.

The Eyes Have It: Eyewitness Testimony

Perhaps the greatest evidence for the resurrection of Jesus Christ is that, as we noted earlier, more than five hundred eyewitnesses saw Him. In addition to Jesus' followers, He also appeared to one of the greatest enemies of Christianity, Saul of Tarsus.

Saul was a Jewish leader who saw to the martyrdom of many Christians, the first of which was Stephen (Acts 7:54–60). Yet, when Jesus Christ appeared to Saul on the Damascus road, Saul was transformed and became one of the greatest defenders and preachers of Christianity. In Acts 26:4–5 and 9–23 Saul, who upon his conversion became known as Paul, gives his own testimony:

All the Jews know my way of life from my youth, which was spent from the beginning among my own nation and in Jerusalem. They had previously known me for quite some time, if they were willing to testify, that according to the strictest party of our religion I lived as a Pharisee. . . . In fact, I myself supposed it was necessary to do many things in opposition to the name of Jesus the Nazarene. This I actually did in Jerusalem, and I locked up many of the saints in prison, since I had received authority for that from the chief priests. When they were put to death, I cast my vote against them. In all the synagogues I often tried to make them blaspheme by punishing them. Being greatly enraged at them, I even pursued them to foreign cities.

Under these circumstances I was traveling to Damascus with authority and a commission from the chief priests. At midday, while on the road, O king, I saw a light from heaven brighter than the sun, shining around me and those traveling with me. When we had all fallen to the ground, I heard a voice speaking to me in the Hebrew language, "Saul, Saul, why are you persecuting Me? It is hard for you to kick against the goads."

But I said, "Who are You, Lord?"

And the Lord replied: "I am Jesus, whom you are persecuting. But get up and stand on your feet. For I have appeared to you for this purpose, to appoint you as a servant and a witness of things you have seen and of things in which I will appear to you. I will rescue you from the people and from the Gentiles, to whom I now send you, to open their eyes that they may turn from darkness to light and from the power of Satan to God, that they may receive forgiveness of sins and a share among those who are sanctified by faith in Me."

Therefore, . . . I was not disobedient to the heavenly vision. Instead, I preached to those in Damascus first, and to those in Jerusalem and in all the region of Judea, and to the Gentiles, that they should repent and turn to God, and do works worthy of repentance. For this reason the Jews seized me in the temple complex and were trying to kill me. Since I have obtained help that comes from God, to this day I stand and testify to both small and great, saying nothing else than what the prophets and Moses said would take place—that the Messiah must suffer, and that as the first to rise from the dead, He would proclaim light to our people and to the Gentiles.

It is a matter of recorded history that Saul was a leader of his day who persecuted Christians. It is also recorded history that Saul went through a radical change in his life, became known as Paul, and was a foundational leader of the early Christian church. What would change such a man from hating, persecuting, and killing Christians to becoming a Christian and defender of Christianity unless it was as Paul said—an encounter with the risen Lord?

Who Wants to Die for a Lie?

It was Paul himself, in 1 Corinthians 15:6, who told any skeptics to ask the eyewitnesses who were still living at the time if they believed they had seen the risen Lord. Those who saw Christ were changed and were willing to die rather than to say they had not seen Jesus alive after His crucifixion. The ones who ultimately died for their faith only had to say, "He is dead," and they could have lived.

Former skeptic and critic Frank Harber correctly points out that people are not willing to die for something they know to be a lie: "Many people have died for a cause they believed was true even though it was false; however, no one ever eagerly dies for a cause knowing it to be false. Christianity could have never endured had these first Christians not believed in the Resurrection. The tenacity of these early eyewitness in the face of death testifies to the truth that the Resurrection must have occurred."[36]

With the exception of John, every one of the disciples died a martyr's death. Tradition says that Peter was crucified upside down at his own request, for he thought himself "unworthy" to be crucified in the same way his Lord had been. Paul the apostle, the one "born out of due time," after several long imprisonments, died a martyr's death in Rome. Thomas, who had been a "doubter" until he saw the resurrected Christ, carried his Lord's Great Commission all the way to India, where he ministered for many years before he was finally martyred.[37]

Would these men die for a known lie or for a hoax they had orchestrated by stealing the body of Jesus Christ? Even if one or two determined to "stick to their guns," it is unreasonable to think every one of them would have died rather than confessing to the lie. We can only conclude that the eyewitnesses to Jesus' resurrection told what they believed to be true and refused to change their story in the face of persecution, torture, and death. As author Tim LaHaye has said, "They signed their testimony in blood."

The Moral Law and Universal Consent

We've looked at the specific reasons to believe biblical accounts about the truth of Christianity, but I believe there is another compelling reason to believe, and it is available to every man, woman, and child who honestly considers this inkling of the truth. Even liberals can avail themselves of this evidence if they are willing to admit it.

A great evidence for an all-knowing, all-powerful, and holy God and Creator is found in what He has placed in the heart and conscious of every human being. This inborn truth is universally known, and it is called the moral law. According to Romans, this moral law is written on our hearts. Thus, when an individual lies, cheats, steals, or commits adultery, there is a feeling of guilt or conviction. In Genesis, we are told that all people—both followers of Jesus Christ and those who have rejected Him—are created in the image of God. Part of what is meant by the idea that people are created in God's image is that each person has been endowed with the moral law inscribed on his or her conscience.

This "inscription" also brings about the near-universal consent that there is a God. The moral law is a reflection of God's character and nature. As I discussed earlier, everything consistent with the character and nature of God is truth, and everything contrary to the nature and character of God is untruth. We don't murder fellow human beings because murder goes against the character and nature of God. We are not to lie, steal, or break any of the other Ten Commandments because doing so would go against the character and nature of God. Romans 1:21 says, "For though they knew God, they did not glorify Him as God or show gratitude. Instead, their thinking became nonsense, and their senseless minds were darkened."

Romans 2:15 says, "They show that the work of the law is written on their hearts. Their consciences testify in support of this, and their competing thoughts either accuse or excuse them." This verse explains that people can either accept the guilty feeling of the law, accusing them of their transgression when they sin, or they can simply excuse the guilty feeling and learn to ignore it. If people ignore the guilt and suppress the truth long enough or often enough, they will become "liars whose consciences are seared" (1 Tim. 4:2).

Norm Geisler explains how this works out in a person's life:

[T]he root cause of the character disorders (moral corruption) mentioned above is directly associated with a person's refusal to acknowledge and act upon what is morally right and reject what is morally wrong. It becomes harder and harder for the individual to get help with his character disorder because of the increased moral depravity. This increase is associated with greater levels of insensitivity in that person's conscience. For example, during the progressive moral deterioration in the life of the person who uses pornography, his sequence of feeling-to-thought-to-deed proceeds with less and less intervention of the inhibitory mechanism of conscience and guilt.[38]

This is the net effect of having one's conscience seared. We can ignore God—even deny God—but because God has made Himself known by creating us in His image and by placing an understanding of the character and nature of God in the heart and conscience of every human being, no one will have an excuse at judgment for rejecting God and following the lie of humanism (Rom. 1:20). Romans 3:19–20 reminds us, "Now we know that whatever the law says speaks to those who are subject to the law, so that every mouth may be shut and the whole world may become subject to God's judgment. For no flesh will be justified in His sight by the works of the law, for through the law [comes] the knowledge of sin."

This verse makes it clear that everyone has broken the law. No one can justify their entry into heaven by claiming they have "lived a good enough life" because God's standard is the law, and no one has kept the law. To further underscore that committing sin is breaking the moral law, 1 John 3:4 says, "Everyone who commits sin also breaks the law; sin is the breaking of law." Romans 3:10 explains, "There is no one righteous, not even one," and Romans 3:23 concludes that "all have sinned and fall short of the glory of God." Need I say more?

The law makes us aware of our sin, and because all but Jesus Christ have broken the law, any who have not repented of their sins and trusted in the death, burial, and resurrection of Jesus Christ will not be pardoned for breaking the moral law. To repent means to turn from sin, to stop practicing sin as a lifestyle. This does not mean you will never again sin because you will. But there is a big difference between stumbling into sin and willingly jumping in. A repentant heart is born out of an awareness of your deep-seated sinfulness and the understanding that you deserve the wrath of God but are pardoned because of your faith in Jesus Christ and His work on the cross.

My friend Mark Cahill speaks for the Worldview Weekend and wrote a great book entitled *One Thing You Can't Do in Heaven*. Mark played college basketball at Auburn University and has a faith like few people I know. In his book, Mark does a great job explaining the real meaning and result of repentance:

> One topic that I believe we must talk about when we discuss sin is repentance. It seems to be a word that we don't use much in witnessing, and a word that some people don't want to use at all. Yet the word "repent" and its various forms is used over one hundred times in the Bible. It must be a very important word then, and something that we must understand.
>
> The apostle Paul tells us in 2 Corinthians 7:10, "For godly sorrow produces repentance to salvation, not to be regretted; but the sorrow of the world produces death."
>
> John the Baptist preached in the wilderness, "Repent, for the kingdom of heaven is at hand!" (Matthew 3:2).
>
> Jesus preached this same message of repentance. Mark 1:14, 15 says, "Now after John was put in prison, Jesus came to Galilee, preaching the gospel of the kingdom of God, and saying, 'The time is fulfilled, and the kingdom of God is at hand. Repent, and believe the gospel.'"
>
> In Mark 6, Jesus sends out the twelve disciples two by two. Verse 12 states, "So they went out and preached that

people should repent." If Jesus sent the disciples out preaching that people must repent of their sins, we ought to do the same.

According to *The Complete Word Study New Testament* by Dr. Spiros Zodhiates, the main word used for "repent" in the Greek is *metanoeo.* That word means "to repent with regret accompanied by a true change of heart toward God. . . . It signifies a change of mind consequent to retrospection, indicating regret for the course pursued and resulting in a wiser view of the past and future. Most importantly, it is distinguished from *metamellomai,* to regret because of the consequences of one's actions." As you can see, repentance is not when we feel bad because we got caught doing something wrong. True repentance is when we change our mind about our sin so our actions will not continue to be the same. . . .

I was sitting around talking one night with a young man I had met at a camp. He was telling me about his life and confessed that he had been using cocaine for the past thirty days. About forty-five minutes into the conversation he asked, "Is this the point where you are going to start talking to me about Jesus?"

I said, "No." He looked rather surprised. "You're not?" I told him that he was not ready for Jesus, and that it was not his day to get saved. He did not hate his sin enough to want to repent and walk away from it. He loved the world way too much. It was very interesting that he didn't argue one bit with me. He didn't want to get saved that day. He wanted to use drugs. He had gone to a Christian high school, so he knew all the right answers. The issue was repentance, and he didn't want to do that. . . . Repenting means to make a turn, and that is what you see in the true Christian life.[39]

I have watched Mark share truth again and again, and he knows what all of us know whose lives have been transformed by truth. The proof of the truth is in the transformation. Truth is not truth if it does not work.

The Transformed Life Is Proof!

When was the last time you heard a humanist say, "As soon as I accepted the fact that I was god, my life was transformed; I was able to overcome the destructive habits and behaviors in my life; I desired to do good; I wanted to serve others, love others; I wanted to put others ahead of myself; I now have a peace in the midst of the storm I cannot explain, and I don't fear death"? You never hear a humanist say that. On the other hand, the worst of sinners who repent and come to Christ are transformed in an amazing way.

One-time slave trader Charles Wesley wrote the hymn "Amazing Grace." Saul the killer of Christians became Paul the evangelist. Chuck Colson, the arrogant White House attorney who went to prison for Watergate, is now the humble, reserved leader of the nation's largest organization that ministers to prisoners.

The power and validity of truth can be seen through the transformed life.

MinCaye is one of the Auca Indians who killed missionaries Jim Elliot, Nate Saint, Ed McCully, Roger Youderian, and Peter Fleming in 1956. MinCaye now travels the world with Nate Saint's son, Steve Saint, preaching salvation through Jesus Christ alone. There are untold lives that were once filled with evil but made righteous through their encounter with, acceptance, surrender, and practice of the Truth. Only Truth can totally transform a life.

Our Final Answer: Christianity (True Conservatism)— the Truth; Humanism (Modern-day Liberalism)—a Lie

Dr. Erwin Lutzer is the pastor of the historic Moody Church in downtown Chicago. He has spoken for the Worldview Weekend and is an outstanding author who speaks on many topics. In 1994, he attended in Chicago a major symposium on the religions of the world. Dr. Lutzer walked the convention center, visiting with some of the seven thousand individuals in attendance. In his superb book *Called*, he describes his experience:

> I walked through the display area in search of a sinless prophet/teacher/Savior. I asked a Hindu Swami whether any

of their teachers claimed sinlessness. "No," he said, appearing irritated with my question, "If anyone claims he is sinless, he is not a Hindu!"

What about Buddha? No, I was told, he didn't claim sinlessness. He found a group of ascetics and preached sermons to them. He taught that all outward things are only distractions and encouraged a life of discipline and contemplation. He sought enlightenment and urged his followers to do the same. He died seeking enlightenment. No sinlessness here.

What about Baha ullah? He claimed he had a revelation from God that was more complete and more enlightened than those before him. Though he was convinced of the truth of his teachings, he made few personal claims. He thought his writings were "more perfect" than others, but he never claimed perfection or sinlessness for himself.

When I came to the representatives of the Muslim faith, I already knew that in the Koran the prophet Mohammed admitted he was in need of forgiveness. They agreed. "There is one God, Allah, and Mohammed was not perfect." Again, no sinlessness there.

Why was I searching for a sinless Savior? Because I don't want to have to trust a Savior who is in the same predicament as I am. I can't trust my eternal soul to someone who is still working through his own imperfections. Since I'm a sinner, I need someone who is standing on higher ground.

Understandably, none of the religious leaders I spoke with even claimed to have a Savior. Their prophets, they said, showed the way, but made no pretense to be able to personally forgive sins or transform so much as a single human being. Like a street sign, they gave directions, but were not able to take us where we need to go. If we need any saving, we will have to do it ourselves.

The reason is obvious: No matter how wise, no matter how gifted, no matter how influential other prophets, gurus, and teachers might be, they had the presence of mind to know that they were imperfect just like the rest of us. They never even presumed to be able to reach down into the murky water of human depravity and bring sinners into the presence of God.

What did Jesus have to say about His sinless life?

"Which of you convicts Me of sin? If I speak truth, why do you not believe Me?" (John 8:46). He pointed out hypocrisy in the lives of His critics, but none of them returned the compliment.

Judas, an apparent friend turned enemy, said, "I have sinned by betraying innocent blood" (Matt. 27:4).

Pilate, who longed to find fault with Christ, confessed, "I find no guilt in this man" (Luke 23:4).

Peter, who lived with Him for three years, said he "committed no sin, nor was any deceit found in His mouth" (1 Pet. 2:22).

The apostle Paul said that God the Father "made Him who knew no sin to be sin on our behalf, that we might become the righteousness of God in Him" (2 Cor. 5:21).

Jesus was either sinless or the greatest of sinners for deceiving so many people about His sinlessness. As C. E. Jefferson put it, "The best reason we have for believing in the sinlessness of Jesus is the fact that He allowed His dearest friends to think that He was."[40]

That difference, my friends, is what makes Him the Savior of the world. Jesus Christ was and is the sinless Savior. That astounding difference is what makes Him exactly what He is—a member of the Triune God who is the Creator, Savior, and final Judge over all the earth.

Humanism is a lie because Christianity is the truth. Remember, I admitted at the beginning of this chapter that *both could be false*, but I also pointed out that *only one can be true*. Christianity is the truth because Jesus Christ is the risen, sinless Savior—the embodiment, the very Truth Himself. He is the Way, the Truth, and the Life, and all other ways to salvation are wrong. All ideas, values, beliefs, and worldviews that contradict the nature and character of God are wrong and are a lie. They come from Satan, the father of lies.

Everyone Makes the Final Choice

So where does this leave our liberal friends? Thanks to the wisdom of America's Founding Fathers and the inalienable rights they did their best to preserve in the structure of our great country, liberals and other humanists are free to go on believing whatever mix of lies they choose to accept. They are even free to try to convince the rest of us to believe along with them. What they are not—or at least *should* not—be free to do is to manipulate our God-ordained system of government and to undermine the Constitution that protects all our freedoms.

I believe liberals today are mounting an all-out effort to create a social order in which their worldview—no matter how false—is the only one allowed, the only one given credence by those in power, the only one to determine what will ultimately become of our nation and its people. The frightening prospect that they could actually succeed (because they are succeeding remarkably as I've documented in this book!) hardens my resolve to fight them at every turn—from the ballot box to the airwaves, to the speeches I give and the books I write.

My hope is that you, too, will find whatever way opens in your life to contribute to winning the battle in America against humanists in liberal clothing who want to make you after their own image. There is an alternative to being a nation ruled only by the whims of godless men and women wielding power. We've been there before, and we can get there again if we determine we want nothing in this life more than to be one nation fully under the loving, caring God who created the very universe in which we live.

Appendix 1

Test Your Worldview

Do You Think Like a Modern-day Liberal (Humanist) or a True Conservative (Christian Theist)?

The online test offers these possible answers for each statement: Strongly Agree, Tend to Agree, No Opinion, Tend to Disagree, Strongly Disagree. To find out how you would score, go to www.worldview weekend.com. It's free!

(1) God is the creator of all life.

(2) Every person who has ever lived on earth, but Jesus Christ, has committed sins.

(3) The Bible, rightly divided, should be the foundation for all our beliefs, actions, and conduct.

(4) Since God is not the author of law, the author of law must be man. In other words, the law is the law simply because the highest human authority, which is the state, has said it is law and is able to back it up by force.

(5) The Ten Commandments originally provided a basis for our legal and political system creating justice and peace.

(6) Believers should not only base their philosophy in Christ, but they should know how to respond to the critics and skeptics of Christianity with the reasoning and basis of our biblical worldview.

(7) If the research and theory of a group of scientists contradicts the Word of God, the error is with the scientists, not the Bible.

(8) The Founding Fathers had no biblical reason in mind when they made America a constitutional republic instead of a pure democracy.

(9) Under some circumstances Christians are called to disobey the laws of government.

(10) There must be absolutes if there is to be moral and legal order.

(11) The Bible and a biblical worldview played an instrumental role in building our American civilization, original laws, and form of government.

(12) Adam and Eve were fictional characters that never really lived.

(13) Both secular humanism and Marxism are religious worldviews.

(14) All religions are equally true.

(15) The more a government resembles a pure democracy the more disorder and confusion occur.

(16) To know God we must study the Bible and be taught by the Holy Spirit who inspired the Bible.

(17) There are no specific, God-given principles related to law, or if there are, they should not be the foundation of today's legal systems.

(18) Biological evolution (life from non-life to human beings) runs contrary to reason, science, and history.

(19) It is the responsibility of the federal government to create wealth.

(20) All forms of government-sponsored socialism stifle economic growth and prosperity to one degree or another.

(21) The Bible states that money is the root of all evil.

(22) Jesus was crucified on the cross but was not physically raised from the dead.

(23) Individuals must ultimately face the consequences of their actions before a Holy God.

(24) A good person can earn his or her way to heaven if their good deeds outweigh their bad deeds.

(25) One of the greatest virtues one can possess is the virtue of tolerance as defined by our postmodern world; namely, we accept everyone's lifestyles as equal.

(26) The Holy Spirit does not really exist.

(27) The more one discovers about the universe, the more one discovers design.

(28) Family, church, and state are institutions ordained by God.

(29) A God-given responsibility of government is to protect the righteous and punish the wicked.

(30) Legislating morality is a violation of the separation of church and state.

(31) The Bible says, judge not lest you be judged, which means we are not to judge the choices or behavior of a person as right or wrong. We all make mistakes, and thus we should not judge someone's actions or behavior according to any particular standard.

(32) The original intent of our Founding Fathers was a form of government that was free to set its own policy only if God had not already ruled in that area. Our Founders believed that our man-made laws were not to contradict the laws of God.

(33) Individual freedoms would be advanced and protected under a one-world government under United Nations authority.

(34) Our judicial system should allow judges, through their decisions and rulings, to guide and shape the foundational basis of law.

(35) Civil disobedience by Christians is always wrong and unbiblical.

(36) Science, history, literature, and other advanced educational skills and facts can be taught without a religious or philosophical foundation.

(37) American Founding Fathers violated New Testament principles when they founded America.

(38) The Bible is a consistent revelation from beginning to end.

(39) There is a Bible verse that states that God helps those who help themselves.

(40) The wording "separation of Church and State" is found in the U.S. Constitution.

(41) As long as government is serving the purpose for which God created it, government is approved by God.

(42) The Bible is a reflection of God's character and nature.

(43) Physically and mentally healthy adults who do not work should not be protected from suffering the consequences of their actions.

(44) The Bible specifically instructs the people of a nation to base the selection of their judges on biblical principles.

(45) Jesus Christ lived a sinless life.

(46) The biblical purpose for wealth is to provide for one's family, proclaim the gospel, be a blessing to others, test your stewardship and your loyalty to God.

(47) There is more than one way to God.

(48) Ideas have consequences.

(49) If it "works" for you then it must be true.

(50) Biblically minded Christians should look at the issues of the world as falling into one of two categories, the secular and the sacred.

(51) When you study the Bible as a whole, it becomes clear that God is very supportive of an economic system that is based on private property, the work ethic, and personal responsibility.

(52) Pastors should not be allowed to preach against homosexuality from the pulpit, and if they do it should be considered hate speech.

(53) The separation of church and state must be enforced, prohibiting the acknowledgment of God in the public schools, governmental buildings, meetings, and property.

(54) Truth is either nonexistent or unknowable.

(55) While there is evidence for the defense and reason of a biblical worldview and the claims of Christ and Christianity, it is impossible to please God without faith.

(56) There is no evidence for a worldwide flood.

(57) God used the process of biological evolution to create the world as we know it today.

(58) The federal government should fund school-based health clinics that would include safe-sex counseling.

(59) The federal government should require students to pass a national test before graduating from high school.

(60) A Christian can develop a biblical worldview for every major area of life by studying the Bible from beginning to end in context.

(61) Homosexual marriages should be legalized.

(62) Making the incomes of its citizens as equal as possible should be one of the top priorities of any legitimate government.

(63) Ultimately every individual will bow their knee and confess with their mouth that Jesus Christ is Lord.

(64) Truth is discovered by man, not created by man.

(65) Making as much money as you can is more important than whether you have a good reputation.

(66) Salvation is a gift from God that cannot be earned.

(67) The federal government should be directly involved in determining which students go to college and which students go into the workplace and what jobs they hold.

(68) Since it is her body, a woman should be free to end her pregnancy with an abortion.

(69) The federal government should require that only a federally licensed teacher be permitted to teach or instruct a child in an educational setting.

(70) Values clarification courses or situational ethics should be taught to students in our educational system.

(71) If God does not exist, all things are permissible.

(72) The Bible is God's revealed Word and should be the basis of our worldview.

(73) There is no reason why a biblically minded Christian should be opposed to human cloning.

(74) One of the Ten Commandments is, "Thou shalt not kill;" thus it stands to reason that God is opposed to war and nations going to war.

(75) If you want to study the original source of law, then study the previous decisions of judges because our laws are always evolving based on the most recent decisions of our nation's judges.

(76) God had no beginning and has no end.

(77) The most biblically based tax system would be one based on a flat tax system where everyone pays the same percentage of their income in taxes.

(78) God is the Creator of the universe.

(79) Satan is real.

(80) Christians should be directly opposed to a state lottery for numerous biblical and economical reasons.

(81) Your worldview is the foundation of your values and your values are the foundation of your actions.

(82) Life begins at conception.

(83) The federal government should pass legislation allowing doctors and family members to decide when a loved one should be put to death based on the individual's quality of life.

(84) The Bible states that the government does not bear the sword in vain. Numerous verses throughout the Bible make it clear that capital punishment administered by the government, for those that have committed capital crimes, is biblically acceptable.

Appendix 2

The Humanist's Worldview Chart

The chart on the following four pages is by Brannon S. Howse (copyright © 2005) and was adapted and expanded from Dr. David Noebel's basic worldview chart from *Understanding the Times*. It summarizes how the humanists view ten major disciplines of life.

	Education	Science/Medicine	Religion/Church
Theology Atheism—no such thing as God	Secular humanism from kindergarten through college.	Darwinian evolution	Secular and cosmic humanism (New Age movement) is only accepted religion. Heaven on earth.
Philosophy Naturalism	No spiritual or supernatural world	Man has no soul. Survival of the fittest is the rule; therefore abortion, euthanasia, and embryonic stem cell research is acceptable	Humanist John Dewey, signer of the *Humanist Manifesto I,* said there is no reason for religion because man has no soul
Ethics Moral relativism	Situational ethics, values clarification courses	Moral relativism allows doctors to ignore Hippocratic Oath and perform abortions and active euthanasia	Humanists say people are basically good and Christianity is evil and intolerant because it proclaims absolute truth
Biology Darwin's evolution	Darwin's evolution based on natural selection and DNA mistakes	Evolution is taught to the exclusion of creationism	Life devalued by doctors that reject man being created in the image of God. Scientists explore other planets looking for the origin of life
Psychology Man has no soul	Death education and lifeboat values clarification scenarios promote that man dies and that is it	Abortion and euthanasia are acceptable because man dies and that is it	Man can solve his own problems and has no need for religion or God. Cosmic humanists believe man can save himself
Sociology Non-traditional families	Curriculum promotes alternative lifestyle under the guise of tolerance	Artificial reproduction for same-sex couples	Hate-speech legislation threatens pastors and Christians for speaking against same-sex marriage

BORDERS

BORDERS
BOOKS MUSIC AND CAFE
100 DOGWOOD BLVD
FLOWOOD, MS 39232
601-919-0462

STORE: 0472	REG: 02/04 TRAN#: 7319	
SALE	10/05/2005 EMP: 73481	

ONE NATION UNDER MAN
ST T   16.99

Order#:17259

Subtotal	16.99
MISS 7%	1.19
1 Item Total	18.18
CASH	20.00
Cash Change Due	1.82

10/05/2005 04:29PM

Check our store inventory online
at www.borderstores.com

and online at www.borders.com

Opened videos, discs, and cassettes may only be exchanged for replacement copies of the original item.
Periodicals, newspapers, out-of-print, collectible and pre-owned items may not be returned.
Returned merchandise must be in saleable condition.

BORDERS®

Merchandise presented for return, including sale or marked-down items, must be accompanied by the original Borders store receipt. Returns must be completed within 30 days of purchase. The purchase price will be refunded in the medium of purchase (cash, credit card or gift card). Items purchased by check may be returned for cash after 10 business days.

Merchandise unaccompanied by the original Borders store receipt, or presented for return beyond 30 days from date of purchase, must be carried by Borders at the time of the return. The lowest price offered for the item during the 12 month period prior to the return will be refunded via a gift card.

Opened videos, discs, and cassettes may only be exchanged for replacement copies of the original item.
Periodicals, newspapers, out-of-print, collectible and pre-owned items may not be returned.
Returned merchandise must be in saleable condition.

BORDERS®

Merchandise presented for return, including sale or marked-down items, must be accompanied by the original Borders store receipt. Returns must be completed within 30 days of purchase. The purchase price will be refunded in the medium of purchase (cash, credit card or gift card). Items purchased by check may be returned for cash after 10 business days.

Merchandise unaccompanied by the original Borders store receipt, or presented for return beyond 30 days from date of purchase, must be carried by Borders at the time of the return. The lowest price offered for the item during the 12 month period prior to the return will be refunded via a gift card.

Opened videos, discs, and cassettes may only be exchanged for replacement copies of the original item.
Periodicals, newspapers, out-of-print, collectible and pre-owned items may not be returned.
Returned merchandise must be in saleable condition.

Mays
Meet the Fockers
Shark Tale
****

FREE BEVERAGE
When You Purchase a Beverage

Valid at Borders, 10/7-10/10/05,
with this coupon.

Barcode #: 1590049500000000000
POS: S1, S4, barcode #, $ of drink

Limit one free beverage per customer.
Offer applies to least expensive
beverage. Not valid with other coupons
or standard group discounts. Cash
value .01 cent. Not redeemable for
cash. Any other use constitutes fraud.
****

STORE: 0472   REG: 02/04 TRAN#: 7319
SALE   10/05/2005   EMP: 73481
****

	Government	Family	Entertainment & Media
Theology Atheism—no such thing as God	Because there is no God, government is the highest form of authority	Not instituted by God but created by man to be whatever brings pleasure	Sitcoms mock God and Christians and Christian morality
Philosophy Naturalism	Because there is no God, He does not move in the affairs of men and there is no divine providence	Fathers and mothers have no spiritual responsibility to their children	Life portrayed as having no meaning
Ethics Moral relativism	Moral relativism allows legislation for abortions, active euthanasia and other such violations of the Moral Law	Abortion on demand and active euthanasia	Hedonism is the pursuit of pleasure and is the highest pursuit of life
Biology Darwin's evolution	U.S. Supreme Court outlaws creation being taught along side evolution in 1987 decision	Families evolve into whatever society accepts as normal	Evolution promoted as fact and creationism as unscientific and accepted by uneducated Christians
Psychology Man has no soul	Supreme Court legalizes abortion and outlaws ban on partial-birth abortion and refuses case on active euthanasia in 2005	No spiritual heritage to develop and pass on to children because there is no spiritual world	Man can solve his own problems and New Age themes promote that man can save himself while secular humanists promote death is the end
Sociology Non-traditional families	U.S. Supreme Court declares state sodomy laws unconstitutional	Judges and legislatures battle over same-sex marriages	Same-sex marriage and same-sex couples promoted as normal and acceptable lifestyle

	Education	Science/Medicine	Religion/Church
Law Positive Law (moral relativism applied to the law)	Courts don't allow students to pray, read the Bible, be taught creationism, or invoke the name of God at graduations or pray at football games	Laws allow doctors to perform abortions, partial-birth abortions, and active euthanasia in certain states	Separation of church and state lie allows for persecution of Christians and secularization of America
Politics Globalism and World Government	National Education Association promotes loyalty to the United Nations and global citizenship		UN passes tolerance declaration calling for prosecution of missionaries and Christians preaching gospel
Economics Socialism	Radical environmentalism bemoans capitalism and promotes redistribution of everyone's wealth but that of the liberal elite	Attempts to pass national health care continue as means to redistribute others' wealth	Humanists continue to call for churches and Christian organizations to loose tax-exempt status
History Begins by accident through Darwinian evolutionary theory	Revisionist history denies America's godly heritage and providential origin	Advancements and discoveries by Christian doctors and scientists ignored	Founding Fathers that were pastors and the men of their church that were involved in American Revolution are ignored

	Government	Family	Entertainment & Media
Law Positive Law (moral relativism applied to the law)	Supreme Court embraces concept that truth is relative, morals evolve, and laws should do the same. Court looks to foreign law to support decisions	Special rights for same-sex couples. Parental authority undermined by laws that allow minors to have abortions without parental consent	Judges embracing legal positivism held forth as heroes while judges, legislators, and citizens that believe in absolute truth are ridiculed
Politics Globalism and world government	UN and World Court threaten American sovereignty	UN Convention on the Rights of the Child threatens parental authority. U.S. Senate has yet to ratify this	United Nations promoted as noble organization with admirable goals
Economics Socialism	Bigger government, higher taxes, more regulations on business to redistribute wealth	Tax laws punish marriage, reward cohabitation, and higher taxes force moms into workforce and kids into daycare	Materialism is promoted as god and key to happiness
History Begins by accident through Darwinian evolutionary theory	Original Intent of Founding Fathers is ignored by U.S. Supreme Court in making decisions	Godly heritage, history, and legacy is ignored and even discouraged as old fashioned, intolerant, and out-of-date	Revisionist history promotes lies about Founding Fathers, our godly heritage, the separation of church and state, and contribution of Christians

Appendix 3

Historic and Liberal U.S. Supreme Court Decisions (1881–2005)

The Progression of Legal Positivism

by Brannon S. Howse

How the U.S. Supreme Court and Its Justices Are Pushing Us toward Becoming One Nation under Man

1. In 1881, Associate Justice of the U.S. Supreme Court Oliver Wendell Holmes Jr., in his book *The Common Law,* attacks the moral law: "The life of the law has not been logic; it has been experience. The felt necessities of the time, the prevalent moral political theories . . . have a good deal more to do than the syllogism [legal reasoning process] in determining the rules by which men should be governed."[1]

2. In 1907, Charles Evan Hughes, who would later become chief justice of the U.S. Supreme Court, said, "We are under a Constitution, but the Constitution is what the judges say it is."[2]

3. In 1932, Benjamin Cardozo was appointed to the U.S. Supreme Court. Cardozo proclaimed his belief in legal positivism when he said, "I take judge-made law as one of the existing realities of life."[3] Cardozo saw little purpose for the person of faith who believed in the moral law as the foundation of the U.S. Constitution and founding documents when he said, "If there is any law which is back of the sovereignty of the state, and superior thereto, it is not law in such a sense as to concern the judge or lawyer, however much it concerns the statesman or the moralist."[4]

4. 1947, *Everson vs. Board of Education*. The U.S Supreme Court took the Fourteenth Amendment, which addressed specific state powers, and hooked it to the First Amendment. With this decision, the Court took off the handcuffs that had restrained and limited the scope of the federal government's power and placed them onto the states. Now the federal courts were empowered to decide when and what rights the states could practice. So severe was the impact of this ruling that Supreme Court Justice Williams Douglas referred to the 1947 decision as creating a "revolution." It was a silent revolution of which most Americans are unaware even to this day, despite the freedoms that were stolen from them and their states by the high court. The U.S. Supreme Court deliberately took the separation phrase from Jefferson's letter out of context, changed the meaning of his words, and began to propagate a lie to the American people. This case was the first time the Court used Jefferson's letter completely divorced from its context and original meaning.

5. 1948, *McCollum vs. Board of Education*. The U.S. Supreme Court ruled that Illinois could not offer voluntary or elective religious courses to its students despite the fact that parents had picked these courses and signed printed cards that verified that the parents wanted their children to take these weekly, voluntary, elective religious courses. This ruling set national policy for all the nation's public schools.

6. 1958, *Trop vs. Dulles*. Chief Justice Warren declared the Eighth Amendment of the U.S. Constitution could not have the same meaning as it did at the time it was written. Warren stated, "the Amendment must draw its meaning from the evolving standards of decency that marks the progress of a maturing society." In other words, morals and standards evolve over time as does the meaning of the Constitution.

7. 1961, *Torcaso vs. Watkins*. In a footnote to this decision, Justice Hugo L. Black wrote, "Among religious in this country which do not teach what would generally be considered a belief in the existence of God are Buddhism, Taoism, Ethical Culture, Secular Humanism, and others."[5] Despite this finding, judges do not apply the "separation of church and state" standard to secular humanism, which is the primary worldview taught in America's public schools via government funding.

8. 1962, *Engel vs. Vitale*. The U.S. Supreme Court ruled it is unconstitutional and a violation of the "separation of church and state" for

the students of New York Schools to recite a long-standing prayer. This was the first time the Court ruled on a decision using zero precedent—not citing a single preceding legal case to substantiate their justification for such a ruling. In this case, the Court changed the word *church* to mean "a religious activity in public." This decision made corporate, voluntary student prayer in America's public schools illegal throughout the nation.

9. 1963, *School District of Abington Township vs. Schempp.* The U.S. Supreme Court rules that Pennsylvania public school children cannot be involved in corporate, voluntary reading of the Bible at school. This decision set national policy, as U.S. Supreme Court rulings often do, for all the nation's public schools.

10. 1968, *Epperson vs. Arkansas.* The U.S. Supreme Court ruled that Arkansas cannot require that creationism be taught in the public schools.

11. 1971, *Lemon vs. Kurtzman.* This U.S. Supreme Court ruling established what became known as the "Lemon Test" related to church and state interaction. The Lemon Test requires that state policy have no religious purpose. In addition, the Lemon test requires that no state policy create a situation where one religion would have advantage over another or be promoted over nonreligious beliefs. Interestingly enough, despite the 1961 footnote in *Torcaso vs. Watkins* that secular humanism is a religion, the Lemon test has not been applied to secular humanism, which to this day enjoys an advantage over the Christian worldview in America's schools.

12. 1973, *Roe vs. Wade.* This U.S. Supreme Court ruling allowed for abortion on demand.

13. 1980, *Stone vs. Graham.* The U.S. Supreme Court ruled that Kentucky cannot post the Ten Commandments in their public school classrooms. The Court said, "If the posted copies of the Ten Commandments are to have any effect at all, it will be to induce the schoolchildren to read, mediate upon, perhaps to venerate and obey, the Commandments."[6]

14. 1984, *Lynch vs. Donnelly.* In writing her opinion in this case Justice Sandra Day O'Connor created what has become known as the "endorsement test." This test is used to determine whether or not a government policy is endorsing a religion.

15. 1985, *Wallace vs. Jaffree.* The U.S. Supreme Court struck down an Alabama statute that required a moment of silence in classrooms for "silent meditation or voluntary prayer."

16. 1987, *Edwards vs. Aguillard.* The U.S. Supreme Court ruled Louisiana could not require that evolution and creation both be taught side by side.

17. 1992, *Lee vs. Wiseman.* Through this decision, the U.S. Supreme Court made it illegal for a pastor, priest, or member of the clergy to offer an invocation or benediction at a public school graduation ceremony. Writing in this decision, Justice Anthony Kennedy created what has become known as the "coercion test." The coercion test prohibits the minority from being coerced by the majority to participate in a religious activity such as a prayer, the reading of Scripture, or reciting of religious speech in a public setting. Atheist Michael Newdow used the "coercion test" as the foundation of his case in asking the U.S. Supreme Court to make it illegal for public school children to recite the Pledge of Allegiance if it includes the phrase "one nation under God."

18. 1992, *Planned Parenthood of Southeastern Pennsylvania vs. Casey.* In writing the majority opinion, Justice Sandra Day O'Connor, Justice Souter, and Justice Kennedy wrote, "At the heart of liberty is the right to define one's own concept of existence, of meaning of the universe, and the mystery of human life."[7] Author and family advocate James Dobson wrote that "with those words, the Court discarded its historic reliance on 'a law beyond the law,' or a transcendent standard."[8] Author and attorney Chuck Colson wrote that "the mystery passage could mean absolutely anything to a future court, including the right to marry your toaster if you wish."[9]

19. 1993, Ruth Bader Ginsburg is appointed to the U.S. Supreme Court. While serving as an attorney for the American Civil Liberties Union, Ginsburg wrote a paper entitled, "Sex Bias in the U.S. Code," which was prepared for the U.S. Commission on Civil Rights in April 1977. The paper recommends lowering the age of consent for sexual acts to twelve years old.

20. 1996, *Colorado vs. Romer.* In 1992, 53.4 percent of the people of Colorado voted to pass a statewide initiative known as Amendment 2. Amendment 2 was written and put on the ballot as a response to ordinances in several Colorado municipalities that granted minority

status to homosexuals not granted to others. The U.S. Supreme Court declared Amendment 2 unconstitutional. Justice Scalia authored the dissenting opinion in which he chastised his fellow justices stating, "Today's opinion has no foundation in American constitutional law and barely pretends to. The people of Colorado have adopted an entirely reasonable provision which does not even disfavor homosexuals in any substantive sense, but merely denies them preferential treatment. Amendment 2 is designed to prevent piecemeal deterioration of the sexual morality favored by a majority of Coloradans, and is not only an appropriate means to that legitimate end, but a means that Americans have employed before. Striking it down is an act, not of judicial judgment, but political will."[10]

21. 2000, *Santa Fe Independent School District vs. Doe.* The U.S. Supreme Court declared it unconstitutional for students to pray over the loud speaker system before a football game.

22. 2003, *Texas vs. Lawrence.* The U.S. Supreme Court declared unconstitutional the law of Texas that made homosexual acts illegal. Steve Crampton, lead attorney for the Center for Law and Policy, declared, "criminal law is quintessentially morals law . . . . Under our constitutional republic, it is the place of the state legislature, acting through its duly elected representatives, to decide what is moral. For a handful of unelected judges to impose their views of morality is not law, it is tyranny."[11] The Court decision struck down sodomy laws in eleven states. To justify their unconstitutional ruling the Court cited foreign law, which many legal scholars believe was in itself unconstitutional. "Justice Anthony M. Kennedy's majority opinion cited a 1967 British Parliament vote repealing laws against homosexual acts and a 1981 European Court of Human Rights decision that those laws were in violation of the European Convention on Human Rights."[12]

23. June 2005: The U.S. Supreme Court announced its ruling on two cases that involved displaying the Ten Commandments on state property. In the case *McCreary County, Kentucky, vs. ACLU,* liberal Justice David Souter wrote in a 5-4 decision that the displays in county courthouses were motivated by a religious purpose and so were impermissible. However, in the *Van Orden vs. Perry,* the Court allowed a monument containing the Ten Commandments to remain on the grounds of the Texas State Capitol because it was surrounded

by other historical documents and thus the purpose of the Ten Commandments display in Texas was for historical purposes and not religious purposes. The result of these two rulings is that the Ten Commandments cannot be posted on government property if it is for the purpose of acknowledging God or promoting the religion of Christianity.

24. June 2005, *Kelo vs. City of New London, Connecticut.* In a 5-4 decision the U.S. Supreme Court ruled that government can take private property and sell it to another private entity. Prior to this ruling government could only take private property for public use such as building a highway, railroad, and other such necessary public infrastructure projects. Through this ruling the Court has now legalized theft and is encouraging the sin of coveting.

Appendix 4

The Worldview Weekend Experience

Worldview Weekends help you deepen your understanding of the Christian worldview and hone your ability to respond to those who disagree. To find out about the weekend seminars in your area, go to www.WorldviewWeekend.com.

Worldview Weekend also provides a way to develop your worldview at home through the Worldview Weekend Online Institute. Online presentations are given by Josh McDowell, Ken Ham, David Noebel, Kerby Anderson, David Barton, Norm Geisler, Frank Harber, David Jeremiah, and others. The twelve-week course will enrich your knowledge of many of the issues raised in this book, such as:

- What sets Jesus Christ apart from every other religious leader in history?
- What happened to the dinosaurs?
- How to talk to people opposed to your worldview
- Why the Christian worldview is not anti-intellectual
- How to prove there is a moral law for all people, times, and places
- More about the so-called eight hundred contradictions in the Bible
- Why multiculturalism is not the study of many religions
- What is postmodernism, and why is it so dangerous?

See www.WorldviewWeekend.com for complete course information.

About the Author

Brannon Howse is president and founder of Worldview Weekend, America's largest Christian worldview conference. Founded in January 1993, Worldview Weekend seminars are now held in approximately twenty states each year, with an annual attendance of roughly twenty thousand.

Brannon, a trained soloist, has performed in hundreds of American churches, including those of Dr. D. James Kennedy and Dr. Chuck Swindoll. He has also performed at the Anaheim Convention Center for the eight thousand delegates of the Association of Christian Schools International.

Brannon hosts the Worldview Weekend Family Reunion in Branson, Missouri, each spring, an event attended by two thousand people. This three day event features numerous nationally known speakers, comedians, and musicians. Because of the success of the Branson event, the Smoky Mountains Worldview Weekend Family Reunion in Gatlinburg, Tennessee, was added. This will take place in the fall.

Brannon, president of Howse Agency, a literary and marketing firm, is the agent for Michael Reagan's book *Twice Adopted* (released in October 2004). In addition, Brannon serves as the education reporter for *The Michael Reagan Show* and has been that program's guest host on numerous occasions.

He is the cohost of *Christian Worldview This Week*, a weekly radio broadcast heard on more than 225 stations.

Brannon is the author of three books on education, family issues, and Christian worldview topics, including *An Educational Abduction* and *Reclaiming a Nation at Risk*. Because of his expertise in family issues, Brannon has been a guest on more than six hundred radio and television programs, including *The O'Reilly Factor* (Fox News), the News on MSNBC, *Truths That Transform* with Dr. D. James Kennedy, *The G. Gordon Liddy Show*, *The Michael Reagan Show*, *The Ken Hamblin Show*, and *The Oliver North Show*.

Notes

Introduction

[1] David Barton, "Election 2004: A Moral Mandate?," November 16, 2004.

[2] Ibid.

[3] Ibid.

[4] "Keilor: Born-agains should not have right to vote," www.Worldnetdaily.com, November 15, 2004.

[5] David S. Broder and Richard Morin, "Four years later, voters more deeply divided," www.msnbc.com.

[6] Barton, "Election 2004."

[7] Pat Buchanan, 1992 Republican Convention.

[8] Thomas Edsall, "Blue Movie," *Atlantic*, January/February 2003, 36.

[9] Michael Barone, *Almanac of American Politics* (Washington, DC: National Journal, 2002), 7–28.

[10] Robert B. Reich, "The Last Word: Bush's God," *The American Prospect,* June 17, 2004.

[11] Charles Kimball, *When Religion Becomes Evil* (New York: Harper San Francisco, 2002).

[12] Dr. D. James Kennedy, *Lord of All: Developing a Christian World-and-Life View* (Wheaton, IL: Crossway, 2005), 86.

[13] Ibid., 85.

[14] David Barton, quoting John Witherspoon, *The Works of the Rev. John Witherspoon,* vol. 3 (Philadelphia: William W. Woodward, 1802), 46.

[15] Dan Whitcomb, Reuters article, November 24, 2004.

Chapter One

[1] Dan Whitcomb, Reuters article, November 24, 2004.

[2] Ibid.

[3] Kenneth L. Woodward with David Gates, "How the Bible Made America: Since the Puritans and the pioneers, through wars and social conflicts, a sense of Biblical mission has united us, divided us and shaped our national destiny," *Newsweek,* December 27, 1982, 44.

[4] William J. Federer, *The Ten Commandments and Their Influence on American Law* (St. Louis, MO: Amerisearch Inc., 2003), 19.

[5] Ibid. Federer's sources are as follows: Donald S. Lutz and Charles S. Hyneman, "The Relative Influence of European Writers on Late Eighteenth-Century American Political Thought," *American Political Science Review* 189 (1984), 189–97. (Courtesy of Dr. Wayne House of Dallas Theological Seminary.)

John Eidsmoe, *Christianity and the Constitution—The Faith of Our Founding Fathers* (Grand Rapids, MI: Baker Book House, A Mott Media Book, 1987; 6th printing, 1993), 51–53. *Origins of American Constitutionalism* (1987). Stephen K. McDowell and Mark A. Beliles, *America's Providential History* (Charlottesville, VA: Providence Press, 1988), 156.

⁶ Information provided by David Barton's Wallbuilders (Aledo, TX), www.wallbuilders.com.

⁷ Ibid.

⁸ John Jay, *The Correspondence and Public Papers of John Jay, 1794–1826*, Henry P. Johnson, ed., vol. 4 (Reprinted NY: Burt Franklin, 1970), 393.

⁹ David Barton, *Original Intent* (Aledo, TX: Wallbuilders), 214.

¹⁰ Washington's Farewell Address.

¹¹ Bill Federer, *America's God and Country* (St. Louis, MO: Amerisearch, 2000), 247.

¹² David Barton, president of Wallbuilders, speech, "The Practical Benefits of Christianity," www.wallbuilders.com.

¹³ John Eidsmoe, *Christianity and the Constitution—The Faith of Our Founding Fathers* (Grand Rapids: Baker Book House, 1987), 360–61.

¹⁴ Ibid., quoting Martin Diamond, "The Declaration and the Constitution: Liberty, Democracy, and the Founders," *The Public Interest*, no. 41 (Fall 1975), 39–55 at 46ff.

¹⁵ Ibid., 362.

¹⁶ Clarence E. Manion and Verne Paul Kaub, *Collectivism Challenges Christianity* (Winona Lake, IN: Light and Life Press, 1946), 58. Tim LaHaye, *Faith of Our Founding Fathers* (Brentwood, TN: Wolgemuth & Hyatt, Publishers, Inc., 1987), 65.

¹⁷ Donald Kagan, "Nihilism rejects any objective basis for society and its morality, the very concept of objectivity, even the possibility of communication itself," *Academic Questions* 8, no. 2 (spring 1995), 56.

¹⁸ Bill Federer, *3 Secular Reasons Why America Should Be under God* (St. Louis, MO: Amerisearch, Inc., 2004), 66.

¹⁹ Dr. D. James Kennedy, *Lord of All: Developing a Christian World-and-Life View* (Wheaton, IL: Crossway, 2005), 130.

²⁰ Benjamin Rush, "On the Mode of Education Proper in a Republic," *Essays, Literary, Moral and Philosophical* (Philadelphia: Thomas and Samuel F. Bradford, 1798), 8.

²¹ U.S. War Department, Training Manual No. 2000-25, printed November 30, 1928.

²² U.S. Constitution, Article 4, section 4.

²³ Fischer Ames, *Works of Fisher Ames* (Boston: T. B. Wait & Co., 1809), 24; speech on biennial elections delivered on January 15, 1788.

²⁴ L. H. Butterfield, ed., *The Letters of Benjamin Rush*, vol. 1 (Princeton: Princeton University Press, 1951), 454; quoting John Joachim Zubly, Presbyterian pastor and delegate to Congress, in a letter to David Ramsay in March or April 1788.

²⁵ John Adams, "Discourses on Davila; A Series of Papers on Political History," *The Works of John Adams, Second President of the United States*, vol. 6 (Boston: Charles C. Little and James Brown, 1851), 484.

²⁶ Noah Webster, *The American Spelling Book: Containing an Easy Standard of Pronunciation: Being the First Part of a Grammatical Institute of the English Language, to Which Is Added an Appendix, Containing a Moral Catechism and a Federal Catechism* (Boston: Isaiah Thomas and Ebenezer T. Andrews, 1801), 103–104.

[27] John Witherspoon, "Lecture 12 on Civil Society," *Works*, vol. 7 (1815), 101.

[28] U.S. War Department, Training Manual No. 2000-25, printed November 30, 1928.

[29] Noah Webster, *History of the United States* (New Haven: Durrie & Peck, 1832), 6.

[30] David Barton, *Keys to Good Government* (Aledo, TX: Wallbuilders Press, 2000), 8.

[31] John Adams, "Thoughts on Government," quoted in John R. Howe Jr., *The Changing Political Thought of John Adams* (Princeton: Princeton University Press, 1966).

[32] Alexander Hamilton, *The Federalist Papers*, 80, Federalist #15.

[33] Alexander Hamilton, *The Papers of Alexander Hamilton*, Harold C. Syrett, ed., vol. 1 (New York: Columbia University Press, 1961), 87; quoting William Blackstone, *Commentaries on the Laws of England*, vol. 1 (Philadelphia: Robert Bell, 1771), 41.

[34] Rufus King, *The Life and Correspondence of Rufus King*, Charles R. King, ed., vol. 6 (New York: G.P. Putnam's Sons, 1900), 276, to C. Gore on February 17, 1820.

[35] Found at www.barna.org.

[36] Ibid.

[37] Ibid.

[38] Barton, *Original Intent*, 337–38.

[39] Benjamin Rush, "A Defense of the Use of the Bible as a School Book," *Essays, Literary, Moral and Philosophical* (Philadelphia: Thomas and Samuel F. Bradford, 1798), 93–113; addressed to the Rev. Jeremy Belknap of Boston.

[40] Jedidiah Morse, "A Sermon, Exhibiting the Present Dangers and Consequent Duties of the Citizens of the United States of America," delivered at Charlestown, April 25, 1799, the Day of the National Fast (MA: Printed by Samuel Etheridge, 1799), 11.

[41] *The Daily Advertiser* (New York), May 1, 1789, 2.

[42] Henry Gilpin, ed., *The Papers of James Madison*, vol. 3 (Washington: Langtree and O'Sullivan, 1840),1391.

[43] Barton, *Original Intent*.

[44] David Barton, *The Spirit of the American Revolution*, quoting William Blackstone, *Commentaries on the Laws of England*, vol. 1(Philadelphia: Robert Bell, 1771), 42.

[45] This memorable quotation is from Sir Alex Fraser Tyler (1742–1813), Scottish jurist and historian; he was the widely known professor of universal history at Edinburgh University in the late eighteenth century. The quotation is from the 1801 collection of his lectures.

[46] From an e-mail sent by David Barton of Wallbuilders to a small group of Christian and conservative leaders throughout America in the summer of 2004, quoting Professor Olson.

Chapter Two

[1] Soviet Union Constitution, Article 124.

[2] Thomas Jefferson, letter to Danbury Baptist Association.

[3] Page Smith, *The Nation Comes of Age*, vol. 4 (New York: McGraw-Hill Book Co., 1981), 660.

[4] Gary DeMar, *The Untold Story* (Atlanta, GA: American Vision Inc., 1993), 116.

[5] John and Abigail Adams, *Letters of John Adams, Addressed to His Wife*, Charles Francis Adams, ed., vol. 1 (Boston: Charles C. Little and James Brown, 1841), 152.

[6] David Barton, *The Myth of the Separation* (Aledo, TX: Wallbuilders Press, 1991), 42.

[7] Barnes Mayo, ed., Jefferson *Himself—The Personal Narrative of a Many-sided American* (Boston: Houghton Mifflin Company, 1942), 231.

[8] Barton, *The Myth of Separation*, 176.

[9] Ibid.

[10] DeMar, *The Untold Story*, 173.

[11] Gary DeMar, *God and Government—A Biblical and Historical Study* (Atlanta, GA: American Vision Press, 1982),173.

[12] Barton, *The Myth of Separation*, 176.

[13] Joseph Story, *Commentaries on the Constitution of the United States*, 3rd ed. (Boston, 1858).

[14] See Alvin W. Johnson, Sunday Legislation, 23 KY. L.J. 131 n. (1934–35). Sited by William J. Federer, *The Ten Commandments and Their Influence on American Law* (St. Louis, MO: Amerisearch, Inc., 2003), 15.

[15] M. E. Bradford, *A Worthy Company: Brief Lives of the Framers of the United States Constitution* (Marlborough, NH: Plymouth Rock Foundation, 1982), iv–v.

[16] John Eidsmoe, *Christianity and the Constitution* (Grand Rapids, MI: Baker Book House, 1987), 44.

[17] Ibid.

[18] Noah Webster, *History of the United States* (New Haven: Durrie & Peck, 1832), 339.

[19] Benjamin Rush, "A Defense of the Use of the Bible as a School Book," *Essays, Literary, Moral and Philosophical* (Philadelphia: Thomas and Samuel F. Bradford, 1798), 112; addressed to the Rev. Jeremy Belknap of Boston.

[20] Ibid., 93–113.

[21] Ibid.

[22] David Barton, "Either by the Bible or the Bayonet," *Education and the Founding Fathers,* quoting Robert Winthrop, *Addresses and Speeches on Various Occasions* (Boston, MA: Little Brown & Co. 1852), 172.

[23] Ibid.

[24] Ibid., 324–25, quoting John Witherspoon, *The Works of the Rev. John Witherspoon,* vol. 3 (Philadelphia: William W. Woodward, 1802), 46.

[25] Fisher Ames, *Notices of the Life and Character of Fisher Ames* (Boston: T.B. Wait & Co., 1809), 134–35.

[26] Alexis de Tocqueville, *The Republic of the United States of America and Its Political Institutions, Reviewed and Examined*, Henry Reeves, trans., vol. 1 (New York: A.S. Barnes & Co., 1851), 337.

[27] Ibid., 334.

[28] David Barton, *The Spirit of the American Revolution* (Aledo, TX: Wallbuilders Press, 2000), 21, quoting *Reports of Committees of the House of Representatives Made during the First Session of the Thirty-Third Congress* (Washington: A. O. P. Nicholson, 1854), 6–9.

[29] Ibid., quoting B. F. Morris, *The Christian Life and Character of the Civil Institutions of the United States* (Philadelphia: George W. Childs, 1864), 328.

[30] John Adams, "The Right Constitution of a Commonwealth Examined," letter 6, *A Defense of the Constitution of Government of the Untied States of America,* vol. 3 (Philadelphia: William Young, 1797), 217.

[31] David Barton, *Original Intent* (Aledo, TX: Wallbuilders Press, 1997), 172, quoting John Quincy Adams, *Letters . . . to His Sons*, 61.

[32] Ibid., 70–71.

[33] Ibid., 173, quoting Noah Webster, "Reply to a letter of David McClure on the Subject of the Proper Course of Study in the Girard College," *Collection of Papers,* (Philadelphia: New Haven, 1836), 291–92.

[34] Matt Staver, *The Ten Commandments in American Law and Government*, citing *Florida vs. City of Tampa,* 48 So.2d 78, 79 (Fla. 1950); see also *Commissioners of Johnston County vs. Lacy,* 93 S.E. 482, 487 (N.C. 1917).

[35] Federer, *The Ten Commandments and Their Influence on American Law*, 32.

[36] Ibid., 35, quoting the speech given by former Prime Minister Margaret Thatcher, February 5, 1996, New York.

[37] Ibid.; quoting United States District Court (1983), Western District of Virginia, in the case of *Crockett vs. Sorenson,* 568, F. Supp. 1422, 1425–1430 (W.D., Va. 1983).

[38] Ibid., quoting *Wisconsin vs. Schultz,* 582, N.W. 2d 112, 117 (Wis. App. 1998) (Quoting *Sumpter vs. Indiana,* 306, N.E. 2d 95, 101 (Ind. 1974).

[39] Joseph Story, *Commentaries*, 731.

[40] David Barton, *The Foundations of American Government* (Aledo, TX: Wallbuilders Press, 1993), 5.

[41] Ibid., 41.

[42] Joseph Story, *Commentaries,* 2:593, quoted in Robert L. Cord, *Separation of Church and State: Historical Fact and Current Fiction* (New York: Lambeth Press, 1982), 13.

[43] Ann Coulter, *Disestablish the Cult of Liberalism*, June 15, 2001.

[44] David Barton, *America's Godly Heritage* (Aledo, TX: Wallbuilders Press, 1993), 15.

[45] Ibid.,16.

[46] Barton, *The Foundations of American Government*, 10.

[47] Barton, *Original Intent*, 17.

[48] *Walz vs. Tax Commission,* 397 U.S., 701–703 (1970); Douglas, J. (dissenting).

[49] Samuel Adams, *The Writings of Samuel Adams*, Harry Alonzo Cushing, ed., vol. 4 (New York: G. P. Putnam's Sons, 1908), 332, letter to Elbridge Gerry.

[50] Fourteenth Amendment, U.S. Constitution.

[51] Ibid., 198.

[52] *Abington vs. Schempp,* 374 U.S. 203, 215–16 (1963).

[53] *Walz vs. Tax Commission,* 397 U.S. 664, 701, 703 (1970), Douglas J. (dissenting).

[54] Todd Connor, Fox News, August 21, 2003.

[55] Alliance Defense Fund press release, September 23, 2004.

[56] Jerry Newcombe, research.

[57] Torsten Ove, staff writter, *Post-Gazette,* May 7, 2003.

[58] www.Worldnetdaily.com, April 1, 2004.

[59] Ryan McCarthy, *The Sacramento Bee*, October 6, 2001.

[60] Webster, *History of the United States*, 337.

[61] *Only Half of Protestant Pastors Have a Biblical Worldview,* January 12, 2004, www.barna.org.

Chapter Three

[1] David Limbaugh, "Warring with Christianity," September 27, 2003.

[2] Irving Kristol, "American Conservatism, 1945–1995."

[3] John Dewey, *Liberalism and Social Action* (New York: G. P. Putnam's Sons, 1935), 88.

[4] John Bunzel, "Religion and Liberals," *LA Times,* September 14, 2003.

[5] Cited in David Noebel, *Clergy in the Classroom: The Religion of Secular Humanism* (Manitou Springs, CO; Summit Press, 1995), 144, quoting *Journal of Higher Education* 23 (October 1952), 361–62.

[6] Ann Coulter, *Disestablish the Cult of Liberalism*, June 15, 2001.

[7] Phyllis Schlafly, "Who Controls Education Policies?," vol. 37, no. 1, August 2003.

[8] George Archibald, "NEA 'Reaching Out' from the Left to the GOP," July 8, 2003.

[9] Schlafly, "Who Controls Education Policies?"

[10] Ibid., 74.

[11] David Limbaugh, "NEA: Politicizing 'Education,'" July 12, 2003.

[12] Dennis Cuddy, "NEA: Grab for Power," *Investor's Business Daily* (Oklahoma City, OK: Hearthstone Publishing, 73101, 1993), 55.

[13] Peter Brimelow and Leslie Spencer, "The National Extortion Association," *Forbes Magazine,* June 7, 1993, 79.

[14] Cuddy, "NEA: Grab for Power," 11.

[15] Ibid.

[16] Ibid., 49, quoting the August 1995 *Phyllis Schlafly Report.*

[17] Ibid., 51.

[18] Gary Bauer, Campaign for Working Families daily e-mail alert, June 8, 2005.

[19] David Barton, *The Wallbuilder Report*, Winter 2004.

[20] Ibid., 25.

[21] Ibid.

[22] Ibid., 26.

[23] Ibid.

[24] Tim LaHaye and David Noebel, *Mind Siege: The Battle for Truth in the New Millennium* (Nashville, TN: Word Publishing, 2000), 187.

[25] George Grant, *The Family under Siege* (Minneapolis, MN: Bethany House Publishers, 1994), 145.

[26] Ibid., 145; quoting Peggy Lamson, *Roger Baldwin: Founder of the American Civil Liberties Union: A Portrait* (Boston: Houghton Mifflin, 1976), 138–39.

[27] The D. James Kennedy Center for Christian Statesmanship, summer 1995.

[28] LaHaye and Noebel, *Mind Siege*, 188.

[29] Ibid., quoting *Soviet Russia Today*, September 1934.

[30] Grant, *The Family under Siege*, 146.

[31] Ibid., 147.

[32] Ibid., 149; quoting William Donohue, *The Politics of the American Civil Liberties Union* (New Brunswick, NJ: Transaction, 1985), 5–6.

[33] Ibid., quoting the *Washington Action Alert*, August 1993.

[34] Ibid., quoting Donohue, *The Politics of the American Civil Liberties Union*, 36.

[35] Ibid., 140.

[36] Matt Kaufman, "Reverend Barry, Quite Contrary," Focus on the Family *Citizen* magazine, www.family.org.

[37] Ibid.

[38] Ibid.

[39] Ibid.

[40] Grant, *The Family under Siege*, 140.

[41] Ibid.

[42] Ibid.

[43] Ibid., 141.

[44] Education Report, *Eagle Forum*, July 1988, no. 150.

[45] Samuel L. Blumenfeld, *NEA: Trojan Horse in American Education,* NEA Resolution.

[46] Grant, *The Family under Siege*, 139.

[47] ACLU sues over disclaimers, the Associated Press, vol. 91, no. 3, August 23, 2002.

[48] Grant, *The Family under Siege*, 141.

⁴⁹ ACLU Web site, about the ACLU Drug Policy Litigation Project.
⁵⁰ ACLU Web site, Reproductive Rights.
⁵¹ Grant, *The Family under Siege*, 140.
⁵² Ibid., 141.
⁵³ ACLU Web site, Women's Rights.
⁵⁴ Grant, *The Family under Siege*, 139.
⁵⁵ Dennis Laurence Cuddy, Ph.D., *The Grab for Power* (Marlborough, NH: Plymouth Rock Foundation, 1993), 7.
⁵⁶ Grant, *The Family under Siege*, 139.
⁵⁷ Ibid., 140.
⁵⁸ Schlafly, "Who Controls Education Policies?"
⁵⁹ Limbaugh, "NEA: Politicizing 'Education.'"
⁶⁰ Grant, *The Family under Siege*, 141.
⁶¹ ACLU Web site, "Why the Supreme Court Decision Striking Down Sodomy Laws Is So Important."
⁶² Howi Beigelman, "What Kind of First Amendment Is This Anyway?" *Jewish Law Commentary*.
⁶³ Cuddy, 102; quoting Lily Wong Fillmore, keynote speaker, third annual conference, National Association for Multicultural Education, Los Angeles, February 11–14, 1993.
⁶⁴ Susan Duquesnay, "Tom without Pity," *Fort Bend Star*, April 24, 2002.
⁶⁵ Ibid.

Chapter Four

¹ Benjamin Cardozo, *The Nature of the Judicial Process* (New Haven: Yale University Press, 1921), 10.
² Benjamin Cardozo, *The Growth of the Law* (New Haven; Yale University Press, 1924), 49.
³ Final Report of the Joint Committee on the Organization of Congress, December 1993.
⁴ Lino A. Graglia, "Judicial Review on the Basis of 'Regime Principles': A Prescription for Government by Judges," *South Texas Law Journal*, vol. 26, no. 3 (Fall 1985), 435–52, at 446.
⁵ John Eidsmoe, *Christianity and the Constitution* (Grand Rapids, MI: Baker Book House, 1987), 391.
⁶ Ibid., 394.
⁷ David Barton, *Original Intent* (Aledo, TX: Wallbuilders, 1996), 228.
⁸ Oliver Wendell Holmes Jr., "The Law in Science-Science in Law," *Collected Legal Papers* (New York: Harcourt, Brace and Company, 1920), 225.
⁹ Steve Brown, "Fears Grow over Academic Efforts to Normalize Pedophilia," www.CNSnews.com, July 10, 2003.
¹⁰ "Danger from Foreign Precedent," editorial, *The Washington Times*, March 25, 2004.
¹¹ Ibid.
¹² Ibid.
¹³ Ibid., quoting Sandra Day O'Connor.
¹⁴ Gary Bauer, e-mail to "Friends and Supporters" of Campaign for Working Families, March 1, 2005.
¹⁵ Ibid.
¹⁶ *Washington Times*, May 17, 2004, A07.
¹⁷ Ibid.
¹⁸ David Barton, *The Wallbuilder Report*, Winter 2004, 21.

[19] Ibid., 22.

[20] Gary DeMar, *God and Government I* (Powder Springs, GA: American Vision Inc, 2001), 188, quoting letter by Thomas Jefferson to William Charles Jarvis.

[21] Barton, *Original Intent*, 228.

[22] John Dewey, *The Public and Its Problems* (New York: Henry Hold and Company, 1927), 34.

[23] Barton, *Original Intent*, 441.

[24] Thomas Jefferson, *The Writings of Thomas Jefferson*, Albert Ellery Bergh, ed., vol. 12 (Washington, D.C.: The Thomas Jefferson Memorial Association, 1904), 392, letter to Governor John Tyler.

[25] Joseph Story, *Commentaries on the Constitution of the United States*, 3rd ed. (Boston, 1858), 283, 400.

[26] Craig R. Ducat and Harold W. Chase, *Constitutional Interpretation: Powers of Government* (West Publishing Company, 1992), 3; quoting Charles Evans Hughes.

[27] Edwin Meese III, address to American Bar Association, 1985; adapted in "Toward a Jurisprudence of Original Intention," *Benchmark*, vol. 2, no. 1, January-February 1986, 1–10, at 6.

[28] *Family News from Dr. James Dobson*, October 1997, Focus on the Family (Colorado Springs, CO, 80995)

[29] Thomas Jipping, *Intimidated Judges Judge Well*, February 15, 2001, syndicated column, www.Worldnetdaily.com.

[30] John W. Whitehead, *The Second American Revolution* (Good News Publishing, 1985), 89.

[31] Greg L. Bahnsen, *By this Standard: The Authority of God's Law Today* (Institute for Christian Economics, 1991), 264F.

[32] DeMar, *God and Government*, 165–66.

[33] Eidsmoe, *Christianity and the Constitution*, 400–401.

[34] Samuel Adams, *The Writings of Samuel Adams*, Harry Alonzo Cushing, ed., vol. 4 (New York: G. P. Putman's Sons, 1904), 388, to the Legislature of Massachusetts.

Chapter Five

[1] D. G. Lindsay, c1990, *Foundations for Creationism* (Dallas: Christ for the Nations, 1998).

[2] D. M. S. Watson, "Adaptation," *Nature*, 124:233, 1929.

[3] Richard Lewontin, "Billions and Billions of Demons," *The New York Review*, January 9, 1997, 31.

[4] Tim LaHaye and David Noebel, *Mind Siege: The Battle for Truth in the New Millennium* (Nashville, TN: Word Publishing, 2000), 140.

[5] S. C. Meyer, "The Methodological Equivalence of Design and Descent: Can There Be a 'Scientific Theory of Creation'?" *The Creation Hypothesis*, J. P. Moreland, ed. (Downers Grove, IL: InterVarsity Press, 1994), 98, 012.

[6] N. L. Geisler, *Baker Encyclopedia of Christian Apologetics*, Baker Reference Library (Grand Rapids: Baker Books, 1999), 574.

[7] See William Paley, *Evidence of Christianity* (London, 1851).

[8] P. L. Tan, c1979, *Encyclopedia of 7700 Illustrations: [a treasury of illustrations, anecdotes, facts and quotations for pastors, teachers and Christian workers]* (Garland, TX: Bible Communications, 1996).

[9] Walter T. Brown Jr., *In the Beginning* (Phoenix, AZ: Center for Scientific Creation, 1989), 2.

[10] Ibid.

[11] Tan, *Encyclopedia of 7700 Illustrations*.

[12] Frank Harber, *Reasons for Believing: A Seekers Guide to Christianity* (Green Forest, AR: New Leaf Press, 1998), 29–30.

[13] Tan, *Encyclopedia of 7700 Illustrations.*

[14] D. G. Lindsay, c1990, *Harmony of Science and Scripture* (Dallas: Christ for the Nations, 1998).

[15] Harber, *Reasons for Believing*, 33.

[16] Bill Gates, *The Road Ahead*, rev. ed. (New York: Penguin, 1996), 228.

[17] Lindsay, *Harmony of Science and Scripture.*

[18] Michael J. Behe, *Darwin's Black Box* (New York: Free Press, 1996), 187.

[19] Ibid., 160.

[20] N. L. Geisler and P. K. Hoffman, *Why I Am a Christian: Leading Thinkers Explain Why They Believe* (Grand Rapids, MI: Baker Books, 2001), 93.

[21] Lindsay, *Harmony of Science and Scripture.*

[22] *National Geographic,* September 1976, 355.

[23] Lindsay, *Harmony of Science and Scripture.*

[24] D. G. Lindsay, c1991, *The Origins Controversy: Creation or Chance* (Dallas: Christ for the Nations, 1999).

[25] Ibid.

[26] Brown, *In the Beginning*, 3.

[27] Ibid.

[28] Fred Hoyle, *The Intelligent Universe* (New York: Holt Rinehart, and Winston, 1983), 11.

[29] Brown, *In the Beginning*, 34.

[30] Harber, *Reasons for Believing*, 33.

[31] Michael Denton, *Evolution: A Theory in Crisis* (Chevy Chase, MD: Adler and Adler Publishers, Inc., 1986), 328, 342.

[32] Brown, *In the Beginning.*

[33] Robert Jastrow, *God and the Astronomers* (New York: Warner Books, 1978), 111.

[34] N. L. Geisler and R. M. Brooks, *When Skeptics Ask* (Wheaton, IL: Victor Books, 1990), 220.

[35] Henry Margenau, "Modern Physics and the Turn to Belief in God," *The Intellectuals Speak Out about God,* Roy Abraham Varghese, ed. (Dallas: Lewis and Stanley, 1984), 43.

[36] Corliss Lamont, *The Philosophy of Humanism* (New York: Frederick Ungar Publishing, 1982), 145.

[37] Ibid.

[38] Brown, *In the Beginning*, 3.

[39] C. R. Darwin, *Origin of Species*, 6th ed., 1872 (London: John Murray, 1902), 413.

[40] Letter from Dr. Colin Patterson, then senior paleontologist at the British Museum of Natural History in London, to Luther D. Sunderland, as quoted in L. D. Sunderland, *Darwin's Enigma* (Green Forest, AR: Master Books, 1984), 89.

[41] S. J. Gould, *Evolution Now: A Century After Darwin*, John Maynard Smith, ed. (New York: Macmillan Publishing Co., 1982), 140. "Teaching about Evolution," 56–57, publishes a complaint by Gould about creationists quoting him about the rarity of transitional fossils.

[42] S. J. Gould, "The Ediacarant Experiment," *Natural History* 93 (2):14–23, February 1984.

[43] Brown, *In the Beginning*, 5–6.

[44] Oswald Spengler, *The Decline of the West,* vol. 2 (New York: Alfred A. Knopf, 1966), 32.

[45] Charles Colson and Nancy Pearcey, *How Now Shall We Live?* (Carol Stream, IL: Tyndale House Publishing, Inc., 1999), 85.

[46] Gordon Rattray Taylor (former chief science advisor, BBC Television) *The Great Evolution Mystery* (New York: Harper & Row, 1983), 48.

[47] Lee Spetner, *Not by Chance* (Brooklyn, NY: The Judaica Press, Inc.), 131–32, 138, 143.

[48] James F. Crow (professor of genetics, University of Wisconsin) "Genetic Effects of Radiation," *Bulletin of the Atomic Scientists*, vol. 14, 1958: 19–20.

[49] Frank B. Salisbury (Plant Science Department, Utah State University), "Natural Selection and the Complexity of the Gene," *Nature*, vol. 224, October 25, 1969, 342.

Chapter Six

[1] John Eldredge, *Why Christians Should Be Involved*.

[2] Ibid., 9.

[3] "The First Nine Months of Life," brochure, Focus on the Family (Colorado Springs, CO), 1995.

[4] Kerby Anderson, *Moral Dilemmas* (Nashville, TN: Word Publishing, 1998), 3.

[5] Ibid.

[6] Ibid., 3–4.

[7] Ibid., 4.

[8] Ibid.

[9] Ibid.

[10] Ibid.

[11] Ibid., 8.

[12] "Princeton Students against the Hiring of Peter Singer": statement they wrote and distributed.

[13] Anderson, *Moral Dilemmas*, 27.

[14] Ibid., 19.

[15] Ibid.

[16] Ibid., 20.

[17] Ibid.

[18] R. Finigsen, "The Report of the Dutch Committee on Euthanasia," *Issues in Law and Medicine*, July 1991, 339–44.

[19] J. S. Feinberg, P. D. Feinberg, and A. Huxley, c1993, *Ethics for a Brave New World* (Wheaton, IL: Crossway Books, 1996).

[20] Curtis Krueger, *St. Petersburg Times,* October 28, 2003.

[21] David Limbaugh, "A Turning Point in the Culture War," www.Worldnetdaily.com, March 25, 2005,

[22] Anderson, *Moral Dilemmas*, 27–28.

[23] Feinberg et al., *Ethics for a Brave New World*.

[24] Anderson, *Moral Dilemmas*, 27–28.

[25] Neil Chadwick, "A Christian Response to Gambling," sermon.

[26] P. L. Tan, c1979, *Encyclopedia of 7700 Illustrations: [a treasury of illustrations, anecdotes, facts and quotations for pastors, teachers and Christian workers]*, (Garland, TX: Bible Communications, 1996).

[27] Southern Baptist Convention Ethics and Religious Liberty Commission.

[28] Robert Goodman, *The Luck Business* (Touchstone, 1996).

[29] Bob Knight, "Talking Points on Marriage," www.nogaymarriage.com.

[30] Tony Perkins, FRC president, speech to a crowd of more than twenty thousand people from the Seattle, Washington, area who attended a rally in support of traditional marriage.

[31] Stanley Kurtz, "The End of Marriage in Scandinavia: The 'Conservative Case' for Same-Sex Marriage Collapses," *The Weekly Standard,* February 2, 2004, 27.

[32] Theo G. M. Sandfort, Ron de Graaf, Rob V. Bijl, and Paul Schnabel, "Same-Sex Sexual Behavior and Psychiatric Disorders: Findings from the Netherlands Mental Health Survey and Incidence Study (NEMESIS)," *Archives of General Psychiatry* 58 (2001): 85–91.

[33] Peter Sprigg, remarks, World Congress of Families III, Mexico City, Mexico, March 29, 2004.

[34] Scott Shane, "Many Swedes Say 'I Don't' to Nuptials, Unions," *Baltimore Sun* January 16, 2004, 1A.

[35] Timothy J. Dailey. "Comparing the Lifestyles of Homosexual Couples to Married Couples."

[36] OLR Backgrounder: "Legal Recognition of Same-sex Partnerships," *OLR Research Report,* October 9, 2002, 1.

[37] Maria Xiridou et al., "The Contribution of Steady and Casual Partnerships to the Incidence of HIV Infection among Homosexual Men in Amsterdam," *AIDS* 17 (2003): 1031.

[38] A. P. Bell and M. S. Weinberg, *Homosexualities: A Study of Diversity among Men and Women* (New York: Simon and Schuster, 1978), 308–309; see also A. P. Bell, M. S. Weinberg, and S. K. Hammersmith, *Sexual Preference* (Bloomington: Indiana University Press, 1981).

[39] Paul Van de Ven et al., "A Comparative Demographic and Sexual Profile of Older Homosexually Active Men," *Journal of Sex Research* 34 (1997): 354.

[40] "Sex Survey Results," *Genre,* October 1996, quoted in "Survey Finds 40 percent of Gay Men Have Had More Than 40 Sex Partners," *Lambda Report,* January 1998, 20.

[41] Mary Mendola, *The Mendola Report* (New York: Crown, 1980), 53.

[42] William Aaron, *Straight* (New York: Bantam Books, 1972), 208.

[43] Knight, "Talking Points on Marriage."

[44] Ibid.

[44] Timothy J. Dailey, "The Slippery Slope of Same-Sex Marriage," www.frc.org.

Chapter Seven

[1] "Religion," *Webster's New World Dictionary of the English Language—The Unabridged Edition* (New York: Random House, Inc., 1966, 1973), 135.

[2] "Belief," *The Random House Dictionary of the English Language—The Unabridged Editions* (New York: Random House, Inc., 1966, 1973), 135.

[3] Tim LaHaye and David Noebel, *Mind Siege: The Battle for Truth in the New Millennium* (Nashville, TN: Word Publishing, 2000), quoting Ian S. Markham, ed., *A World Religions Reader,* 2nd ed. (Malden, MA: Blackwell Publishers, 2000).

[4] David Noebel, *Clergy in the Classroom* (Manitou Springs, CO: Summit Press, 1995), 9.

[5] Marilyn Ferguson, *The Aquarian Conspiracy* (T. P. Tarcher, 1989), 90.

[6] David Noebel, *The Battle for Truth* (Eugene, OR: Harvest House Publishers, 2001), 37.

[7] *Beliefs: Salvation,* 2004 survey, www.Barna.org.

[8] *Beliefs: Theological,* 2004 survey, www.Barna.org.

[9] Ibid.

[10] Ibid.

[11] *Beliefs: Trinity, Satan,* 2001 survey, www.Barna.org.

[12] *Lifestyle Activities,* 2004 survey, www.Barna.org.

[13] *Unchurched People,* 2004 survey, www.Barna.org.

[14] Ibid.

[15] Ibid.

[16] *The Bible*, survey, www.Barna.org.

[17] Ibid.

[18] Ibid.

[19] Rick McGough, *One Minute Till Midnight* (Moline, IL: New Life Fellowship Association of God, 1988), 26.

[20] Ibid., 7.

[21] *Torcaso vs. Watkins*, 367 U.S. 488, 495, fn. 11 (1961).

[22] Noebel, *Clergy in the Classroom*, 8.

[23] Paul Kurtz, *Eupraxophy: Living without Religion* (Buffalo, NY: Prometheus Books, 1989), 80.

[24] Paul C. Vitz, *Censorship: Evidence of Bias in Our Children's Textbooks* (Ann Arbor, MI: Servant Books, 1986), 1.

[25] Ibid., 2–3.

[26] *A Humanist Manifesto I,* 1933, was first printed in *The New Humanist*, May/June 1933, vol. 6, no. 3.

[27] Curtis W. Reese, *Humanist Sermons* (Chicago, IL: The Open Court Publishing Company, 1927), v.

[28] Curtis W. Reese, *Humanist Religion* (New York: The Macmillan Company, 1931), 53.

[29] Roy Wood Sellars, *Religion Coming of Age* (New York: The Macmillan Company, 1928), 125.

[30] Ibid., 252.

[31] Ibid., 270.

[32] Charles Francis Potter, *Humanism: A New Religion* (New York: Simon and Schuster, 1930), 3.

[33] Ibid., 114.

[34] John H. Dietrich, *Humanism* (Boston, MA: American Unitarian Association, 1933), 11.

[35] Noebel, *Clergy in the Classroom,* 143; quoting Harvey Cox, *The Secular City: Secularization and Urbanization in Theological Perspective,* rev. ed. (New York: Macmillan, 1965, 1966), 18.

[36] Tom Minnery, *Why You Can't Stay Silent* (Carol Stream, IL: Tyndale House Publishers, 2002).

[37] David Barton, *Original Intent* (Aledo, TX: Wallbuilders, 1996).

Chapter Eight

[1] Frank Harber, *Reason for Believing* (Green Forrest, AR: New Leaf Press, 1998), 61.

[2] Michael D. Lemonick, "Are the Bible's Stories True?" *Time* magazine, December 18, 1995, 67.

[3] Josh McDowell, *Christianity: Hoax or History?* (Wheaton, IL: Pocket Guides, Tyndale House Publishers, Inc., 1989), 83–84.

[4] For more details on these texts, see Norm Geisler and William Nix, *A General Introduction to the Bible* (Chicago: Moody, 1982), 285, 366; Bruce Metzger, *The Text of the New Testament* (New York: Oxford University Press, 1964), 30–54; and Archibald T. Robertson, *An Introduction to the Textual Criticism of the New Testament* (Nashville: Broadman, 1925), 70.

[5] McDowell, *Christianity*, 52.

[6] Archibald T. Robertson, *An Introduction to the Textual Criticism of the New Testament* (Nashville: Broadman, 1925), 22.

[7] Benjamin B. Warfield, *An Introduction to the Textual Criticism of the New Testament* (London: n.p., 1886), 154.

[8] Norm Geisler and Peter Bocchino, *Unshakable Foundations* (Minneapolis, MN: Bethany Press, 2001), 254.

⁹ Ibid.

¹⁰ For more details on these texts see Geisler and Nix, *A General Introduction to the Bible*, 285, 366; Metzger, *The Text of the New Testament*, 30–54; and Robertson, *An Introduction to the Textual Criticism of the New Testament*, 70.

¹¹ Geisler and Nix, *A General Introduction to the Bible*, 268.

¹² Geisler and Bocchino, *Unshakable Foundations*, 255–56.

¹³ Ibid., 258.

¹⁴ Ibid., 258, quoting Geisler and Nix, *A General Introduction to the Bible*, 285.

¹⁵ Josh McDowell, *The New Evidence that Demands the Verdict* (Nashville, TN: Thomas Nelson Publishers, 1999), 45–46.

¹⁶ Ibid., 46.

¹⁷ Ibid., 55–56.

¹⁸ Ibid., 60, quoting Norm Geisler.

¹⁹ Ibid., 371.

²⁰ Ibid., 373.

²¹ Ibid., 380.

²² William F. Albright, *The Archaeology of Palestine* (Baltimore: Penguin, 1949), 127–28.

²³ *Archaeological Confirmation of the New Testament*, 331; quoted by Dr. Norm Geisler in his book *Unshakable Foundations*, 271.

²⁴ *What Mean These Stones?* (New Haven; CT: American Schools of Oriental Research, 1941), 1, quoted by Geisler, *Unshakable Foundations*, 271.

²⁵ *The Bearing of Recent Discovery on the Trustworthiness of the New Testament*, 222; quoted by Geisler, *Unshakable Foundations*, 272.

²⁶ Geisler and Bocchino, *Unshakable Foundations*, 270.

²⁷ Tim LaHaye, *Jesus Who Is He?* (Sisters, OR: Multnomah Books, 1996), 176–77.

²⁸ Ibid., 178.

²⁹ Geisler and Bocchino, *Unshakable Foundations*, 302.

³⁰ Ibid.

³¹ *Charlotte Observer,* December 30, 1993; quoted by Norman L. Geisler, *Baker Encyclopedia of Christian Apologetics* (Baker Book House), 615.

³² LaHaye, *Jesus Who Is He?*, 259.

³³ Ibid., 245.

³⁴ Josh McDowell, *The Resurrection Factor* (Nashville: Thomas Nelson Publishers, 1981), 6, 8.

³⁵ David Strauss, *The Life of Jesus for the People*, E.T., 2nd ed. (London:, 1879), 412.

³⁶ Harber, *Reason for Believing*, 119–20.

³⁷ LaHaye, *Jesus Who Is He?*, 265.

³⁸ Geisler and Bocchino, *Unshakable Foundations*, 358.

³⁹ Mark Cahill, *One Thing You Can't Do in Heaven* (Atlanta, GA: Biblical Discipleship Ministries, 2002), 131–36.

⁴⁰ Erwin Lutzer, *Christ among Other Gods* (Chicago: Moody Press, 1994), 62–64.

Appendix 3

¹ Oliver Wendell Holmes Jr., "The Law in Science—Science in Law," *Collected Legal Papers* (New York: Harcourt, Brace and Company, 1920), 225.

² Final Report of the Joint Committee on the Organization of Congress, December 1993.

³ Benjamin Cardozo, *The Nature of the Judicial Process* (New Haven: Yale University Press, 1921), 10.

⁴ Benjamin Cardozo, *The Growth of the Law* (New Haven: Yale University Press, 1924), 49.

[5] *Torcaso vs. Watkins,* 367 U.S. 488, 495, fn. 11 (1961).

[6] *Stone vs. Graham,* 449, U.S. 42 (1980).

[7] *Planned Parenthood of Southeastern Pennsylvania vs. Casey, Governor of Pennsylvania,* 505, U.S. 833 (1992).

[8] "Family News from Dr. James Dobson," Focus on the Family (Colorado Springs, CO: October 1997).

[9] *BreakPoint,* Chuck Colson, March 11, 1996.

[10] Scalia, Dissenting opinion, *Romer, Governor of Colorado et al., vs. Evans et al,.* (94–1039), 517 U.S. 620 (1996).

[11] Center for Law and Policy press release, June 26, 2003.

[12] "Danger from Foreign Precedent," editorial, *The Washington Times,* March 25, 2004.